I0224572

Crumbs from the Master's Table

**I overcame the Pain of
Poverty, Prejudice, and Addiction
On Grains of Faith.**

Van McKellar
Transformational Memoir

Copyright © 2024 Van B. McKellar. All rights reserved. No part of this publication may be reproduced, for sale or distribution, by any means without the prior written permission of Van McKellar, except in the case of brief quotations embodied in critical reviews and certain other noncommercial uses permitted by copyright law. For permission requests, email: vmckellar@comcast.net.

Library of Congress Copyright Registration Number: TXu 2-435-227.

eBook Cover by **Leah Berhe**

Paperback Cover by **Van McKellar**

To protect privacy, some names have been changed.

Except for my photo in the author's bio, all graphics in this book are from online stockpiles inserted through Microsoft Word 365, and from Canva, and istock.com. Although they depict actual scenes from my life, I did not create them. They are used for illustrations only.

First, this Book is dedicated to the memory of my parents, Van Sr. and Geneva McKellar, who were fine examples of how a person ought to live.

And, to Roslyn (Roz) McKellar for insightful criticism and encouragement. Then, equally to Charity Berhe, Vanda McKellar, Eileen Underwood, Saundra Bayson, and Sharon (Peaches) Newman-Stanfield, for being intrepid readers of the early work.

My sincere thanks to all others who contributed to bringing this Memoir to life.

Van McKellar

Table of Contents

Prologue

WE FELT THE DRONING, THROBBING SOUND in our bodies. The deafening noise rattled the old three-room shotgun shacks as the gleaming behemoths came over the horizon. Sitting sideways on the full bed in the front room, shock, and fear, transfigured Mama's worried face.

Her round shape shifted as she cried out nervously, "*Lawd* have mercy!" Wringing her hands, she finished with, "They *gonna* kill us one of these days."

The rising, pulsating, and shaking of everything in the house increased the fear in me, too. The fear in my little 10-year-old heart that I might miss the heavenly parade of silver giants. Little chance of that. I darted through the gauntlet of rickety objects that lay between me and the tattered screened front door. Bounding off the porch onto our rock-strewn yard, I broke out into the sunlight and looked up in wonder, mouth agape. A long, loud "*Hooorаaayy*" escaped my throat as I caught sight of the squadron of B-36 Very Heavy Bombers flying low over *Baptist Hill.* The gigantic six engine airplanes were so huge that I could see the outlines of the massive bomb bay doors. As they passed with terrible thunder, they had the appearance of long-necked geese, climbing up to *kingdoms in the clouds.*

Not only on *The Hill*, but across Fort Worth, our country flexed the muscles of its might in the skies above. This was 1949, and the sprawling *Consolidated Vultee Aircraft Corporation* and the *Carswell Airfield* complex, on the northwest side of town, was the home of the largest airplanes in the world. Ever Since America's entry into WWII, government subsidies made it possible for every White person in the nearby *Liberator Village* addition to feel ecstatic in their newly built two and three-bedroom homes. However, such lucrative job opportunities at the *Bomber Plant* were nonexistent for the Black people we knew.

The result was these flyovers provoked in Daddy and many others of our race a blend of annoyance and longing to be included. But aggregate prosperity for *coloreds* was unthinkable by Whites because of *Jim Crow laws.* These laws and customs gave Whites extraordinary power to control the destinies of Negro peoples. Today, in the post *Jim Crow Era,* it is told that a trickle-down portion of the funds reached individuals like us who provided menial services to the White middle-class society. But a trickle is a consistent flow from its origin. What we received from the prosperous citizens was more like intermittent lingering drops that tested our resolve and brought the usual nothing to our culture's dinner tables.

This contradiction in equality existed because a great gulf was fixed between the economically strangled inhabitants on my side of the segregated societies and the well-off residents in the shining cities of our towering young nation. Marginalization seemed all so natural, as if *endowed by the creator*, but it was not. Its inception, like the intricate celestial machines, was crafted by human hands long ago.

Section I: A legacy of Poverty

Beginning July 4th, 1776, the *Grand Old Men of Liberty* proclaimed a season of feasting fit for all who hungered for freedom but called only their privileged class to dine. Having gorged themselves on the main course of *Men's Unalienable Rights*, they withheld the scraps from those who toiled in obscurity. Next, *The Fathers* locked the *Old Chattel* outside the banquet hall. There, they suffered from hunger, like Lazarus, the biblical beggar. (Luke 16:19-21)

Following an amended *Constitution and Bill of Rights*, I was born one hundred sixty-three years into their merrymaking. I am an eyewitness to those consequent days, when:

at the table of the master, no place was set for the servant.

It seems only yesterday in my memory.

My parents settled on *Baptist Hill* in Fort Worth, Texas, two years after leaving my birthplace in the small town of Weatherford, twenty-eight miles to the West. Delivering a child of Black itinerant fieldworkers was not worthy of recording then. It is officially June 11th, 1939, now.

During the boom years (1946–1964) following the war, when our nation led the world, the Whites flourished under the Law while the Black citizens famished for want of Justice. But our nation, grown fat on the one-sided laws, continued to embrace White Supremacy and inflicted injury on its impoverished citizens. We were so constrained into our ghetto trap by *Jim Crow* tactics that no genuine avenue of escape into the middle class and up existed for most who lived there. As a result, killings, prostitution, and squalid living conditions plagued my little community on Oak Street at T*he Bottom of The Hill.* Nevertheless, my timid soul survived the hardships, bullying, bigots, and heartbreaks that are the heritage of the underclasses.

Before I came of age, I too, felt the irresistible magic that called me to the skies. As I grew eager for outside adventures, knowledge unshackled me from the Earth. But, in my flight for freedom, like Icarus,

I flew too close to the Sun.

I fell many times, but I did not utterly despair.

My story is timeless.

Chapter 1: Tales of pilots begin this way

Credit: istock.com/PCH-Vector

I yearned to fly airplanes when I was a little boy in the 1940s. I didn't know where the airborne machines came from, but I pointed and cheered as they passed overhead. My youthful infatuation had little to do with aviation as the highest achievement of civilization. It was the magic of something moving high in the sky. Once I learned that there were people in them, I longed to be up there. I wanted to look down and see the vast wonders of the whole wide world.

Throughout my formative years, I went through a prolonged period of wondering what makes an airplane fly. I found out the hard way that jumping off the house with cardboard wings wouldn't make me fly; it just leads to a painful crash. Also, my hand-held propeller that spun in the wind needed an engine attached to it. I bought ten-cent balsa wood gliders, made rubber band-powered paper-covered wooden models, and continued flapping my arms like a little birdman. The part that proves God is good is that I never seemed to have enough money to buy the big fireworks rockets and Roman candles to build a rocket ship large enough to ride in. Miraculously, I never caught my flying cape in the tree branches and broke my neck as I dropped like a stone from the upper limbs of the big mulberry tree in Mrs. Cressie's front yard. To make matters worse, it was before the civil rights era when the flying fantasies of a near-penniless Black youth living under oppression had little hope of maturing. However, my simple faith trusted that one day when I became a man, my dreams would soar.

In my private world, flying fantasies abounded, still, struggling to get off the ground could be disheartening. But it wasn't the most disconcerting hindrance to taking a meaningful step toward the life I craved. From those closest to me, there were the inevitable heartbreaking frowns that greeted the first word coming from naïve lips. How dare I whisper about topics beyond the expectations of colored people? Embarrassment washed over me as the rebuffs sung me.

"Van Jr., You're crazy, man. Why don't you get real?" "It's stupid for you to talk like that!"

My head sagged as I formed with their lips the last cut, "Life is too short; you need to grow up!"

I had no peers to share my thoughts of flying with, so I learned to keep it all in, both the dreams and the slanders, along with the countless times that excitement caused me to commit the social gaffe.

My playground

When I was growing up, the Black citizenry expected, but rarely got fair treatment from the White community. Through the years, the time-honored battle lines between the Whites and Black people remained fixed. The war was heavily tilted in favor of the overwhelming number of armed White citizens, who pressed their advantages continuously, with little real opposition from us beyond weak complaints. When we dared to protest through legal channels, the police came out against us with deadly effects. Besides everything else, White mobs destroyed the economic progress of Black enterprises, just like in the *Tulsa Race Massacre in 1921*.

I will never forget the rigid ground rules. Regardless of political beliefs or social standing, all Black people had to address White adults as mister, mistress, or miss and use sir and ma'am while speaking. In response, Whites openly referred to us as either *colored people* or *niggers*. When meeting Whites while walking, blacks had to give way, stepping off the sidewalks when necessary. The small minority of Whites who claimed to dislike these double standards appeared contented with pretexts that racism was essential for the economic survival of their race. However, inequality was so ingrained in all our lives that fear of competing with us wasn't a valid reason for the added effort to keep their "knee on the black man's neck."

As I mentioned, not all Whites practiced narrow-mindedness, but I didn't personally know anyone who openly objected to racist doings when I was a boy. No matter how other Whites may have felt, it was too dangerous for anyone to buck the prevailing mindsets tolerated across the country. It seemed nothing ever changed, so I took it all in stride.

By 1950, Fort Worth's population was 278,778. It ranked as the 38th largest municipality in the United States. Besides the *Bomber Plant* in the *White Settlement Addition*, the White economy flourished through oil exploration and development, the meatpacking industry, and other businesses peculiar to urban communities nationwide.

White men also hogged the good-paying unskilled work while in many of their modest households, their women stayed at home. They could afford a *colored house cleaner* and babysitter as symbols of their privileged lives. The *colored maid's* salaries were significantly lower than those for the White's menial labor because they were only allowed to pay *coloreds* a miniscule amount of the monies they made from the widespread prosperity.

The dark side of this growth resided in our city's *Jim Crow* mentality, which slighted most black citizens. Compounding the insult to well off Black people, the average White person viewed Black culture as monolithic. However, a clear distinction existed between the sophisticated middle-class Black Americans and my class of uneducated field workers.

On the bright side, a limited few relatively prosperous black people had gained footholds on the edge of the White middle-classed south-side residential district. This minority of black people: schoolteachers, doctors, and dentists, had degrees from southern black colleges (HBCUs). Some owned properties and small businesses that catered to a black clientele. Others on *The Hill* made good "*colored boy wages*" and were as refined as anyone anywhere.

Originally called *Chambers Hill* by the Whites in 1910, the centerpiece of the neighborhood was *Chambers Hill High School.* The large brick building became *I.M. Terrell High School for Colored Students* in about 1931 when the

Third Ward district shifted to predominantly black. As the district became populated with middle-class and poor black residents, they called it *Baptist Hill.* The area at *The Bottom of The Hill* on Oak Street, where I was raised, was a mess. The two and a half sloping blocks ran just north of East Lancaster Street. Most of this underlying section of *The Hill* was overgrown with a variety of gnarled trees, hearty bushes, and stubborn undergrowth. Surprisingly, good style houses were partially hidden down the trails that had street names. Overall, the roughness made it just the right environment for an adventurous lad like me. Along all these unpaved surfaces, lightning-fast lizards scampered. *A moment of fear as a blade of grass twitched and the odd snake retreated into the vegetation.* As I patrolled my domain, at about eight years old, I was an intrepid, barefooted jungle adventurer; eager eyed, with slingshot at hand. I was happy!

At that time, a ramshackle juke joint called the *Jitterbug Inn* sat at the lowest point of the rough and rocky intersection of Oak and Kennedy streets. To people outside, in the mini counter cultures that included the juke joint crowds, such dives were seen as hangouts for the worst people in our race. No self-respecting Black people came near the old tavern at the *Bottom of The Hill* for fear of being tainted. However, nothing went on behind closed doors at the *Jitterbug Inn* that was unheard-of by oppressed people. In all my years, I had never seen Daddy and Mama enter the door for any reason. Except from time to time, Mama sent scathing words inside to Grandma who had the corner near the juke box lit up with vulgar dance gyrations.

I didn't like the shootings and cuttings that were so common, but Fat Daddy and the hustlers had a twisted role model effect on me. Fat Daddy had my regard because like any hustler he was a con man. However, he treated Mama with respect, always speaking with cultural courtesy and passing a few minutes when she was on the front porch catching a breath of fresh air. As he approached our house, old fedora hat in hand, he stepped slower, as if Mama was the queen mother, and him, a nobleman of distant family relations. Of course, Mama had no hand in the street scene, but it may have been that Fat Daddy's respect came from a guilty feeling that something righteous saw him through Mama's eyes.

Although hard and muscular, he softened as he voiced the greeting, "Good *mornin'* Miss Sister, how are you today?

"Fine, Gene, a little touch of the asthma." she answered, unemotionally.

I noticed Mama did not inquire about his wellbeing. There was no overt tension between them, but it was obvious that Mama was highly displeased that Fat Daddy had sent his lady-friend scrambling through the night in tears over something unknown.

Seeing his attempts at civility were making no headway with Mama; and having put in his appearance, he made a long step for a man of his build. Then he floated away and disappeared silently without further comment.

Fat Daddy always called me by my given name, and I called him by his street name, cheerfully. although he did not seem to recall who some of the other urchins were. On that basis, he became the sort of person to be imitated by me. I didn't think of my respect for him as the obvious leader of his cronies, but I admired the respect everybody gave him. I should have dismissed him as a gangster as I did the others, but I saw him as a person of importance. In later years, I would be conflicted when I saw his true nature in action. I believe that this idolization, like the white's tolerance of the status quo, was responsible for my acceptance of wrongdoing by my neighbors as necessary to endure the trials we did. It would cause me to fall into a way of life that trapped me into backsliding into the wrong mindset.

Many street hustlers and prostitutes lived in the old shotgun houses around the three-way intersection. However, my family was one of the few exceptions that were forced to make our home there because we were large and poor.

On the upper part of *The Hill*, the city moved progressively along racial lines, but only by baby steps. They built the red-bricked *Ripley Arnold Place Housing Project* for White residents on the northwest side of town, and on the east side, its mirror image, the *Butler Place Housing Project,* for *colored people*. *The Projects* were more than my family could afford. Their leasing price varied from $9.00 - $15.00 a month, which was the affordable rent rate for poor Whites. Even so, we fell behind with the $5.00 a month rent for our wooden house. A few other civic amenities expected of a separate but equal social order existed here and there across the town. However, in the segregated societies in America, the Whites came up with a substantial share of monies made, which greatly increased their family wealth as they grew.

Photo for illustration only

DOWN IN THE SHOTGUN HOUSES WHERE I WAS RAISED, we struggled for a living all the years I lived there. Our part of town was like a dead end for the world's lowest of the lows, where food was always insufficient for our needs and sometimes wholly absent. The "Welfare" of the day deliberately slighted black communities. Every few years, when there was a considerable surplus of goods, government commodities such as dried kidney beans and powdered milk popped up briefly. Now and then, hard, tasteless pasta and a few other excess items also found their way to Oak Street. I don't remember getting them when we were hungry for long days at a time. Nevertheless, the smell of pinto beans and cornbread was as much a feature of the house as the steps leading to the front door.

Ours was typical of *shotgun* dwellings in the South. Nine people would eventually be packed into this unpainted little hovel: my father, mother, five boys, and two little girls. Despite the hardships, joyous laughter was no stranger to our home. From my earliest memories of the cramped living space there was still enough room for my older brother Ray, to pump the high tricycle with me standing on the rear pedestals. Valuing his privacy, Don, the third of the boys, was always hidden somewhere in the house. Asthmatic, little Robert Dewey was the crawling baby then. Each of the girls, Jacqueline (Jackie), bright little Genevieve (Jill), and my final sibling, Louis (Laddy Boy) arrived every two years. Although we lived on *Baptist Hill*, our family wasn't religious. Family Bibles with colored pictures and the works were in the house, but we never once went to church services as a family. So, serious prayer was absent from my upbringing, and God was a mystery to me as I grew into a man. He was not something I normally turned to in times of stress. However, I don't know when it started, but before I attended school, I talked my problems over with an imaginary inner confidant, whom I referred to as "Old Friend." Somewhere, as I left those early years, I grew out of such childish thoughts.

I also remember the house wasn't dilapidated, but patches of new wood showed its years of use. Two lateral inner walls with doors separated the place into three square-shaped ten-foot rooms with no closets. There was no insulation between the wallpaper-covered thin inside planks of the house and the exterior walls. The front room had a full-size bed and a wood-burning stove. The middle room also had a bed and connections for another stove (sometimes a kerosene heater), and the kitchen Range with an oven also burned wood. The stoves were basically cast-iron metal boxes that held fire and burned anyone who accidentally contacted them. Although the stoves kept us cozy during the day, when the heat died at night, the ones in the sleeping rooms barely kept us warm enough while we slept. And, on deep-wintry nights, the water bucket in the kitchen and the family slop jar froze. But quilts, blankets from the army and navy surplus stores, and used army footwear, fatigues, and field jackets made the detestable weather bearable.

In the seventh grade, some boys openly teased me about my brown Army Air Force bomber jacket and brogan boots. Like the would-be cowboys' western fantasy clothing, my garments revealed my secret dreams of joining the Air Force and flying the planes. For the moment, I could only do odd jobs and work in the fields alongside my family.

We didn't have electricity until 1952, but the light of family love never let the interior of the house seem dark and dank. My older brother, Ray, and

I swept and mopped; we fought over who would wash and who would dry the dishes but ultimately did them to Mama's satisfaction. I remember using the washboard on the back porch, and the nostril tingling smell of the big bars of laundry soap. I was so small that I couldn't wring the water from the blue jeans.

When I was in the sixth grade the skinny, stooped over, German-Jewish handyman from the landlord's office came and wired the ceiling of each room with a single hang-down light socket. His accent was so coarse we could hardly understand his rudimentary instructions on the use of electricity. He explained how to use the screw-in multi-plugged socket and light bulb receptacle without getting a shock.

In those days, the cramped kitchen was dominated by an icebox. It resembled a small refrigerator and substituted as our only appliance. The top compartment held a fifty-pound block of ice. Against the north wall was an ancient, once white cupboard. Plates and various drinking vessels were housed behind the glass panes of its doors. On the countertop sat a well-worn canister set containing flour, cornmeal, and sugar. The salt and pepper shakers rested on the oilcloth covered makeshift table in the corner. Beneath the furniture were small wood and coil spring mouse traps. The sight of these caused me to shudder, but I always looked, hoping I wouldn't see a dead mouse mangled up in them.

There was no hot water or sink in the kitchen, just a large wash-pan on a wooden table where a water pipe stuck through the back wall from the mainline, which also connected to the enclosed cast iron commode on the back porch. There was nothing in the toilet except the bare pot and an overhead tank with a pull chain for flushing. Sitting in it was misery in extreme temperatures! Bathtubs and showers existed for those living in *Butler Place* and the upper part of *The Hill.* We hung curtains in place of the missing middle room door for bathing, but the galvanized number 2 and 3 wash tubs were woefully inadequate for larger family members. *I escaped bathing as often as I could.* The wooden floor in 2202 Oak Street raised our standard of living above that of a teepee or a hut.

Infrequently changed linoleum carpets from the neighborhood furniture store overlaid the unfinished wood flooring throughout the house. Whenever Dad and his friend came home with a colorful new one rolled up in a paper tube, Mama's spirits were high as she oversaw the replacement. As she supervised their work, she had my dad rearrange the few pieces of actual furniture so that the end effect brought compliments from Mama's friends. I, too, liked the new colors and smell of the paint as I lay on them and read. Such were the infrequent pleasures of a poor household in the shotgun homes.

Despite the negative aspects of ghetto living, from the earliest, I remember moments of being a happy boy lying on my sleeping pallet, comforted by a child's innocent thoughts. I recall feeling proud to live in the "Biggest state of the biggest [Richest, I fantasized], country on Earth." I did not know how underprivileged I was and that I lived as the disdained of the world lived. When the term Texan is used, the image of a black person rarely comes to mind. Yet, it delighted me I had some part in Texas, and for the time, the childlike understanding of the young shielded me from the pain of the darkness beyond the glow of our kerosene lamps.

In the middle room, under Pop's bed, I stashed a cardboard box of various reading materials. The printed words on the pages became easily understood by my nine-year-old mind. They did not pass through my thoughts without a child's inescapable "Why?" to all that needed clarification. "Why" was a cry for information to broaden my understanding. I fantasized a lot, not realizing that my imaginings were a coping mechanism that allowed me to escape the harsh oppression by the dominant society. There, too, were jabs of You're strange! from my black friends who also acted in more real-world fashion. My make-believe scenarios were so real to me I did not long for many of the material objects segregation kept just beyond the reach of my peers. They could not acquire the new cars, motorcycles, and a myriad of things that the Whites owned matter-of-factly. So, my friends' wants were never satisfied, but my illusions were always fulfilled in the very way that satisfied my soul.

Pages from the Family Album

I was somewhat bullheaded when I was about nine years old! Although I was bashful around people I didn't know well, I was downright mouthy when dealing with family and friends. My brothers and sisters were obedient and well-behaved children. But I was the final authority on everything with everybody except Mama.

My father, Mr. Van Buren McKellar Sr., was referred to by our neighbors as Mr. Van. He was a light brown complexioned man at forty-five, just under six feet tall and a little less than two hundred pounds. His graying temples revealed he had reached a softened maturity. Pop, as I sometimes called him, occasionally drank bourbon whiskey. But he was not a violent man and, like Mama, highly respected by all.

Pop's daily wear consisted of light brown khaki work pants and old worn-out brown shoes. However, when he was working, and the times were good he jumped sharp on Saturday after payday. Then, his McKellar men's rugged handsomeness shined when he donned one of his two dress suits, put on his highly polished oxford shoes, and mouthed his huge *John Ruskin* cigar. Neither Mama nor I lavished upon him the compliments he looked for as he straightened his tie before the big mirror on the dresser in the middle room. Mama, without exception, threatened him concerning "High yellow women," and I followed him outside and hurled insults at him as he opened the door of his old green *Hudson Super Six*. I wasn't miffed because he was leaving, like Mama was. I was angry because he didn't take me with him to his penny poker game with the boys from the job. As a child, I couldn't understand why my older brother, Ray, would always rough me up whenever he could get away with it. I know now it was because of my closeness with Pop. Ray always sat next to Pop, whom he called Daddy, when we jumped into the company's stake body Ford truck. He honored his father with a son's respect, which Pop returned to his firstborn son. Perhaps Pop saw me as a reincarnation of himself, as he was before he settled down. Mama saw it too and frequently urged Pop to take a stronger hand when dealing with me. But he was not a disciplinarian of his children. Neither Pop nor she showed any favoritism except for the baby, whomever that was at the time. But Pop and I spoke of dreams and adventure as if I were an old buddy. From these stories, I saw in Pop the spirit of the heroes in my books, although accounting for his fifth-grade education and present circumstances. Before meeting Mama, Pop had been a traveler and had seen many things. I had questions, and he had explanations, that's all [At least that's the way I saw it].

Mama, Mrs. Geneva McKellar, a well-rounded, deep brown-skinned, no-nonsense lady, was called *Little Sister* by her close friends. She was twenty-seven years old then and after her own fashion, more resolute than I was. No one doubted she ran a tight ship, where any sign of arguments or disrespect from anyone received a swift rebuke from the captain. So, when we boys had scores to settle, it was out somewhere where Mama didn't get word of it.

Naturally, Mama administered one hundred percent of the capital punishment in the family. Mama's strict hand supplied the impetus for me to find [later] within me the ability to respect all people. It wasn't only because of the fear of a painful lick, although not a professing Christian at the time, Mama was a splendid example of true character in action. I knew that the things she instilled in me were important, regardless of how I also saw the way others outside our family behaved.

When Mama wasn't laying down the law to me, she was a Mother Hen to the neighborhood girls (my grandma included) that hung out at the *Jitterbug Inn.* The juke joint sat diagonally across the street from our house. These fascinating women hung out with Grandma, who was older, but Mama, who neither drank nor smoked, was the cooler head. Perhaps, because Mama took no part in their doings, she represented an anchor of respectability they turned to when the seas of life were stormy.

[I remember them as mostly gayly painted, fun filled girls who loved to tease me, saying that I had old folks' sense, and that because of my many explanations I was going to be a con man when I grew up.]

We children could not have wanted better parents, and they were thrilled enough with us to boast of our good individual characteristics. If there was a contradiction to this assessment, it was me, bumping heads with Mama from time to time.

Whenever Mama caught me overstepping the line, my father would look down at me, shake his head slowly, and say disapprovingly, "Now, BOY, you *knowed* better than that."

He gave me the cold shoulder for a bit. Knowing I had disappointed, my pop was worse than the few little licks Mama gave me. To be sure, I still had my naughty moments and a bit of a temper, but the harmful antics of my bullying neighbors repulsed me as much as the ones by the Whites did. Overall, I grew up well-mannered of my own free will. Many people found this a weakness, but it became a great power that opened doors. Had it not been for the ever-present food insecurity and Mama's bouts with chronic asthma, our family would have been happier, even with the demanding times.

WHILE NOT A GIANT AMONG METROPOLITAN CITIES, Fort Worth still had much for a tween to experience. My wonderful world unfolded as fast as I could grasp the reality of the things in it. I grew up in an old western town where most of the Whites desperately clung to a cowboy image. Many businesses, private properties, parks, and other public places bore a Wild West motif or name. Fort Worth was renowned as *The Queen of the Prairies* and said to be *Where the West begins.* Whether actual wranglers or only posers, the White men dressed in blue jeans, cowboy boots, and wide-brim hats. We all did now and then, but for the Whites, it was the uniform of the day. Their everyday casual wear and work clothes gave them the appearance of ranch hands. They also cut their formal attire in the style of rich stockmen. Pretentious cowgirls of the era sported their frilly leather jackets, wearing tight pants, wide skirts, and slightly smaller cowboy hats. Last, ornate boots rounded out their costumes. This horse opera extended to luxury cars decked out with long cow horns across the hoods.

Many working cowhands who made their *Home on the Range*, punching cows around Fort Worth and the West, have always been black. In fact, they were as much a part of actual history as the renowned *Buffalo Soldiers*, like my maternal great-grandfather. My daughter, Vanda McKellar, discovered that after retiring from the *10th Calvary* for medical reasons in 1877. Robert (Bob) Hopkins worked for the *McFarlin Cattle Ranch* in Aledo, a beef Producing community south of town, until he passed away in 1926. But there was no acknowledging these things by *Drug-store cowboys*, even though actual White cowboys who worked side by side with Black ones knew better.

These phony types still deny that bit of *Black History* today, objecting loudly:

"There ain't no nigger cowboys!"

It was as if they feared acknowledging Black people were competent cowhands would consign them to some less than near-Negro status to fade away out in the back pasture. To their credit, they tried to fight off extinction, but not against the approach of civilization, which was the root of the entire ruckus. Misguidedly, they were hostile to the people at the bottom, wide-eyed people like me.

Most of the rough and rugged cowboy craziness happened across town in the *Stockyards District* on North Main Street. However, up in the eastside business section of "*Old Cowtown*," another AKA for Fort Worth, there were a few honky-tonks with flashing neon lights, where shootings were common and shootouts occasional.

One day I was walking home from *Brandon's Grocery Store* on East Lancaster Street. My eleven-year-old bare feet were hot against the sidewalk. I was carrying a small rolled-up cotton rope in my hand. When I was just outside the entrance of a Bar nothing seemed suspicious or kicked my senses into high alert. I only heard the country jukebox, subdued voices, and smelled the funky odor of cigarettes and beer. That's when the Whites played a dirty trick on me.

A tall, sly looking, cowboy-type character leaned against the inside of the door. The color of his face blended with the red flowers printed on his cream-colored shirt.

Grinning, his high-pitched western drawl distinct from the background noise; he extended his hand, "Hey kid, you want this hanger to put *cher'* rope on?"

Stepping slower, I considered the several reasons he said I might need the coat hanger.

I listened and shook my head "No" each time, then finally. "No, thank you, Sir," I replied courteously and walked on past him.

He leaned further out of the doorway and insisted firmly. "*Cum* on back here and *git* this hanger!"

The eyes on his smug face gleaming as he extended the wire toward me.

A White man insisted; I had to obey. I came back and grasped the hanger. Instantly, I was jolted by enough electricity to cause me to fall against a parked car. A blue aura enveloped me as the current passed through my slender young body. As the pain subsided, I heard several voices from the room roaring with laughter.

They defiled me with this cowardly act against a helpless child. I did not know if I would be all right. I couldn't tell my dad because he would have to come up and do something about an insult of this magnitude to his family. Although he was a mild-mannered man, he would walk right up to the forbidden front door and challenge them. More than a few heated arguments between black people outside the *Jitterbug Inn* at the *Bottom of The Hill* erupted into gunfights. So, I knew confronting these Whites, who could not tolerate a black man speaking to them on equal terms, meant war.

In my mind, I could see Pop standing, knees bent, leaning forward, his craggy face upset, his khaki work pants starched and ironed as if dressed up for the occasion. His big apple cap tipped slightly upward in the front, tragically shooting it out with them in their skinny britches and ten-gallon cowboy hats. Even though I imagined the loud bark of his old *Iver Johnson Owl Head 38 Revolver,* he would be in a no-win situation against a room full of *Colts* and *45 Smith & Wesson handguns.* So, on the way home, I quickly put the thought away. but the evil deed festered inside me!

Credit: istock.com/Magnilion

THE *NINETEENTH OF JUNE* WAS AN INFORMAL Black peoples' holiday that celebrated the 1865 release from enslavement of African Americans wrongly detained (Ostensibly, so they could get one last crop in). *Juneteenth* was a celebration among Texas Black citizens, but as far as Texas Whites were concerned, it was a farce. They mockingly referred to it as "*Nigger Day.*" They joked about Black people's ravenous craving for *red soda water*, watermelon, and fried chicken. Some White employers took perverse pleasure in refusing to give Black employees the day off, even without compensation. But we Black youths were delighted when the gates of *Forest Park Zoo* swung open on the long-awaited morning. We flew to our favorite amusement rides. In the evening, like good little *colored folks*, we left when ordered out by the attendants. We were saddened that the magic moments had vanished but vowed to return next year on *Juneteenth*.

The rest of the year, whenever we drove by the enormous city park, we heard the White children's shrieks and laughter coming from the amusement rides. We imagined their joy as they ran to the entrance gates but felt only the slap in the face of exclusion. Rolling on, we glimpsed enormous African animals through the shrubs and surrounding fences.

Whenever we caught sight of any creature, the car would explode with, "Wow, did you see that?"

"Boy, I wish we could go in." "Why can't we go in?"

My dad's only explanation was, "The White folks—won't let us."

I would then tell what I presumed the creatures we saw were.

Prohibiting our admittance into the park denied us access to symbolic ties to our ancestral home. Such fleeting looks as we sped by only sowed into my fertile young mind the seeds of imperfect dreams. The beasts in my African fantasies became as ludicrous as my movie idols. When we Black children went to the *Ritz Theater* on Saturdays, we cheered as Tarzan, or some "Great White hunter" rescued poaching ivory traders from the clutches of allegedly savage African peoples who were only defending their homeland from robbers.

The most frustrating, to me, thing about these once-a-year colored people's days was that we could only visit the downtown *Fort Worth Public Library* annually. And not as patrons, then. I have never forgotten the time my class toured the forbidden library when I attended *Gay Street Elementary School.* Since it was an important event for Black students of a specific grade, fifth, I think now. We practiced for the upcoming field trip.

Our principal, Mrs. Hamilton, an indomitable woman, was middle-aged, and loved by us all. Her heart was as big as the lime green *Buick DynaFlo* she parked in front of the 19th Street entrance. She gave us a long talk about being on our best conduct, because we knew the Whites would watch us! Then, Whites judged all *colored people* by their perceived negative actions of any within the Black race; sadly, we accepted their presumptions. However, this was only outward condemnation; internalization severely damaged our amenable young minds.

When rationalized, the final accusation was, "You coloreds are not good enough to have these things that we show you, but we Whites are."

Also affected by the negativity, I reasoned, "Since I knew how to behave, my less educated, crudely speaking Black relatives and friends must be the offenders." I accepted the devious message as articulated because I was disappointed that I couldn't peruse the books. In later years, when used against me in another context, I would still struggle with the underpinnings of racial self-hatred.

The principal went down a lengthy list of things expected of us and things forbidden.

Calling out particular boys as she said sternly, "Gilbert, be sure and wear clean clothes." "Alfred, Thomas, if I have to so much as look at you, I'm going to take you to the book room when we get back." That stiffened my spine because I had gotten the book room treatment with other boys for talking in my fourth-grade class. However, her spanking wasn't that hard and was over quickly.

The principal picked girls and boys to ask questions about the library's history but wagged her finger at those who were to say nothing during the trip. She didn't assign me anything to do, which was alright with me, but I was eager to look at the library's stash of books.

A little later, an off-duty city bus arrived at the Water Street entrance to *Gay Street Elementary.* The White driver and Mrs. Hamilton spoke quickly, and we packed in, girls seated first. Some boys and I stood in the aisles while holding the bars to the back of the seat.

When we were downtown, we gathered at the bottom of the steps and our guide came out and gave us a welcome speech and some historical facts about the *Fort Worth Public Library.* I have never forgotten how the tone of that speech impressed me that we were outside guests. However, I listened for anything that would allow me to read this treasure trove of books but didn't hear it. She said nothing that would lead me to believe we had any visiting rights to the library. Our escort lectured us on library use. Uselessly, we learned about the Dewey Decimal Classification System and used the microfiche viewer to find other media. She said schools could use the system to order books, but I needed to browse.

City leaders' twisted rationale for banning Black people from the accumulated knowledge was not a public subject. Unfortunately, the downtown library was my only path to costly reference volumes and classical books mentioned in other readings. Black schools in the district were issued new hardcover class books infrequently. I remember *Gay Street* getting the marked-up, hand-me-down books from the White schools. It was something about justifying the expenditure. In societies divided along racial lines, testing biased in favor of White students with the new materials skewed the results of such testing to their credit. These tests supplied sham evidence that Black students trailed White ones. All this was not a mistake that could be credited to innocent reasoning.

The White community knew the pain they caused us! They knew we, like them and all humanity, suffer from ill-usage, just as their ancestors agonized under the heel of conquering empires from the early centuries of the first millennium. During World War II, American Whites died in Europe, fighting to set other White nations free from the very oppression they visited upon Black people here. Since they fought for the high-minded ideals handed down in *The Constitution of the United States,* racism clearly must be the reason for denying the same to Black people. Yet, they persisted in their cruelty and created for all children a heritage that must eventually play out in fire on future city streets. I know they knew better because I read it in the marvelous old books they wrote.

It would be years before the Black churches and college students would move to the forefront of the fight for actual equal status. During these trials, particular White people, (Not a systemic effort) like the abolitionists during slavery, yielded to their higher values, losing their lives in defense of their noble convictions.

Chapter 2:
Summertime Days

Credit: istock.com/Gorodenkoff

Although the White communities had the best of tangible things, I found no reason to envy them. I revered the heroes and martyrs who came to life in my stack of old books. My critical young mind was like *Socrates*, the ancient Greek truth seeker. I would not reconcile their illogical justification for their shortcomings with the thinking of those I respected as actual people of wisdom.

I also avoided my quick-fisted peers, who refused to accept me on a live-and-let-live basis. So many people lived heartlessly. Violence in adult society trickled down to the children. I couldn't completely evade fights and ended up in a couple of unforgettable scrapes. In the first one, I was punched in the nose, which swelled noticeably. I didn't win, but I did all right. A black eye in a later scuffle caused a flurry of awkward talk and uncomfortable questions for weeks. To be a good brawler, you must take punches, which, to me, is stupid. I did not like the pain! Although I could be pushed into a scrap because there were limits to what my pride would take, I realized fighting was not for me. Wisely, I shied away from the manly art of fisticuffs as much as possible.

Keeping above the fray, I was prone to reading and seclusion but not isolated or low-spirited. When I was not working, my small circle of less quarrelsome friends and I lived adventurous lives. At twelve, I was slender, a little less than five feet tall, and had a light brown skin tone underneath my dark seasonal tan. A soft blue ring blended with my brown eyes, but it was not as noticeable as it is now. In my pockets were a magnifying glass, a few marbles, a scout knife, and the junk of the day. Every day, I went barefoot and wore blue jeans over white briefs. Occasionally, I wore a polo shirt and tennis shoes. My brothers and the other boys dressed similarly.

Baptist Hill was the stomping ground for the kids living in the shotgun houses. It also included the *Ritz Theater* in the eastern downtown part of the city, near the *Santa Fe* railroad tracks, that separated the commercial district from us. It was wise then to go in groups when we ventured beyond our neighborhood, so we traveled five or ten at a time accompanied by four or five dogs. They were not vicious dogs; to be sure, some of them would bite on cue, just as the tougher boys would fight when provoked. These were *good ol' summertime dogs*! Undeterred by the high humidity and the summer sun, the canine crew was as full of spirit and adventure as we were. Shag was a yard dog but ran with the pack whenever he was off the rope. He was a mixed Collie, the big dog, and like his master, Rat, (The little guy of the band), fancied himself the alpha of the gang. The other assorted mutts, like the two-legged members of the pack, changed as seasons passed. I didn't own a dog myself, but sometimes my canine companion was a little black, short-legged ball of fur, who struggled to keep up with me. This was Scotty, who came along for the good times. We ran everywhere, talking smack, dogs barking, our bald heads glistening with sweat in the oppressive heat.

Just south of the *Ritz Theater* was the *Jones Street Produce Market* (a large farmers' market), where we rummaged through the waste bins out back, looking for fruits that were too ripe to be sold but good enough for us. However, it was no less hazardous snitching thrown away bananas, peaches, and plums from the trash cans than it was sneaking over the vigilant-eyed fruit grower's fences out in the country. In either case, we ended up running with the goods.

When the thermometer climbed above 100 degrees Fahrenheit, it grew too hot in the house. So, I put away my books and toy airplanes and headed out with the bunch to *Sycamore Creek*, which flowed out of the White districts into a wooded area less than two miles east of where we lived. Looking down from the underbrush across from *I.M. Terrell High School*, two scraggly green lines in the distance marked the minor tributary's East and West boundaries as it wandered northward. At the end of its journey, it surged from a patch of thick reeds to join the West Fork of the Trinity River as it turned eastward to meet the Elm Fork at Dallas. Where it went after it left Dallas was a mystery to me. The kids used a steep secret trail behind the school on Chambers Street to get there. The popular pathway lay further southward near the bridge at the bottom of East Lancaster Street, where the old trees along the banks were thickest and the water deepest.

Sometimes I carried my single-shot 22-caliber rifle and hunted small game. Moving stealthily through the trees and bushes along the banks, I pretended I was in Africa, carrying an enormous gun while stalking gigantic prey I saw in my books that lived eras before the coming of man. Truthfully, I didn't shoot rabbits or any other living thing when I was alone. I only watched them scamper about.

The slow-flowing *Sickimo*, as we called it, was the neighborhood kid's favorite hangout. We made rafts that came apart or sank as often as they floated. Boys and some girls skinny-dipped and carried on, as did the free-spirited White youths depicted in stories of the South. However, instead of a backdrop of childhood freedom, free from harm, the *racial caste system*, by its nature, wove bias threads through the tapestry of the Black characters' lives.

Hallowed were the carefree summertime days. By the time I arrived at my thirteenth year, I was unstoppable in the sunshine; things fell into place by chance. I didn't have money in my pockets all the time, but I earned sufficient cash to buy used books and enough candy to develop cavities. Roaming around, I met the very people I needed to achieve my projects. Cleanup and lawn mowing jobs were available for the asking.

One morning, while dressed for work in a buttoned-up shirt and old tennis shoes, I confidently rang the front doorbell of a White person's house on the South Side: my straw hat in my hand.

A stern face came to the door. "Yes, boy, what do you want?"

"Excuse me, ma'am," I piped up politely, in the voice to quell any fears she may have had of being close to a *colored boy*, "Would you like for me to cut your yard, or do this or that?"

"Well—come on to the back door," she responded, her face still frowning.

When she appeared at the side door near the fence, where the dog snuffled under the planking, she looked different. This time, she smiled courteously, unlatched the yard gate, and gave me instructions while introducing me to her canine friend, who still had reservations about me. *Old Butch* knew me; he had seen me through the cracks in the alley fence. He usually managed a few threatening barks, along with the other yard dogs, each time I walked by with some noisy contraption. However, *Butch* was no pup. He quickly lost interest and turned away to lie near his doghouse to let the heat from the sun soothe the arthritis locked in his bones.

I stood under the eaves of the house, and surveyed the backyard, my left arm resting on my hip and the right at my side, as I formed an image of the finished work. As I contemplated the task, I felt taller than when hanging with the guys. Basically, it was a simple clean-up job, which had become nightmarish for an ultra-tidy older white-collar couple. They kept up with most of *Butch's* droppings, but to them, the rest of the backyard was in shambles. I mentally sectioned the work into smaller bits and then fitted them into one big project. I thought first to sweep out the old shed, put away various things lying around, and stack away bits of lumber. As I took on the duty, a good feeling spurred me on.

Early on, *Butch* and I saw Mrs. Taylor peek from the rear window twice. He stood erect each time to show he was on the job watching me, and I stayed on course. She may have had second thoughts and wondered if the enormity of the tasks was too much for a boy my age. But it was not, and I was confident enough to expect compliments. After that, I didn't see the curtains move again. Just past mid-afternoon, I was singing softly as I wielded the yard broom rhythmically. Gradually, the serenity of the old place came back. It was gratifying to do a job well. The work Mrs. Taylor wanted was easy for a boy, tempered by hard work in the fields. Finally, I cleaned and set up the unused yard furniture, reclaiming a bit of charm that had gone missing for a few years.

I called her around five o'clock, when I finished and Mrs. Taylor fairly bolted out the back door, looking officious as she inspected everything. She did a poor job of containing her excitement over how pleased she was. Being intimate with a Negro in the South was unthinkable. When we settled-up after my tasks, my employer and I addressed each other more familiarly. Instead of "boy" and "Ma'am," it was now Van and Mrs. Taylor. It was not the same closeness I felt with elderly Black women I worked for, but it was not a strained feeling either.

She gave me fifty cents extra for doing a "fine job" and food treats in a bag. Ironically, if I had been a White boy the same age, performing the exact level of work for her, Mrs. Taylor could have been openly pleased that I had such a "Good Christian Work Ethic." She could have given me a dollar more, served me milk and cookies at her dining table, and bragged to her friends about me. However, for Whites, belief in the doctrine of *the natural order of things* was the order of the day. She could ascribe no such work ethic to, as it was commonly thought, an inferior child. How sad that this kindly older woman was forced by a stupid convention to be outwardly gruff toward Black people. Upon seeing that I had followed her instructions to the letter, she could only show her approval of me offhand. Mrs. Taylor's behavior toward me revealed she was delighted with my work.

But her cultural conventions would only allow her to tell her friends, "Girls, I have found me a *good little nigger* now."

All that aside, I had a few dollars and was ready for fun.

WHITES OPPRESSED BLACKS, AND BLACKS OPPRESSED OTHER BLACKS in a way that gave credence to the vulgar adage that explains why those at the Bottom of The Hill are in deep trouble. Then, as now, anyone could kill an underprivileged Black person with near impunity. These *Misdemeanor Murders* carried a $200.00 fine, and a suspended sentence. As a young child, I saw too many killings.

Late one summer night, as I slept on our high front porch, I awakened to angry voices coming up from the street below. The door of the *Jitterbug Inn* was closed, so the box thumped at a lower volume and did not drown out the argument.

I recognized the voice of Fat Daddy growling, "You got the rod, man; gimme the rod, man."

This time, his soft but vulgar voice was chilling. It sounded so different from when they gave the usual beatings over the Girls, a street corner dice game, or any pretext for thrashing unfortunate outsiders.

I peeked through the planks bordering the porch to the shadowy scene below and saw the short stout figure that was Fat Daddy, and three other street hustlers holding Mr. Otis, a man I knew, by both arms. Silky, another frequent visitor to our house, handed Fat Daddy a huge pistol.

With mounting trepidation, it came to me why Mama and her friends whispered, "You never wanted to cross that big fat gangster."

Then, as if pronouncing the sins of the world upon him, they all cursed Mr. Otis loudly with final damnation, "You dirty mother so and so," and "You're a no-good son of a so-and-so!"

A tall lanky shape floated out of the other members in the group and gave Fat Daddy a pillow, which he shoved against Mr. Otis's stomach and fired once. The pillow didn't mute the pop of the big gun; the sound reverberated loudly.

No doubt many other eyes saw what was happening, but no lights in the houses came on. Mr. Otis's body slumped slowly down. As they dragged him over to the bed of a pickup truck, my spirit, in pain from his bloodied wound, sank with him. It was as if I, too, died at that moment!

The next day, the Cops found the dead man less than a quarter of a mile from our house in a foul stream called *the greasy branch.* As the word of the shooting went around the neighborhood, it was no secret to us who the killers were, but like Mr. Otis, the deed died there. The police asked questions but didn't investigate further. A murdered insignificant Black man was just another matter that the police never brought before a judge.

I moped about for a while but found no inner answer to "Why Mr. Otis?" that offered a rationale for his murder. The thought of a dope deal gone bad never entered my mind. There were no religious or psychological counselors to help me deal with the grief; I agonized over these things alone.

Crimes against most Blacks were often ignored by the courts. Our self-esteem was harmed in ways not wholly understood. Being undervalued by the legal system confused many of my friends and neighbors. We behaved as though we were responsible for our inability to mesh with the contemptuous society around us. Confused about our predicament, we acted as if we didn't deserve the fundamental rights of human beings, presumably because we were children and grandchildren of enslaved people. We had to know better but feebly accepted the White's open allegations: we were nothing but *niggers.* In ignorance, we called ourselves and each other *niggers.* However, unlike today's affectionate word, *Niggas*, it was not from the dignity of a people of presidential stock but from shame. Lacking few avenues for our pent-up energies because of prejudices galore, we foundered, drank, fought, picked cotton, and suffered.

Dear old Golden Rule Days

My journey continued; it became more philosophical than physical, an escape route from the poverty of the mind. From the stories I read in the encyclopedias and the Bible, I saw throughout history that the nature of men to make war upon other men was a common occurrence. Therefore, subjugation did not cause me to feel my people alone were beneath all humanity. I read about many heroes, particularly young boys, who overcame obstacles while under an enemy. The typical self-loathing that downtrodden people sink into while under persecution did not taint me. I identified with the great deeds I read. I found the freedom to engage in a life of discovery.

Because my family was needy, I wanted more and better food, clothes, and shelter. However, I didn't accept life as a struggle to escape being a *Negro*, or ache to move from dismal surroundings to an allegedly better way of life on the White side of town. I never believed that being among those who had things without effort or even to have them effortlessly would satisfy my developing mind.

Basking in privilege seemed deteriorating, doing little to help the heart. Moving into adolescence, as an active kid, only planning and achieving could satisfy my young yearnings. In my tween years, I physically conquered the world around me. I climbed the highest trees, sprang across trenches, and vaulted rock to stone across waterways. I traveled by myself and took in the wonders beyond the shabbiness of *The Hill.* Life was much too exciting to boast about one's personal possessions, which I didn't care that I didn't have. I was so happy that my poverty never lingered in my thoughts. It was time to explore, and I had sturdy legs and two sharp eyes to unravel new mysteries.

I was a dreamer, to whom adversities were but temporary annoyances along the road to actualization; the thought of what could be, became a greater reality than the discomforts of my existing situation. Through the years, I learned that no matter who you are, each vision comes packaged with the certainty that the dream is within your reach.

All the same, I performed less than required in school with English, Arithmetic, and History. I only received Cs and Ds on my report card, but I was a whiz at taking the yearly knowledge comprehension tests. Except for one girl in my class (Dorothy Napoleon), whose results bested mine, my scores were considerably above the rest of the students, outperforming the straight "A" scholars. I could not account for the enigma then, but it delighted me.

The achievement tests probably were a factor in me not becoming a total washout over low grades. Still, they couldn't save me from the whipping that came with not turning in homework or when the teacher felt students weren't making the required effort. Then, the *rod of correction* became the best learning aid. I received a most unforgettable application by the strap at *Gay Street Elementary* in sixth grade. It was a time when I joined my class in the second semester after the cotton season. I wore new clothes, had a jingle in my pockets, had a bald haircut with bangs, and, though bashful, was popular with the girls.

Before class, some proper talking, hip-dressing ones from The Projects mockingly teased me, chiding in a lighthearted manner: "Van McKellar, you big round head!"

When I didn't respond quick enough, they made a down-turned smile and quipped: "*Mmm*, you're so shy."

I would grin and mutter something silly back. The class howled at the high *jinx*.

During the lesson, the teacher, a highly respected Black man, called me up to the blackboard to point out the "verb," or "action word," as he called it, in the sentence, "The steamboat puffed gaily down the river." The class had covered verbs earlier, but I had not caught up to them.

He lost his patience as I kept guessing incorrectly! "What is the action word, Mr. McKellar?" he demanded sternly.

I knew what was coming and showed signs of fear before the class. "I don't know," I said.

"Well, you ought to know, sir," he replied, moving over to his desk and opening the top drawer. "Didn't you work on your assignment?"

"I did, but I didn't understand it."

I trembled as I saw the doubled-up brown belt in his hand! As the first lick came, I turned back to the blackboard. WHACK! Each time he raised the strap high momentarily, then swung it swiftly down and around in an arching motion that brought forth shock, shame, and burning, searing pain to my buttocks. (The most brutal anyone had ever hit me as chastisement.)

"What did the steamboat do, McKellar?" his voice rising higher. He immediately countered each wrong guess with the accursed phrase: "What did the steamboat do, McKellar?"

And another hard lick from the Professor, as everyone affectionately called him.

Embarrassed, I tried to keep my face on the blackboard as I continued answering with phrases instead of just one word. After an eternity of [actually, five or six] more punishing strikes from the belt, I cried piercingly, and he stopped. He seemed satisfied he had broken me before the class. I realized I would leave school; I just didn't know how to do it because it would break Mama's heart when I did.

Humiliated because I couldn't do the class work, I vowed to leave somehow. For being whipped and embarrassed before the other students, I dreamed darkly of retaliation for years. I have forgiven him now, but his "sin is ever before me."

After that, I lost interest in how the teachers presented the information and the techniques taught to make sense of it. I continued learning in my own way. The teachers were competent, and the other children understood satisfactorily, but I grasped the things I read outside of the class better. This does not mean I became some child prodigy, jam-packed with the buffet of cultural history, which I am quick to spout-out today, but I burned to know what made a thing what it was. I lay amid my own books and took my time putting it all together. When one writer was unclear, I turned to others. I would not leave the object of my interest partially understood. It was essential to my grasping of the workings of anything that I understood how it was originally conceived. In my mind, the scenarios shifted from reading words on a page to hearing what the writers revealed to me directly. As that ability grew, I saw clues to what I wanted to know in similar circumstances everywhere. Because I was mechanically inclined, my rocky path, interspersed with many erratic experiences on the way to inner fulfillment, was smoother.

AS A YOUNG TEEN, I DELIVERED PAPERS for Fort Worth's two leading newspapers before and after school. My customers on *The Hill* included the businesses on East Lancaster Street, the city bus depot, and other shops in the industrial district on Pine Street. The people in the front offices were decent enough when I brought the paper through the back entrance, referring to me as a *colored boy*. I wasn't offended. The White workers in the shops were the problem.

Racism of the period brought out rank silliness in White men. The moment they saw me come in, the showoffs grinned and danced around awkwardly while pretending to talk like a Black person. After I left the front, they were waiting to taunt the little, *nosey nigger boy*. To call me nosey was an exaggeration; I did glance around when I came through the back to bring the papers. I wanted them to tell me about the various machines and what they did, but that didn't happen. Often, their teasing was dangerous. They threw objects at me when I left and shouted racial insults.

Although they didn't call me *nigger* directly all the time, they did it slyly when they made stupid inquiries like, "How-*cum niggers* love watermelon so much, boy?"

Like the jokes of failed old comedians, "They had a million of-*um*." They would feel my head, tell me that kinky (as they called it) hair was bad hair, and rub my brown skin to see if the black would come off.

Something sinister was rooted in this bullying; perhaps it was fear of competing with Black men equally. These southern Whites, who were around us all the time, knew from experience that we could do any job they could do. They promoted the lie that we were too ignorant for anything but the most menial "*colored boy work*." However, they knew my inquisitive nature was on point, but they quibbled rather than respond truthfully to my questions. On a level beyond the racial cracks, their rejection of me as a human being offended me darkly. They could tell by my keen interest in machines that I could understand an exact explanation. If they had believed I could not comprehend such information, they would have boasted about their superior ability to appear more intelligent than they were. But they didn't; they either mocked me or changed the subject. I dared not respond to them as I did to someone my age, hurling insults and racial slurs to match theirs; they were adults, and I would lose my paper carrier job.

Admittedly, not the purest of motives, but I decided I would turn the tables on people like them. From then on, when I tackled the most complex jobs, like my reading habits, I made sure that I abandoned no project; I left no job unfinished. Whatever task I put my heart to, my hand accomplished. Throughout my life, I proudly referred to myself as a self-educated man. I found reasonable success without a formal education, but it always troubled me that I had failed at school.

Chapter 3: Crumbs from the Rich Man's Table

Mama had an elderly aunt who was "in service" to a judge and his family on the lower south side of Fort Worth. To be in service meant she lived in a tiny [one-room] apartment behind their four-bedroom house. They paid her only a little money. While not as wealthy as one in a similar station today, this family was rich compared to us. My great-aunt was available twenty-four hours a day. Her duties mirrored those of the *lovable old plantation house nigger* who served in many roles. She showed her best behavior as she cleaned, washed, cooked, and did other chores they wanted of her. Now and then, she intercepted a box of trash-bound junk and brought it to us. When she came by with the assorted rubbish, she praised the judge's family in such a way as to let us know how pitiful she thought we were compared to her "*White folks*." She scolded us and told us in foul language that we were low-class.

Now that she was back in the slums and away from her "*White woman's*" eyes, she let her hair down. She was tall and heavyset, marked not only by her graying hair but her face bore the weight of the hard years. By the time she had finished distributing frayed items from the near-useless care package, she was halfway through the half-pint bottle drawn from her oversized purse. The old woman was born in the late 1800s to formerly enslaved parents. Possessing no education to speak of, she had survived the tumultuous years through deviousness and prostitution. Time eventually turned against her; now, she served the judge's family for what amounted to food and shelter for many years. She perceived their wealth and power and how they kept the law and moved freely, without restriction. She spoke glowingly of them, not understanding that the same rules that made the Whites prosperous were rigged to keep minority races outlawed and wretched. Many Black people of the time misunderstood the dual standards in the legal system. They believed our punishment was justified when we broke unjust laws, such as sitting in the wrong public place or stealing a can of food. Although she pointed her finger at us then, I now know that it was her own conflicted sense of self-worth, commonplace on *The Hill* but despised by the duplicitous White society in which she was forced to live, that she crucified in alcohol.

She rose to her feet and began dancing awkwardly without music and reminiscing about former good times. Her mood grew sadder as the gin worked its ill effect on her. But she stood erect, wrapped her old, hand-me-down fox fur around her neck, and lectured us kids on the facts of life. We all giggled, but I listened closely, hoping to learn something to improve my meager knowledge about the mysteries of sex. Mama stopped her when the language became too vulgar, and she slept it off on the full-size bed. Aunt Australia was funny then. But in the coming years, I also would fall into an occasional drunken stupor, trying to ease the strain of living as an ideal Black person. Sadly, the old housemaid's belief that we would never amount to anything was commonly in evidence among people of both the Black and the White races. While no legitimate studies proved Whites were unequivocally superior to us, many Blacks and Whites clung to this belief as if it were an unwritten truth.

Another likely source of this flawed thinking lay in the belief that people who did not speak proper English lacked the mental power of White people. Our English was as varied from American Whites as theirs was from British English. Although the poor Whites around us spoke crude southern-affected English, Black men with only a slight education often looked to them for the last word on any matter. Not all Black people dismissed their intellect in the face of the dominant tongue, but too many did and far too readily.

Lying by the kerosene lamp

Books were among the discarded things Aunt Australia brought from the judge's house. I don't know who included *Walden and Civil Disobedience* by Henry David Thoreau (His name was so unfamiliar that I distorted it when I sounded the end vowels).

Indeed, would the judge?

Many superficially enlightened *Rebels* and fledgling me also did not understand what the deep-thinking philosopher truly meant. Had they known, they might not have so readily claimed him as their own.

In his work *On the Duty of Civil Disobedience,* Thoreau used a known motto: "That government is best which governs least." Perhaps, Conservatives of the period assumed it echoed their beliefs concerning *laissez faire,* which opposes governmental interference in the free market. Had the judge considered Thoreau's work revealed the writer's abolitionist views, he would not have intentionally planted such thoughts in the mind of a Black child.

I remember reading, *"I am too high born to be propertied, to be a second at control, or useful serving-man and instrument to any sovereign state throughout the world."* Through my budding self-esteem, I was hooked. Some other views in the books also seduced me, laying the peculiar personality that defines me. The books my aunt brought were not solely mine but became my treasure as I enjoyed reading with more depth. The timeworn hardcovers, dictionary, tattered Family Bible, and copies of *Popular Science* and *Popular Mechanics* from the used bookstore found their way into the box with my collection of bubble gum cards of WWII airplanes. In the beginning, I looked at the colorful pictures, but in due course, the written stories became vivid and as cherished as the artwork.

Chapter 4:
A Legacy of the Wind

Photo for illustration only

I was never ashamed that I was a field hand. It was only a hard job, but when the term cotton patch came up around *Bougie* (bourgeois, middle-class) Black people, the conversation suddenly bordered on taboo. *The old cotton fields back home* recall the ongoing tragedy of slavery in our country. We have never been adequately compensated for our and our families' part in developing this nation's wealth through enforced subjugation. No wonder an unmindful *Brotha* or *Sista* becomes highly unpopular with their fellows, when they do anything other than affirm, they would die before they have a thing to do with cotton.

Out of pride for their race, some poor Whites also vehemently protested:

"No free White man will ever pick cotton!"

However, they chopped it!

Chopping cotton is to do the backbreaking work of using a hoe to clear weeds from around the young stalks. It is lowly servitude, and the distinction between picking and chopping is no different. All this nonsense really wasn't about whether *cotton pickers*, rather than *potato peelers*, were the lowest in social status but about a denial of the other race's humanity.

The Southern Knights in *Gone with the Wind* were a far cry from the dingy, rumpled-dressed old cotton farmers who sought my father in late summer to gather field hands. Our house was at the bottom of a rocky hill at the Oak and Chambers Streets intersection. It sat perched on top of a slight embankment. We didn't have a phone or electricity in the 1940s, but the news went out when a well-worked pickup truck showed up and parked in the grassy area across the street from our front door. Soon, neighbors appeared from the shabby houses and gathered on their front porches. After my father climbed into the truck with the planter, onlookers passed around bottles and sacks, and the guzzling began. As if by some secretive cue, the jukebox in the tavern across the street started thumping out a bluesy number. Taking advantage of the distraction, a few of us younger boys sneaked under our high front porch, away from Mama's view. We gazed through the front door of the juke joint. The sun was high; it helped us see into the dimly lit interior. Grandma and the working girls swayed and swung their big behinds to the tempo of slow music.

They snapped their fingers and moaned sultry sounds of joy like: "Yeah… baby."

Occasionally, sharp whacks, then boisterous male voices bellowed out. A domino game had begun. Though far off, business just picked up. The *hullabaloo* was medicine for the everyday drinkers who had to get it out of their systems then. After we pulled out, supposedly, there would be no getting drunk until we returned. This meant the low bass emanations would throb therapeutically until the morning light.

Meanwhile, Daddy and the White man laughed and drank in the truck's cab; the porch scene was festive. The noisy little crowd grew as regulars from elsewhere caught word of the deal's completion. Neighbors who never went to the fields showed lighter spirits. It was not that we loved pulling cotton; nobody did, but it was relatively quick money for those who could. Common laborers, like my father, made around forty cents to fifty cents an hour. At forty hours per week, including overtime, this maxed out at around $25.00 a week. The wages paid for cotton pullers stayed at $2.00 per one hundred pounds from the time I was nine years old until I left the fields as a young man. Typically, if I pulled about four hundred pounds a day (Some pulled eight-hundred pounds daily), I made $8.00 a day, which could amount to $40.00 a week. The two months we were in the fields promised a sorely needed cash flow. In those lean years, when we returned, it would be equivalent to the fleet coming in with loaded pockets.

These were incredibly liberating times for me because I hated school, which meant I wouldn't have to attend until after the Christmas break. Many of my friends felt the same. After my brothers and I gave Mama some money, which we were proud to do, we had a few dollars left in our jeans. It was good to say, "I gave my mother some of the money I made." We were little men, after all. So little that I don't remember our ages when we began to work in earnest in the fields. Through the years, the vision of my younger brother, Don, and I draped in burlap bags remains in my recollection. I remember I helped Grandma, and Don helped someone else. We went to the cotton patch every year. I was about thirteen years old and clearly remember this particular trip In 1952.

The time for departure rolled around, and Mama had our old house cleaned enough so the mice wouldn't have a play day after we left. She took bedclothes, pots and pans, some dry foods, and a few condiments. My siblings were four brothers and two sisters; there were always small children and a baby under Mama's care. I never saw her pick a cotton boll, nor did my dad. However, as a former sharecropper, he had previously experienced all aspects of cotton farming. Even with his history, it would have seemed bizarre to see him dragging a sack with the rest of us. I was the second of the three older boys who did the fieldwork for the family. I don't know how much the planters paid Daddy for his role; Mostly, he drove the trucks. However, it was more than the top field hands made. Besides the pickers in the truck, others came in their private vehicles. Sometimes, they included women with children so small that they walked beside their mothers, putting little handfuls of cotton in her sack or riding on it as she worked. Although we lived in town, in some ways, families of itinerant field hands were like gypsies, covering all four quadrants of Texas during the season.

The first small towns we came to after leaving Fort Worth were often called *Sundown towns*. This was because Black people were not allowed in town after dark. We cotton field workers were tolerated because we were the lifeblood of their segregated communities, although it was never acknowledged.

A murky sea of pink faces met us when we jumped off the truck and piled out of the cars to buy supplies. My inquisitive nature promptly kicked into gear as I tried to understand what we had done to make them dislike us so much. I wasn't afraid of these storekeepers but did nothing to draw their attention to me or provoke their hostility.

They watched me all the same.

These *die-hard Confederate* folks didn't want to live with us but needed our business in the stores that sold cotton sacks, gloves, kneepads, and such. When they "owned" us, they were eager enough for us to live with them, but only as domestics. These segregated ones would allow a *nigra* to work all day in their homes, especially as cooks, but wanted us out of sight by sundown. Their discriminatory mindset labeled us as lying, thieving, rascally, and always up to no good. It was, however, a mistaken one, still it cautioned them to be wary. Regardless of the stern faces and the impenetrable veil that separated us, these country folks spoke to us like any other customer. They adopted the pseudo-polite manner of southern Whites, which bordered on courtesy.

As the store manager shadowed us, he would ease up beside one adult, conversing with them while glancing leisurely at several others. Oddly enough, he was dressed in the same clothes that were stacked in neat piles on long tables in the middle of the store. I suppressed a chuckle as I believed he saw himself as a cotton field fashion model, ready to explain the virtues of his wares.

"Where *ya'll* from," he drawled slowly but at a high volume, … *"Foat Wuth, huh?"*

He wanted us to know he was watching us.

"*Yas Suh*," his target would respond at a lower volume.

"I got a nephew *livin'* up there in Richland Hills; he got a big *ol'* tire shop up there," A pause, (shifting his position), and then, "I guess he's *doin'* alright; they got a great big *ol'* house an all."

As he spoke, the woman behind the counter was stationary, her eyes transfixed on another one of us; she appeared ready to pounce. But seeing nothing amiss, she relaxed in a few minutes. All the while, the White man worked the floor as if he were the host at a cocktail party, moving graciously from guest to guest, but there was unspoken tension in the air: We all wanted to scream, "We're not thieves; you are the one overcharging us for this cheap junk, and we're not stupid because we pay your prices. "You thieves have us so squeezed up that we can't complain or go anywhere else."

But we didn't protest outright. We knew that would bring swift retaliation from the entire White community because they thought the same as the storekeepers did. Complaining didn't mean the other merchants on the block wouldn't do business with us. They would, however, jack up their prices in retaliation for our supposed ungratefulness. Still having no other alternative, our situation would be worse.

When I made my purchases, I went to the truck and watched his antics through the plate-glass window until our crew came out.

When the last of us came out, and we loaded up to leave for the fields, there was an explosion of "Goodbyes," and "*Ya'll* come back when you need anything else."

Sadly, this all too familiar cat-and-mouse stereotype scenario only widens the racial misunderstanding gap. It is even more unfortunate that the shadowing of Black people in stores survives today.

The Cotton Patch

The *cotton patch*, our colloquial name for the cotton fields I worked in, was long lines of closely planted green and a few brownish-leaved plants. They stood straight and stiff, over three feet high. The planters separated the rows about a yard apart to accommodate the workers. The ripened cotton bolls' shimmering color was eye-catching; at a distant glance, they appeared to be white shrubbery. The stalks sometimes were so full of fluffy bolls, they touched each other across the rows. These ran about a quarter of a mile long on average but varied in length to accommodate the plots chosen by a crop rotation scheme. The field's extended rows were beautiful, but they often looked heartbreakingly long to a picker crawling in the Texas summer heat!

Cotton bolls are green colored, round firm capsules fully impregnated with fibers and new seeds. They grow on the branches extended from the vertical stalk. By harvest time, the bolls have busted open, revealing tufts of white raw fiber. There also are still green, unripe bolls on the limbs. The pointed ends of the busted bolls are quite sharp.

Cotton picking differs from *cotton pulling*. Pickers grasp the fibers in the open boll with the tips of the fingers, remove the tufts, and leave the empty husk attached to the limbs. The cotton with its seeds goes into the sack. Cotton pullers catch hold of the bottom of the boll by sliding the stem between the fingers; it is pulled off the limb with the palm side of the hand. The entire dried boll is kept intact. The ginning process separates the hardened shell from the cotton fibers later. In both methods of extracting, the sharp edges of the capsules occasionally cut my hands enough to bleed.

Old paintings of former days showing enslaved people picking cotton were different from our reality. The skimpy stalks in the pictures bear little resemblance to a robust plant grown for production. The images show pickers, lined abreast or in a small group, ambling as they work. Their nice clothes falsely depict the rough demands of the task and the heartlessness of the slave masters that clothed them. Some workers stand slightly bent at the waist, with their hands on the top of the plant. Others carry cotton in baskets or small sacks, which barely touch the ground. Even pictures with the overseers and their whips do not capture the truth of the grueling labor of fieldwork. Essentially, the artist has portrayed a false atmosphere of serenity in the unhurried *Old South.*

Today, the media would not publicize raw footage of armed men forcing other men, women, and small children clad in soiled rags to work under hot, wearying conditions. There would have to be a suitable warning or disclaimer that the images shown may negatively affect some viewers. Enslaved Black people were forbidden to learn to read and write, so few people on the receiving end of the whip could record the anguish and injustice of enslavement. Pictures illustrating the horrors of the period cannot make it into school history books today, and the truth fades. If I hadn't worked in the fields when I was young, I wouldn't have understood how our people suffered from centuries of abuse.

Of course, our work was hard, but there was another aspect that attracted us young boys. Sometimes there were swimming holes in the creeks that meandered through the area. One warm morning, I looked forward to exploring these hidden gems. Animals, which had sought shelter or hunted other creatures during the night, ran away as we walked through the field. We shouted back and forth. Our crew was about twenty pullers. We worked an average of two three-foot-wide rows, cutting a swath about one hundred twenty feet wide. The disturbance affected the wildlife, like the uproar of beaters, flushing out lions for a Rite of Passage ritual for twelve-year-old African *Masai* boys. As intoxicated as I was about wanting to experience the magic of Africa, it sobered me somewhat to know I was far more afraid of the garter snakes and other small critters in the field than *Masai* boys my about age were of savage lions.

As the sun climbed higher, the light nutty odor of the oily seeds in the cotton, reacting to the heat, was in the air. The scent of the field and the feel of the soft gray soil beneath my bare feet were exhilarating. For now, I was glad to be back in the country and away from the city and its clamor. The only naturally noisy sound heard was the far-off cawing of crows somewhere in the trees beyond the field. The air was clear, and the unfamiliarity of the scenery held the promise of new adventures later when time allowed. Although there was strenuous work ahead, I accepted it all. I didn't realize back then that facing the difficulties in working in the fields helped me develop resilience to overcome life's challenges. The days ahead mercilessly bore the reality of a life of labor on my knees. The earth beneath me seemed to grow hotter with the passing years, increasing my displeasure with each return to the fields.

WHEN I WAS THIRTEEN, WE RODE IN THE TRUCK TO THE FIELDS before daylight. This time we started miles from the farm's bunkhouse. Most of us young teens were dressed in loose, worn-out clothes and had a hat, kneepads, and gloves. Sometimes, work crews from Mexico were in the fields. They were outfitted as we were, and we were friendly to each other. We did not intermingle because of the language barrier, but we greeted each other sincerely.

We put the cotton into our canvas sacks as we went up and down the rows. The best pullers had ten to twelve feet long sacks, eighteen to twenty-four inches in diameter. By the time I was a teen, I had gone from a short four-foot sack to a six-to eight-foot one, which was sufficient for a mediocre cotton puller. Some girls used longer ones and had bigger tallies than I did. They never let me forget it. Undeterred by my ineptitude, they still flirted with me, but I was way too shy for cotton field romance.

My timidity didn't stop Velma Jean! She was shy of sweet sixteen, but well-seasoned and determined to cure me of my ignorance of the ways of the world. To classify her intentions as bullying is ridiculous now. Still, she was adamant and did not take no for an answer.

I remember one time when the vehicle that carried her family arrived at the field before our truck. She was a fast worker and was far up the pickers' line when I started.

She picked one row instead of her usual two to the end and was now coming in my direction. When she was about thirty feet across from me, she stopped, unhitched her sack, and sauntered towards me with an "I *gotcha* now" look.

She stood above me, her hands on her hips. Then, with an exasperated expression, she looked down and boldly asked me if I was going to kiss her.

I was so embarrassed that I am sure there was redness beneath my sun-tanned face and, for some unknown reason, was near to confessing out loud, "I love you, but I don't know what to do."

Thank God I only blushed and stammered something goofy like, "Well, I guess I better get back to work."

So, she responded by trying to bounce a green boll off my head. It was twisted, I know, but I enjoyed being the object of her interest, although I didn't let on that I did. We became good friends in later years, but the magic we could have known disappeared with our youth.

Credit: istock.com/SongSpeckels

The furnace of humiliation

"Work on the farm is hard enough, but the cotton fields are still plantation drudgery at its core. Sunup to sundown, toiling in the merciless sun, a lowly thing beneath the hot heavens. Sweat pours out of your body and down your face. Your back aches whether you walk while bending or you are crawling. Blasts of burning wind stir the stifling dust. You stink, and you sting while the sun roasts you all day long. Unlike the shimmering shapes rising in the heat, you are tethered here in the now, but God knows your daydreams, though they are as fragile as cottony clouds in the sky, which vaporize wistfully into the stream of time. As you add cotton to the sack, it becomes heavier and more difficult to drag along the ground. When you are ready to return to the scales, the lengthy sack can weigh over one hundred pounds. It is a long, cruel burden for a young back to carry."

LOOKING BACK AT IT NOW, I SUPPOSE I COULD HAVE BEEN A TOP FIELD HAND if I had not been extra cautious as I went about my task. I feared snakes might be coiled up around the bottom of the stalks. When illiteracy is a factor, superstitious prattle usually attaches itself to myths about nature.

These traditional tales stoked much of the apprehension I went through. When the adults sat and chatted at night, they swore snakes did things that would earn them Olympic Gold Medals today. I believed them since many of the older hands did. The snakes we saw were harmless, and some of the other workers, whom we thought were foolish, would seize them without ill effect, but there were still other potential perils.

In North Texas, near the small towns of Denton and Crum, six-inch reddish-orange and black centipedes dominated the fields. The experienced cotton pullers believed they delivered a poisonous bite. I went carefully because the *creepy crawlies* were on the tops of the stalks and scuttling along the ground. In other fields, giant multi-colored spiders spun their webs in the plants. They, too, existed in alarming numbers everywhere; occasionally, I killed scorpions. Whether these insects were deadly or only venomous, they could deliver an excruciating bite. These tightfisted cotton farmers refused to spend a few more dollars, which they kept back by paying low wages to desperate people. They should have sprayed the crops with chemicals to kill these creatures. This disregard for the welfare of one's fellowman caused me to question the morality of people who placed so little value on our lives and safety.

Eventually, the summer days shortened, and I knew the season was changing. The Sun still blazed, but not fiercely. Overhead, the puffy cumulus clouds, which had given us little shade during the afternoons, became more extensive and obscured heaven's flame for brief periods. Rarely did they sprinkle enough for us to leave the field for the day, but now and then pleasant light breezes accompanied them. As Autumn crept closer, the work was still long, but our agony became tolerable. The heat subsided now and then as if to announce that winter would finally bring the cotton season to its finish.

A brief break followed the first picking of ripe cotton bolls. I was ready then, but it wasn't time to put our gear away for the year. We would return after the green bolls we left on the stalks finally bloomed.

Stripping time came around in mid-Autumn, and because the air was chilly, the snakes and other pests went underground to seek shelter before the first frigid blasts came from the North. The cotton was easy to pull because the leaves had fallen off, and only the ripened bolls remained on the stalks. While wearing gloves, our fingers encircled the end of the branches nearest the stalk using both hands. Pulling sharply, we stripped all the fluffy bolls on the stem into our open hands and into the mouth of the sack in one smooth, rhythmic motion.

Spirits were high, and again the field resounded with joyous singing. Our minds pictured high times at home, and feelings of triumph made us giddy. Corny greetings from the jubilant pickers were matched with equally nonsensical responses. We picked with fervor as if we had the lion cowed before the tribe. Never the songbird, I croaked out a spiritual or made-up rhythm and blues verses to set a cadence when no one was within earshot. I pulled my four hundred pounds easily. I was deft!

Usually, the money I made disappeared soon enough when we went home after the first trip, and I would be penniless before Summer. But before that happened, my pockets would bulge for Christmas. The only dark spot on the horizon was that I would have to report to class for the second semester in January.

At fourteen, nothing was said, but I was expected to carry my own weight financially with at least a part-time job. It was an old and necessary custom. There was no break from toil. Black families who had to labor in the fields for a living in those miserable times were economically only a little better off than their enslaved ancestors. The White cotton producer cleared enough money to buy supplies and new farm machinery at the end of the season. His purse was bulky, and his household took their ease for the winter. Their holidays were lively times for feasting. Life was splendid for them, as well as the entire White society's economy and those who prospered personally and indirectly from our virtually free labor.

Only the enslaved were blameless for the question of the righteousness of slavery.

From the earliest days, the mills in the free states in the north never ceased to spin cotton threads and make cloth for lower-priced clothing here. The country also dealt with global cotton commerce, making this land one of the most prosperous in the world. At a meager 2 cents a pound paid for picking the near weightless puffs, the cotton pullers were flat broke within a short while and back in the grind of poverty. There was never any increase in Black family wealth, just a change in how we dealt with insufficiency. I did not understand the sheer devilry behind these things initially, but I perceived they were not moving in the direction I needed to go.

Fruit of the toxic tree

Historical documents and handed-down stories bear witness to the needless brutality the overseers and slave masters inflicted upon the people under their heels. Few questioned the validity of those narratives during the flourishing of national *Jim Crow* institutions and laws that governed public policy and practices. Instead, a smug, superior pride chiseled the tobacco-stained stubble-bearded faces of the White cotton growers we worked for.

However, in the twenty-first century, those who repudiate and bluntly deny the facts about slavery are rewriting history. They want to expunge or contradict the teaching that detrimental effects to African Americans caused by the system of chattel slavery and *Jim Crow laws* continue unintentional into today. They reject all notions that slave codes, similar rules, and policies give disproportionate present-day legal advantages to Whites over Blacks. These critics protest against teaching the "Critical Race Theory" (CRT), which candidly shows how slavery still influences society. I saw firsthand the various farms and estates, the wrecks of the slave cabins where the prisoners lived, and the rock walls they set up as they cleared the fields. These were the same lands we, their offspring, still toiled on in the same Texas sunlight, picking cotton as they did. Slavery and its continuing legacy has prevented the Black community from fully taking part in America's progress by generating almost no systemic Black family generational wealth. It seemed clear that the White cotton producers who held the land at that time were descendants of the people who had subjugated our families. It was accepted knowledge in East Texas, where my father was born. During my time in the fields, feelings remained far too tender to discuss such matters. The Whites would say nothing, and I didn't inquire into the issue with them.

The older workers, whose parents were enslaved, knew but were hesitant to talk about the crime as readily as I do now. It is a heinous deed that has befallen us. Sensing little had changed since emancipation, I wanted to investigate further but gave the due respect. However, I, too, was emotionally distraught.

Chapter 5:
Before dropping out

Continually unhappy over how matters were at school, I had played hooky for the first time in the seventh grade. I rarely attended class after that, but the school promoted me anyhow, so I slipped through to the 9th grade. Approaching the age of fifteen, I was still small in stature, perhaps five feet seven inches tall and 120 pounds, so a career of hard labor didn't seem right for me. About then, my desires changed. I fell in love with motorbikes and cars. Being poor, I became acutely aware of how education affected my ability to earn sufficient money to buy the things I wanted. So, I worried about my low grades and skipping school. I didn't know what would happen to me without education. Some of my friends worked backbreaking jobs or were in criminal life at that age. Ordinarily, my predicament would not be a problem for guys I knew since social condemnation was never a factor among hustlers. But Mama warned me that hanging out with "the crowd" would eventually lead to the penitentiary. The uneasiness in her expressions was real, so they affected me with uncertain concern.

I wasn't a thief or dangerous. But I believed skipping school was committing an offense serious enough to get me locked up in the notorious *Gatesville State School for Boys.* Several teen boys came back from *Gatesville* with scary stories of how terrible life was there. It was a continuation of the slave plantation system for the Black boys. These, and similar horror stories of getting whippings from the staff and unrestrained fighting among the detainees had come down through the years. I feared I wasn't hard enough or could work at the level that would prevent me from getting into a lot of trouble with the overseers. Somehow, the schools never reported my truancy, so I tried to hold on to the feeling that I would be all right. (I know now that the reason they didn't care about my skipping school to work in the fields was actually an old legal custom. Harvesting the crops was more critical than a colored boy's education.) Despite all the barriers surrounding my dreams of flying, I never let them go. □

The rumor was that you could finish high school in the Air Force, so I hurried to the recruiting station to get the facts. The recruiters said it was true, but I was too young to enlist. That disappointed me, but at least I had a workable strategy if I could hold out a few more years. The real problem was that I felt out of place in the world. I was near the bottom of our rough and tumble social structure, which was grounded in practical things, but the things I wanted were unrealistic for the times. My reading habits had taught me I was more than my environment made me. Despite my lack of formal education, I knew I could learn any job because I understood what I read. I was good at repairing cars and other vehicles. However, the Black garages were mostly one-person enterprises, and the White shops rarely hired Black mechanics. Then, by a bit of luck, I learned that *I. M. Terrell High*, offered auto mechanics as a technical training course. I skipped picking cotton the following school year and began high school in the fall semester.

Better days

A young Black man of high moral character frequented the *Bottom of The Hill.* He knew the street hustlers but was not one himself. Everyone respected him not only because of his straightforward nature but also because he could repair cars as well as they did in the big garages. He became an instrument for my escape. *Lee Andrew Shaw* knew of my burgeoning ability to solve car problems and asked me to fix an old car he had parked near his family's house. Then he did a remarkable thing. One day while I was watching him work on a car, our conversation became one of mechanic to mechanic. (It was at the level I wanted from the bus mechanics a few years ago.) As we delved into the mysteries of the craft, his comments lifted my self-esteem because he took my explanations and questions respectfully man to man. Before he left to go home on the Southside, he left me his expensive box of tools and a copy of the *Motors Auto Repair Manual.* I became a person of attention on *The Hill* when the word got around that *Lee* had trusted me with his tools. This brought a double endorsement as far as I was concerned, because I admired how *Lee Andrew's* easy manner brought him respect from all quarters. I secretly disdained the deceptive cruelty of fat Daddy the street hustlers, so there were no authentic role models among them. I could, and did, admire *Lee* with a clear consciousness. His faith in me gave me the confidence to consider myself a trustworthy technician. I never totally repaired his old car because it needed more than engine work, but my devotion to the task had unexpected future benefits.

Things changed radically when I attended the tenth grade at *Terrell High.* I improved my calling in Auto Mechanics. The professional tools, publications, and machines provided an environment for overall growth. Again, I was a whiz and quickly assumed stature, becoming a young man of notable regard among my peers. In my first year, a classmate and I were chosen to represent *Terrell High* in the auto mechanics division of a state conference for *Negro Schools.* It was the *26th Industrial Arts Conference* at *Prairie View A&M College.*

Soon I was on my way to the Conference with the top scholars in school. Mama dressed me and packed my bags for the three-day trip. The borrowed sports coat was a little too big, but unless you looked closely, I looked as sharp as I ever had when the car with the other students came to get me.

Being a school representative grew into pressure I had not known before. However, the new situation didn't overwhelm me. At first, I was unsure if I would fit in, but I was steady because my academic standing had risen a small amount. I worked harder to avoid getting kicked out of auto Mechanics because of low grades in other classes.

Our instructor, Mr. Sullivan, told the class he was "pleased to select me as *Handy Brown's* [A senior's] teammate."

I liked school at that time and became attentive to my studies. I became proficient in algebra and geometry because they were puzzles to solve, similar to diagnosing and troubleshooting. My grades in those classes rose to Bs quickly enough.

The circumstances that catapulted me to the top of my auto mechanics class occurred before I was in high school. I consumed the *Popular Mechanics* magazines I bought from the used bookstore on East Lancaster Street. They were packed with information about cars. I explored them without the pressure of being in an academic setting. My favorite article was *Gus's Garage*, in which Gus, a mom-and-pop garage owner, shared his genius at solving auto repair's most difficult problems. While reading the article, I visualized a friendly old White man explaining things to me the way I wanted the guys in the shops on Pine Street to do. In my mind, I created the perfect atmosphere for learning. Although it was fictitious, I became an excellent troubleshooter from old Gus's secrets. Besides Gus's mythical tutoring, I gained my understanding of electrical systems from in-depth instructions in the *Motors Auto Repair Manual.*

This Photo by Unknown Author is licensed under CC BY-SA

The competition

THE AUTO MECHANICS COMPETITION AT THE CONFERENCE was held in a spacious room with rows of car engines on test stands and all the necessary equipment. It wasn't so well attended by spectators as I previously feared. I still hadn't fully accepted that my skills back at home and *Terrell High* were more than some sort of fluke. The thought of being found out and humiliated in some way was not completely gone. So, the absence of a huge crowd served to settle my jittery nerves, enough to allow me to admire how impressive my surroundings were.

Officials wearing long white shop coats and carrying clipboards told us to pick an engine, diagnose why it did not work, repair it, start it, and then call them over and explain the problem. The first person to make his engine run correctly was the first-place winner, and so on.

Despite a bit of residual social anxiety, I followed my troubleshooting techniques. I pumped the carburetor and saw that the fuel delivery was okay. I then checked the timing, and it was correct. When I moved on to the ignition wires, I saw they were out of sequence. A quick check found nothing else. I was ready to repair the machine and make it run, but I did not realize two students from *Jack Yates High School* in Houston were watching me. Like predators, they sensed the time to move in. They asked me casually what was wrong with my engine; naively, I told them.

Then, one bully leaned hard against me, whispered intimidatingly, "Okay, you move over to that one," pointing to the engine they had just left.

Their surly manner let me know they would deal with me later at the barns, where we bunked during the conference. Surprisingly, the bullies couldn't get the engine running, even with my explanation of the problem. Meekly, I went to their old engine and solved the problem at once. The carburetor pumped fuel, but the timing was off. So, I set the timing to 3 degrees BTDC, as stated written on the timing cover.

The judges, walking around the testing floor, came to me when I signaled them; I started my engine and explained how I had solved the problem.

Then, one Judge asked me, "What does BTDC mean?"

I became nervous and could not remember.

Another Judge said, "When you remember, call us."

Feeling dumbfounded and cheated as the backs of the white coats moved away, I was nearly devastated.

However, above the backfiring in the background, a low voice spoke clearly to me and said, "*Before Top Dead Center.*"

I quickly called the Judge back and blurted out, "*Before Top Dead Center!*"

I was the first contestant to get his engine running correctly.

At that moment, I was self-conscious but relieved as the Judge announced loudly, "We have a winner!"

I cannot tell you how much I grew at that moment, but it was substantial.

I saw the ruffians from *Jack Yates* later, but they said nothing to me. I suppose they were embarrassed about the whole thing.

After my triumph at *Prairie View*, attending school became less vexing. I believed I could graduate with my dignity intact. Before the win and the prestige that came with it, school was just another place of maltreatment. Because I felt I didn't belong, I moved in the background through the halls and classrooms of the upper campus. I saw my classmates as members of cliques in which I did not fit. I was only a ghostly presence that responded softly when addressed by those who belonged. Of course, I wasn't as backward to my fellows as I was to myself, but we shared no dreams in common. By high school, lifelong personal friendships had set in, and I had not been there to grow as one with them. So now, I was well known, but not as intimately as I needed to be. I desperately lacked socialization. In today's jargon, I was a nerd!

But there was more than fitting in with my school fellows that whetted my appetite for more knowledge. It was a thing I perceived more than I heard. I caught wind of it in the spirits of the undergraduates at *Prairie View*. They moved and spoke with the expectancy of the well-educated Whites in my books. I saw the Black scholars from the corner of my eye, but I felt them with my soul. In elementary and junior high school, learning was all theory and was tedious. The reward for completing endless classroom assignments was superficial, only compliments and a pat on the back. However, by my mid-teen years, the return on my investment in study held the potential of transforming me into the man of my dreams, and knowledge was ever goldened to me. As we traveled back to Fort Worth, I recalled that an official at the conference had told us winners about the likelihood of scholarship eligibility. I reflected on my experiences at the college and mentally vowed to do what was necessary to return to Houston and be on campus.

Once home again, I set about improving my entire situation. I attended the other classes regularly, but desires and personality changes couldn't get the job done. I had no separate economic support because racism still held a grip on southern Black people, and my dad could not bring in enough to afford me the luxury of further education. I dropped out of school after the 10th grade and worked two steady jobs. I pumped gas and wiped windows at a service station. It was somewhat more encouraging, that I cleaned parts at a White owned, six bay garage on south Main Street, but they would not allow a *colored boy* to work on the cars. Eventually, I accepted that college was out even with scholarship support. Yet, I did not fear I would sink into obscurity. I had grown resilient through a diet of old books that fell into my life as crumbs from the feast of formal education just beyond my reach. So, indifferent to the dark poverty I had known, I came of age and dared to seek my dreams. At that time, I was old enough for a branch of the service.

In the fall of 1956, I left for the Air Force and the planes.

Chapter 6:
A Dream of the Heart

If daily, you trudge through endless mire,
Faceless among your many peers,
But dream of stoking your inner fire,
By burning the one-size-fits-all careers

Then, you were chosen for special deeds.
Selected in the beginning to fill the part,

When the Sower's choicest seeds
Fell on the fertile ground of your heart.

You have all that you need to make it,
Achievement far outweighs the cost.
Never fear that you will not take it.
A Dream of the Heart will never be lost.

Just as Faith is a sure reflection
Of unseen things, the hopeful receives,
Your Dream is the selfsame projection
Proceeding from a heart that believes.

The power that moves a mountain peak
will make your cherished ideas soar.
Persistence is the key to what you seek
and will lay success at your door.

Step out upon your own true quest,
Following that star that brightly beams,
For deep within your indomitable breast,
There beats a heart that dreams.

Section II: The Seeds of Prejudice

Chapter 7:
Undertaking the Odyssey

When we arrived at the *Love Field* terminal, the raindrops had gathered into bubbles on the enormous plate glass windowsills outside *Braniff International Airways*. Upon entering the waiting area, my anticipation of making my first flight was high. I toned it down so as not to be conspicuous. I knew the score. Southern etiquette demanded that I behave so that no one noticed the colored boy sitting among them.

The White passengers, too, were calm and reserved, muttering softly, if at all. Most of the men dressed in suits, and the women wore expensive-fashion clothes. Like some of the other recruits, I didn't wear a suit. I never owned one, but I dressed in my best clothes, which were clean. Sitting quietly by myself on one side of the waiting area, I went over the events that had brought me there.

I had looked forward to this flight since the Recruiter said we would travel by air from Dallas to Lackland Air Force Base in San Antonio, Texas. However, I kept my excitement to myself for fear that it would cause more teasing by my friends.

To say that I survived the hardships and bullying bigots of my youth does not imply that I was unaffected by them. Looking back at it now, I see how severely damaged I was from the ill-treatment I received from Whites and Blacks. It was to the degree that it altered my thinking and behavior. I became so fearful of ridicule that I bypassed many prospects. I stayed defensive about things close to my heart, which I longed to share but dared not to.

Only my father knew my dream of flying was uppermost in my thoughts of volunteering for the Service. Still, neither of us realized I was contemplating a near-impossible task for a *colored boy* without formal schooling. It is providential how ignorance causes the young to step out in faith. My first bold step carried me back to the window of the *Joint Recruiting Office* on Main Street. I mustered my courage and marched inside to inquire about the Air Force.

Things moved quickly in the two weeks after I walked into the Recruiting Office. So fast, I hardly took time to listen to the little inner fears that suggested waiting until later or backing out altogether. Too late, several people saw me riding in the front seat with the White Sargent as he drove me home the day I passed the preliminary test. Backing out now was unthinkable.

My self-esteem rose to just short of arrogance as the news got around.

"Van Jr. is going into the Air Force."

Most of the time, they said it was the Army, and now and again, the Navy. More importantly, I was a man now, and I was leaving for what was to us at *The Bottom of The Hill*, a giant leap up the economic ladder. For a White family of the times, and today as well, entry-level pay in the military enlisted ranks is at their poverty level. As a Black person accustomed to unfair wages, the Air Force salary put me in the money and catapulted me upward into the social hierarchy.

I made my way around *The Hill,* spreading the good news. For the first time in my life, I grew somewhat sad at the thought of leaving the only life I had known. Now, I was free from the coping mechanism from childhood, which allowed me to see a world I imagined rather than the true one. After my father got involved, we sat in the recruiter's office as the Sargent talked about how all races shared equal opportunities in the newly integrated military. I had scored extremely high on the test he gave me at his office. He seemed genuinely impressed.

"Van won't have any problem with the battery of tests in Dallas." The recruiter said firmly to my father as they looked each other straight in the eye.

[A breach in *Jim Crow* code of behavior] "He scored higher than most others *Negro* or *White*."

That statement caused Pop to sit up a lot straighter as the Sargeant spoke,

"But we've got to get a legal record of his birth before he can enlist."

My birth date had not been a significant problem before; not a word when I got my driver's license. People were who they said they were unless an issue with federal regulations arose. They talked on as I glanced at the posters in the office, glimpsing the most at the ones with airplanes. I recognized them all: the fighters, P-51s and P-38s, the B-17 and B-29 bombers. All I needed now was proof of my citizenship, so Dad and I were on the way to *Mount Pisgah Baptist Church* in his blue and white Buick.

The pastor's secretary gave my dad the Baptismal Certificate; it said I was born June 11, 1939. Dad gave the preacher $5.00, and we sped back downtown. Now that I had proper validation, I was old enough to enlist. That settled it. I left for Dallas in three days.

Mama cried! "I was too young," she said. Affected by her tears, my younger brothers and sisters sat quietly. Acting the part, I was full of swagger and professed to be braver than I was, but my courage held as dad drove me to the bus depot.

MY FELLOW PASSENGERS' HEADS ROCKED ABRUPTLY FROM SIDE TO SIDE when the rear wheels of the blue and silver *Texas Motor Coach* fell off the curb in a short-left turn as it left the downtown terminal. In a few blocks, it made another left turn at Lancaster Street. I sat on the driver's side, pressing my face against the cold window so that I could see our house as we passed. No one was outside! While the last of the old familiar places went by, I felt the touch of emotion that comes with first experiences. Like every inexperienced person who leaves home for the first time, I became acutely aware that I was alone in the world. I began to appreciate that a young person's responsibility for his safety was not a simple matter. Before, I was all right, because I followed my parents' instructions about where to go and what to do. I realized now the original decisions were mine, and that I did not know as much as I had supposed. There could be unseen snakes in this unfamiliar terrain, waiting to strike at a careless misstep. However, trouble was unlikely to raise its head so close to home, so I sat back and thought of the future.

The battery of tests and induction ceremonies in Dallas lasted two days. We stayed in the YMCA for three days and went by taxi to *Love Field* on the third day. A soft rain fell during the drive. Now, I was impatient for the call to board. Finally, the rain let up, and the call came! The ground was still wet as we strolled out to a DC-3, sitting on the parking apron.

My departure was in October 1956. Across the South, transportation terminals remained racially separated despite ICC regulations. However, there was no way to prevent Black and White commuters from sitting close to each other on the planes. So, breaking with the tradition of Whites first, I went in without respect to any particular order to my seat in the middle of the plane. No one sat beside me, but in my heart, I felt the long frigid winter yielding to spring, and these small steps were the first few drops to thaw.

The cabin inside was about what I thought it would be. I sat back at an angle as we taxied to the head of the active runway. The take-off was not the super high-speed dash I expected, though it was not a letdown. As we gained speed, the tail came up. We rose gently, and the sound in the cabin became lower; the vibration stopped; it was clear that we were flying. The temperature inside the plane became chilly. I couldn't see objects on the ground because it was night now. Just the orange glow of clusters of lights from the small towns and communities that went by slowly. I had thought there would be the sensation of speed compared to the ground; it wasn't a let-down, just an awakening to how things are when seen from high up. The night flight itself was smooth enough; the big air instability maker, the Sun, had gone down, and with it went the thermals that caused most of the disturbances. These were the sharp rising and fallings we know as turbulence. Flight attendants served a small but excellent steak and lobster tail meal, even though our in-flight time was two hours or less.

After a while, a small bell went ding, and I noticed we were coming down. I saw the wing flaps extend outside my window and felt a slight, gentle jerk as the "Gooney Bird" lost speed. When [I guessed correctly] the landing gear came down, it made a sound that could be felt as well as heard as it locked in place. Now objects on the ground were visible and speeding by. Lower, lower; the tires barked when she touched down, and I heard the fast-rolling wheels growling as they slowed down on the runway. We had arrived in San Antonio, the loudspeaker announced. The flight attendants were up and moving, giving instructions for deplaning.

Photo for illustration only

Basic Training

THE SAN ANTONIO TERMINAL WAS BUSTLING! A somewhat quiet guide met us, and after a moment, we traveled in a blue school bus-type vehicle past bars and pawnshops to the base gate. Unlike Fort Worth, most people I saw through the bus window dressed in a more conventional style. I was calm. I felt no apprehension, but a rotten tooth was aching.

My dad and I had agreed: "They'll fix it when you get there."

I'll let them know sometime tomorrow, I thought.

Soft mumbles and mutters interrupted the silence as we passed under an enormous sign that read, "Welcome to Lackland Air Force Base, The Gateway to the Air Force;" we were there at last. After many twists and turns, I realized my new home was enormous. Almost all my thoughts of joining the Air Force were focused on the planes. They were peaceful reflections, but I hadn't considered basic training. We stopped in front of a barracks building where a uniformed figure in a helmet with a baton stood waiting; the bus door opened, then suddenly pandemonium!

Loud screaming and cursing filled the bus. I didn't know if it was hazing or a fight, but I became so scared I froze for a moment.

The airman with the baton was in the face of a White boy screaming, "Get off the damn bus right now."

The maniac looked directly at me as he continued barking orders. By the time I was outside, two other screaming airmen with batons and armbands had the newcomers in formation.

The nearest airman came toward me, yelled, "Are you stupid, JERK?"

"No, Sir," I croaked from the throat.

"Then get that damn stupid look off your face," and then he turned to give someone else his attention.

Unharmed, I realized that basic training had begun.

The next few days were filled with rushing and instructors screaming at us. They held an urgency that defied reason. We constantly moved at double-time, got chewed out, and threatened for unclear infractions of unclear rules. I wasn't afraid of bodily harm from our Tactical Instructors (TIs), but each dressing down made us look incompetent, and I got a few of them. Eventually, I recognized my fellow basic trainees as individuals; we kept forgetting each other's names but remembered our home states or cities. Each time one of us told which state he came from, the TIs made a condescending remark about it and referred to the person by his home state's name. There were too many Texans for any one of us to be called "Tex," so my AKA was simply "Mac," a short for McKellar.

Here we were, a mixture of Blacks, Whites, and Mexicans jammed together and working under constant pressure from our TIs, but no nightmare scenario of integration reared its ugly head. It was all so natural that I completely forgot about racism. Missing were the overt signs of racism. I noticed none of the assumptions that usually go with stereotyping. No one prejudged Black airmen in any way that singled us out as being unqualified or of lesser ability. It seemed the Air Force had it all together, and for the moment, it was good and right.

Basic training continued, with me none the wiser that covert racism even existed. Many Whites were withdrawn or outwardly hostile in the life I left behind. I did not have to wonder whether racism was a factor in their behavior towards me; it was plain. However, here, a fellow trainee's quiet moment could be nothing other than a thoughtful reflection or a touch of homesickness. If I had dwelled on it, I would have put it together.

Throughout basic training, we watched episodes of *The Air Force Story*. It was a small thing, but I couldn't remember seeing Black heroes or accounts of the distinguished service that Negro troops performed for our country. We saw film after film about the exploits of White soldiers in the Army Air Corps.

Also, I don't remember seeing *Daniel Chappie James* and other Black aviators among pictures and paintings of renowned warriors and flyers anywhere. Nothing comes to mind about seeing accounts of the valiant flying of the *Tuskegee Airmen* or the stories of the heroic actions of other Black persons. Since a good deal of such information existed, I can only surmise that the oversite was intentional and for no good purpose toward Black people. I didn't realize that many candidates for officer rank were treated horribly in the past. And that the higher-ups winked at that practice in the current services. Nevertheless, the missing accounts of Black pilots during basic training did not negatively affect me because there was no clear negativity. There is little doubt now that military historians' lack of recognition of Black service members' feats was a snub toward the Black race.

As the days became weeks, I was pleased with my progress by how well I competed with others in physical competition. I couldn't climb the social ladder back home because I was a dud in school sports. Although I could swing across the creek on ropes, climb the trees, and cross the rocks in the streams with surefootedness, I received no accolades for actions off-campus. As we marched to various places in the first phase of basic training, we noticed an obstacle course nearby. It was constructed of wooden telephone poles and resembled a giant three-story ladder amid riggings, hills, and ditches filled with water. Trainees from other Flights (groups) were hustling about to loud threats and intense urgings. Some in our Flight seemed apprehensive, but I was eager to play this game of climbing ladders, which I knew well. In my private moments, I named the biggest one, *My Stairway to the Stars.* Our time at the obstacle course came. It was as I knew it would be. I sailed through it quickly and effortlessly. I wasn't the best in the bunch, but I was in the top few. I was giddy.

My past years of social awkwardness never came to the forefront in the following days. Behind me were hours spent merely dreaming of possibilities of how a machine or device could work. I was rather good at visualizing this way. It showed in the conceptions of my flying machines and the modifications I made to my bicycles, skateboards, and other toys. Equally important were my designs of customized and hotrod cars, fantasies only because I lacked the money to create them. Now I had entered the society which flew the fantastic machines in my card collection. I was more than pleased about it, even though it vexed me because I did not have the formal education to be an Air Force pilot.

Eventually, my aching teeth became so bad that I had to break training to get dental work on several of them. I missed too many vital training sessions, which meant that I would not graduate with my class and was held over for 2nd Phase of basic training. My total time in basic training was three months. This unforeseen happening deflated me some, but my teeth needed the work done.

THE 2ND PHASE OF BASIC TRAINING WAS NOTHING OF THE SORT. There was little training, mostly work and guard duty. It would have been boring if it had not been for the eighteen times I pulled KP (Kitchen Police). KP is kitchen work and dreaded because of the fast work pace, but it is child's play compared to fieldwork. Besides, I was there so often that the Mess Sergeant picked me to drive the truck for quick pickups, which was *Cadillac duty*.

While driving the Sergeant on an unfamiliar side of the base, I saw four uniquely dressed men marching briskly, not in the manner that we marched, but at attention and in tight formation.

As they approached the corner, from somewhere in the group, a command rang out: "*Expreeesss* halt!"

Heads turned smartly in both directions of the street.

Then, "Express forward, *harch*!" as the group snapped into motion.

I have never forgotten the scene.

I asked the Sergeant about them: "Who in the Hell are they, Sarge?"

The mess sergeant was an easygoing old veteran and not a T.I., so we had the habit of speaking casually in the truck.

"Who in the hell is who," he said, looking to see who I was speaking about.

Pointing to the unfamiliar marchers, I spoke louder, "Those guys!"

"We're in the cadet area; those are cadets in officer training," he muttered softly, "College kids, *gonna* be pilots."

My heart skipped several beats, and my chest muscles tightened; I asked him more questions.

"Don't worry about them," he said disinterestedly, while pulling a suspicious-looking flask from his pocket. I knew Lackland was not a flight-training base, but I had not considered Pre-Flight instruction for pilots and navigators. My head rang with a newfound interest in me flying. It was more than daydreaming; I clutched the thought tightly, thinking, "there must be someway…."

My 2nd Phase basic unit was a mixture of other trainees held over for assorted reasons. We were beyond the need for drilling and hazing, but we attended classes for other things. Besides, I was genuinely tough now. Enduring the rigors of first phase basic had catapulted me upward in status. At last, I knew what it meant to be one of the best. My self-appraisal was not born of daydreams, but of competitive actions. Here, our intellect counted as much as our physical ability, and I had become a good all-around military trooper.

They moved us to a new barracks in the former cadet area in the last few weeks.

I learned nothing about cadets, but I thought,

This is more than a coincidence, as was the field trip to the *Fort Worth Public Library*. This must be mockery by some unseen forces to dangle a long-desired dream before me, only to deny it.

Had I been a speaking acquaintance of God, he would have gotten an earful then!

My First Phase aptitude test showed I was best suited as a Radio Operator and slated for that school. The thought of this dismayed me because it was not an aircraft mechanic's job, although I learned afterward that it could have been an aircrew member's job. However, when I read the assignments after 2nd Phase, I drew the aircraft hydraulic repairman's school at Amarillo Air Force Base in Amarillo, Texas. That made me happier because it would lead to a technician posting on the flight line and the planes.

The following remarkable feature about going through 2nd Phase had to do with getting my first stripe. (Airman First Class or E-2 in rank) The first stripe meant an airman was no longer in training. If I had left with my 1st Phase class, I wouldn't have gotten my first stripe until completion of six months of tech school. When I began tech school at Amarillo, my new fellow students were Airman Basics (E-1), fresh from 1st phase training. Because I completed the 2nd Phase, I already had my first stripe and more liberties.

Between Basic and Tech School, I went home to Fort Worth for a few days' leave and saw what a change of three months made in how I saw my lifelong home. At Basic, we cleaned and polished everything vigorously. Wherever there was a surface, either in the barracks (especially the latrines) or outside the building, we scrubbed it to hygienic perfection. Any spot or speck brought a tirade of vilifying language and a round of pushups. The number was determined by the offense.

While I was on leave, it became noticeable that the shotgun houses on Oak Street were repulsive. Nowhere was the neatness and order I became accustomed to in the Air Force. I felt some shame in how I had lived. Living in the world outside the slums of *Baptist Hill*, I could now understand another of the ills of economic inequity and enforced poverty. The damage to me was that I had become mentally snobbish in the short three months I was away. What I had loved before as a *colored boy* did not match my new self-image.

Looking back, I can see that it was not personal growth because, as I had learned from my old books, change is appreciating good traits in all people. I could not see at that moment that I, like many today, was deceived into comparing others to my false image. I wore fine clothing, dined on proper food, and no longer struggled to survive. My contract with the Air Force laid life out for me. I had privileges I did not have before I left. It was not perfect, but it carried a level of freedom that people on *The Hill* did not enjoy.

I remember writing to Mama when I was in basic. Writing proudly about my uniforms, I boasted: I have a lot of clothes now, three suits [my first ones], an overcoat [also my first one], two pairs of shoes, a pair of boots, and the caps and hats. I sounded like a country boy in the movies, writing to his folks after getting his first wardrobe. On the screen, those scenes are worth a few good chuckles. These things happen all the time, but when poverty from enforced racism creates the bumpkins, the shame falls on privileged onlookers. I did not know what to do about it!

My ride to Amarillo on the Greyhound Bus grew dull as the routine of lengthy stretches of flat plains and grimy little whistle-stop towns became monotonous. When there was nothing unusual to look at, I reflected on what was nagging me; it was not vexing but one of those trivial things that keep sneaking into quiet moments. I recognized the nature of the problem and had to resolve it and handle my reaction before I could completely dismiss it.

Earlier, my bus stopped at a small town an hour north of Fort Worth. The driver got out and handled the baggage, a box, or a package. He pulled off but stopped again about a block from the pea-sized station and snapped open the door.

"Well, come on!" speaking to someone standing on the curb.

I straightened up to see why we stopped so soon after we left the station. A medium-sized Black man, about 45 years old, stepped slowly onto the bus. He carried a small box sealed with tape and wrapped with cord string. The cautious way he moved drew our attention, looking as if something harmful might be on board. There was disgust on the driver's face as he took the ticket.

"Find you a seat back there and sit down!" He snapped.

The man, obviously accustomed to a segregated lifestyle, moved with care as he made his way to the back and sat down. During this time, the driver rolled slowly, then faster as he returned to the highway. As he moved, the man nodded his head to unreciprocated greetings from the other riders. I noticed the driver had not spoken discourteously to any of us as we boarded at Fort Worth. He wasn't entirely pleasant to me, but I saw he noticed my Air Force uniform and nodded his head slightly as I stepped onboard. There was no trace of the sneer he gave the new Black man we picked up at the corner. Since neither of us Black men created an incident, my blue uniform was the only difference between us as passengers.

That was the source of the little thing that needled me!

I witnessed an innocent man, clearly Black like me, accorded less courtesy because the driver could get away with it. I have experienced the sting of two-faced behavior from Whites pretending to be friendly to others but suddenly becoming rude to Blacks. We had to take it, things being what they were. What troubled me was how willing I was to accept the White driver singling out the other Black passenger to be the butt of his uncivil attitude.

It's the status quo for the moment. But things are changing now, I thought glumly! I was the same race as my fellow passenger, but my blue uniform conferred upon me a little more privilege. I was ashamed of myself for being willing to accept bad treatment of someone else that I wouldn't put up with. I could have spoken but I didn't because it wasn't happening to me. Before the Air Force, I believe I would have spoken up, but I just sat there just like the White people even though I knew that it was wrong to keep silent.

Chapter 8:
Airman's life

"

Photo for illustration only

Tech school's atmosphere for growth exceeded that of my high school auto mechanic's class. The extensive military budget supplied whatever tools, mock-ups, and books were needed for the best learning process. Waiting for necessary parts or specific tools in high school often impeded the flow of an exciting project. The sense of failure attaches itself to an uncompleted task. Here, these interruptions in the learning curve did not exist. Again, I left no project unfinished and grew into an accomplished technician, repairing the world's finest planes. There is so much satisfaction in bringing an essential job to its conclusion.

Three annoying things happened to me in Tech school

First, I passed the test for my high school GED. I received the certificate but did not get the diploma from Texas because it would mean that I was graduating before my class. Texas promised they would send me the credentials after my class graduated in 1958, but they didn't.

Next, Price Daniels, the governor of Texas, was visiting the city of Amarillo, but parked his plane at Amarillo AFB. I was selected for the *Honor*

Guard to greet him when he landed. While we were receiving instructions for our duty, a Sargent came into the room and called me aside. He was replacing me because someone felt that a Black man in the *Honor Guard* for a southern governor might be seen as an offense. I could not agree more because if that was his opinion, it was offensive to me.

Last, I had my first beer at the base service club. I was relaxing in my room when one of the other students I hardly knew invited me "down to the service club beer garden for some 'suds." It was not my first time being in a drinking establishment, but the old *Jitterbug Inn* back home was nowhere as lovely as this place was. I swallowed a whole mug of the icky liquid but did not like the taste or the accompanying buzz, which had slightly impaired me.

I took a sip of each; beer, wine, and whiskey that night but had no desire to drink further. The beer tasted nasty, and the whiskey was dreadful. Plus, the stigma attached to drunkenness concerned me. If there was a positive aspect to being drunk, I didn't see it. It made no sense that people would endure the disgusting taste of liquor to behave foolishly and do detestable things. So, I did not touch the stuff for a long time after the beer garden instance.

Tech school went by at an average pace. I suppose I did well because I was assigned to Holloman AFB near Alamogordo, New Mexico. I arrived a few months before the Air Force named the base *The Air Force Missile Development Center*. It was near the site of the first atomic bomb test in 1945, at the edge of the *White Sands Missile Range*. From 1946 through 1951, it was also the area where captured WW II German V-2 rockets were tested. My assignment in 1957 came in the early years of the *Space Race*, and the place was abuzz with exciting activity. Secrecy surrounded everything. But I believe I can say now that Holloman not only supported the *Space Race* activities but also did considerable testing of its own. As an aircraft and missile hydraulic and pneumatic technician, I worked on the planes and other machines involved in the mission. Holloman was a plumb posting for a young *grease monkey*, and I reveled in it.

Pilots are not the only people in aviation that love the mystique of flying. Designers, builders, navigators, air controllers, and mechanics are but a few that make up the environment. For many of us, just being around these marvelous machines is its own reward. Within one year, from the drudgery of the cotton fields and harsh oppression, I was doing an essential job of keeping the planes flying and learning things like those featured in my *Popular Science* books.

At this point in my life, I still was not amorously involved with any particular young woman. Not that I didn't wish to be, but so far, girls my age weren't around in numbers large enough to trickle down to the geeks. Few mothers allowed their daughters to hang out with our rough bunch when I lived on Oak Street. I was a romantic dud in school because the athletes beat me out. Now I was in the middle of the desert where there were relatively few Black people. These were tiny New Mexico towns. For the moment, I ignored my love life and engaged myself with other interests.

After getting the routine down at work, I found several White friends in the new trainees at the shop who had similar interests. So, we tested ourselves while exploring the nearby natural attractions. We crawled through caves in the *Sacramento Mountains* and explored the dunes at *White Sands*. Some nights, we hunted jackrabbits in the desert while riding on the fenders of *Shipley's* old Nash Rambler Wagon. He struck every ditch and mound with a jolt. It was an adventure sufficient to satisfy any young man's heart.

We discussed various topics when we weren't spending energy on physical pursuits. Naturally, race and race relations came up. We tried to respect each other enough in those moments to lay aside wise-cracking and tired old jokes that seem to find their way into conversations between people that have fundamental differences. I sensed that my newfound White friends sincerely wanted to understand these impediments to genuine friendship as much as I did, so I bared my soul truthfully to that end. But as they said: "The Devil is in the details." The old demon had worked his work well through generations of bigoted sayings that had become part of our perception of our fellowmen. No matter how hard you try to keep them down, these things surface about race, religion, or other things we hold dear and privately.

I pointed out that some Blacks had reservations about things for which we had been mocked by Whites before. Blame that one on *Ol' Jim Crow!* And many Whites' reservations about Blacks had to do with fears of what people hitherto personally unknown to them think or will do. We learned the no-noes and sensitive areas, such as a White person, must never touch a Black one's hair because Whites maintain that their hair is better than a Black person's. So, the Black person feels it is an offense to his dignity and an insult, and he is ready to fight. Or a Black man should never bring up the subject of intimacy with White girls. Again, *Ol' Jim Crow* had burned stereotypical caricatures of lusty big-eyed Black creatures stalking White girls. But we made it through, and for the first time in my and their lives, we developed a working relationship that was good enough to be called a friendship. I suppose that my friends also felt, as I did, some satisfaction in believing that they were not racists after all. Still, things being what they were, there were obstacles to true friendship that could not be overcome.

Distracted by the natural world, I did not burn with the same fire to fly the planes which brought me into their midst. Then, I heard about the *Holloman Flying Club,* where several airmen aviators on the base flew small civilian airplanes. I checked with them, but I didn't have the money for lessons, and I did not pursue it further for some unknown reason. I seemed to have been in one of those puzzling times when you are nearest your goal, and your ambition drops off. It's not about giving up, but rather about being like a sailing ship that becomes motionless when the wind that propels it temporarily ceases. However, I was not deeply asleep, just in a stage of softly dreaming.

EVER SINCE I JOINED THE AIR FORCE, my investigations into me flying yielded no promise of success. So, it seemed the old great gulf still lay between a high school dropout and becoming a pilot, but what wide-eyed eaglet fears the impossible? I did not! Fortunately, in my comings and goings, I discovered how to take flying lessons quite by chance.

It began the day I came out on the second-floor stair landing of my barracks. I was startled to see two small, propeller-driven planes sitting on the parking ramp directly across the street. I didn't know their type, but they had Air Force insignias. There was a slender-built civilian behind the fence, looking them over. I skipped across the street and asked him, "Are these planes going to be based here?" I had many questions. Through our conversation, I learned the T-34 Mentors were primary training planes that now belonged to a new aero club on base. *The Holloman Aero Club* hired *Jim Stallings*, an aircraft inspector for the Air Force, to convert them into their general aviation designation of *Beechcraft A-45s.* I told him about my work on the flight line. *Jim* was a tall, slim, salt-and-pepper-haired White man with an easy-going manner. He reached down to the key ring on his belt and effortlessly opened the fence gate to let me into the parking area. He and I felt an instant liking for each other. After talking for a while, he agreed to ask the club to allow me to help him with the conversions.

My thoughts that night went from the club said "No!" to "visions of sugarplums dancing in my head." As I waited for *Jim* to appear across the street, the days dragged on, and then he did. The club's answer was better than I had hoped. They said that if I joined the club, they would pay me an hourly wage for my work, and I could then rent the planes and pay for my instructor, as any member did. It was a simple matter. I went to the next meeting, *Jim* nominated me for membership, and the club put it to a vote and accepted me unanimously. Introductions and hand shakings followed. As for finding an instructor, the *Aero Club* members were primarily military pilots, and civilians whose job was equal to officers. These professionals wanted to fly the T-34s for recreation or a break from the more powerful planes they flew at work. Some members were world famous, but I found in the days to come, they accepted me as a member. That should have been a tipoff that they were familiar with other Black people flying, but I missed it.

The planes were already serviceable military aircraft, but the modifications to get them licensed by the FAA for civilian use took us about two months to complete. Physical work was simple enough, but waiting for parts and paperwork took the longest. The most complex part of the process was tearing the engines down to install a unique piece on the piston connecting rod to avoid scraping damage to the cylinder walls. Other workers installed a bungee cord under the floorboard, which tied the rudder to the ailerons. The FAA said this modification helped coordination between the two flight controls, but we learned it did not. It did, however, mildly interfere with cross-control maneuvers, but was safe. A strobe light to the bottom of the fuselage completed the major work. Then, I buffed both planes with *Never Dull* aluminum polish until they shone like stainless steel. Next, I put three stripes of dayglow orange reflective tape around the fuselages, which was also a requirement. Last, one of the club pilots performed a test flight on each plane, and they were ready for club rental.

As they went to other airfields and events, the word came back that the "*warbirds*" drew crowds wherever they went. Meanwhile, I read everything I could about flying lessons and bought a logbook and the usual handheld navigation instruments. Both planes were so popular with the club flyers that it took a while to find an instructor and take my first lesson.

I don't recall the instructor, but I remember my first takeoff. The dramatic first takeoff of the student in the blue and white *Aeronca Champ* ahead of me made the most remarkable impression on me that day. The runway of the forgotten airport was red earth with small embankments on each side because a road grader had recently worked on it.

We pulled up to the end of the active runway as number two for takeoff, just as the *Champ* started its takeoff run.

As the student pilot gunned the engine, dust flew from beneath the propeller, and it went to the left embankment, dipping the right wing and making for the right side to repeat the bank-hitting, wing-dipping maneuver. Then down the runway, still wobbling, but eventually getting into the air. The whole thing was like that of a chicken escaping a fight in the barnyard. No doubt my pulse was racing, not from fear of crashing, but from wanting to do better than that.

My headphones came alive as the instructor spoke. "Clear the runway before you move out."

I craned my neck; nothing was landing, and the champ had made its left turn-out, so I said. "Clear" and moved to the center of the runway.

The instructor asked, "Ready!"

I said, "Yes," and pushed the throttle forward.

To my relief, the T-34's tricycle landing gear produced a slightly better takeoff run than the little Tail dragger. The plane darted to the left. Fearfully, I kicked the right rudder and lurched toward the right but straightened up.

A few seconds later, the instructor barked, "Nose up!"

We were airborne, where the streamlining of the ship made efforts less problematic. I felt cold all over, as if I had escaped the meanest dog on my paper route. Had I been flying the *Champ*; my first takeoff would have been a repeat of the one before me that day. My problem the first day was flying straight and level, but when the lesson was over, I knew I would achieve my dream of becoming a pilot. Still, I have wondered occasionally, if I had not seen the wild takeoff of the plane ahead of me, would I have been dismayed over my own poor results? Would I not have come back for my second lesson? Given my timidity, then, it is a question I cannot answer to this day.

In the next three flights, I made minor progress. I learned, but something was missing. I would have enough money on the books for a lesson and then book a flight with a different instructor each time. The situation was that the T-34s had over 200 horsepower engines, a constant-speed propeller, and retractable landing gear. The mentors were high-performance aircraft. However, the Air Force used them as primary trainers, so I knew they were not too complicated for me.

The eaglet takes wing

I FLEW WITH AN INSTRUCTOR NAMED *ED EISLER*, who said I was missing too much time between lessons, but if I took them at once instead of piecemeal, it would better my chance of soloing. Determined to do so, I became a new person. Normally talkative, I would have bent everyone's ear about the wisdom of my plan, but I fell into a secretive mood and told no one. I became near miserly, stockpiling each penny. I cut out trivial expenses and put away enough money to take a series of lessons with *Ed.* Soon the time came. The lessons with *Ed* went well. I became like a fat young bird that had grown comfortable sitting in the nest. I suppose a co-pilot's mindset had eased in on me.

I greeted my instructor on the parking apron for another flight. We took off on a fine fall morning, but *Ed* was grouchy! He demanded absolute perfection in every change of altitude or heading as we flew from Holloman AFB to the small airfield a few miles away. I didn't let on visibly, but he was on my last nerve. As we entered the traffic pattern, he told me to make a full-stop landing and let him out about halfway down the runway. I turned onto the taxiway and killed the engine.

When he got out, he asked for my logbook. He had chewed my behind so much that I did not know what he was about to do. I was in the front seat, and he was on the ground, looking up at me, remarkably full of pride and speaking softly.

As he wrote in the book, I was taken aback by the words coming from his mouth. "I want you to go on around the pattern and make two touch-and-go landings. . . ."

Still mildly stunned, I remembered to smile as I listened to him intently.

He continued speaking, ". . . if I give you the thumbs-up on the second one," gesturing, he stuck his thumb high above his head, "go on out and come back for me in about a half-hour."

What I wouldn't give for a photo of our two faces as he handed the logbook back to me.

"You can turn around and go on to the end of the runway, and I'll be walking down to the hanger and get me a cup of coffee. But you'll see me; questions?"

A no from me, and I fired up the engine.

I was so nervous that my left foot was shaking as I taxied back to the takeoff point alone. When I gave *43 Cocoa* the throttle, I was busy and forgot about the foot shaking. The 225-horsepower Continental O-470 engine screamed like all of Hell's banshees, and the wheels were thumping as she gathered speed. As the flight controls became responsive to the airflow, the grip of the stick was swaying like the head of a cobra in my hand; I applied back pressure to it—and lifted into smoothness.

I yawed slightly to the right to compensate for a bit of crosswind. In a momentary downward glance, I noticed an enormous crowd had gathered along the flight line. Some were still running to get there. I do not know how they knew I would be soloing. Perhaps it wasn't about me. It could have been anyone's inaugural flight, but I attribute it to the prevalent racism beyond the base.

The thing went well. I was elated. I wished Mama could have seen me! Later, I felt sorry for the people in the crowd who had marveled, even then, and their rush to see a Black teenager fly an airplane.

Like the people who ran to the flight line, history had remained hidden from the little dreamer in Texas. No word filtered down to me of the *Tuskegee Airmen* or the daring of *Bessie Coleman*, the Black American female wonder pilot and wing-walker, from the pioneer days of aviation. I knew that other

Black people flew airplanes, but there was nothing in the news about them. It was as if such knowledge was hushed in those days. If it was a conspiracy to hold me down, it was a vain one.

My brothers and I skipped the first half of each school year to pick cotton and attended class in the second half. But, neither lack of formal education nor the weight of systemic racism forestalled the consummation of my childhood dream of flying.

I would not be turned away!

Since the Saturday morning in 1958, when I pulled the shiny *Beechcraft* off the red dirt runway in Alamogordo, New Mexico, and passed over the heads of all the onlookers, *I have had no masters.*

Once I had my solo ticket and was cleared to take off and land from Holloman, I became well-known among the crews on the flight line and elsewhere on the base. I built solo hours in the T-34s, perfecting maneuvers in the practice area southeast of the base. After Ed signed me off for cross-country flights, I explored when the range was open for civilian traffic. I flew to Albuquerque, north of the *Tularosa Basin*, to El Paso, Texas, in the south. And from the *San Andres Mountains* in the west to the *Sacramento Mountains* on the other side of the range. After learning the intricacies of mountain flying, I flew beyond each range several times. During this period, the construction company that Pop worked for had a job at *Sandia Base* near Albuquerque. I flew to a small airfield nearby to let him see me with one of the T-34s. It was a proud meeting for both of us, especially since he had supported my dream of flying. As we stood speaking, I realized for the first time that we both were men. I wasn't twenty-one, but no child could have come as far as I had. It was a satisfying moment. One that he talked about for the rest of his life.

The club bought a 1941 *Beechcraft Bonanza.* It was a beautiful blue and white plane with a fast-cruising speed and a V tail. There was everything to love about this old luxury plane.

They wondered if it might be too "hot" for the low-time pilots, but since it was the basic design that the T-34s were built upon, they decided to see if I could fly it safely. Usually, that would be a concern for a pilot who only had a few solo hours in one of the small, low-powered trainers. Still, except for the V tail and seating arrangement, I was flying virtually the same aircraft. They gave me a couple of check rides and released me to fly the *Bonanza.*

I had logged about 35 flying hours toward the 40 Hours minimum time needed for my Private Pilot's Certificate. I had not yet completed enough ground school to take the test, but I wasn't a student in flying experience. The look of youth was still on me when I took one of the T-34s down to El

Paso International Airport. After I landed, the tower gave me progressive taxiing instructions to the ramp outside the place where I went to pick up a part for the *Bonanza*. I put chocks around the wheels and went inside for a short while to get the part. When I returned, a crowd of people had gathered at a respectable distance from the plane. As I drew near, they turned and scowled at me as I walked past them, pulled the chocks, and performed a brief walk-around- inspection. I was still about five feet eight inches tall and had a baby face then. They were eerily silent as a Black teen opened the canopy, climbed inside, and said loudly, "Please stand clear of the props." I saw they stood rooted in the same spot as I taxied out to the active runway for takeoff. In retrospect, I suppose I should have spoken to them about the plane, but conversations on an equal level didn't happen between Blacks and Whites outside the military.

The trip to El Paso was another rite of passage for me, an acceptance of my status as a free man. The time between my leaving Oak Street and its near abject poverty to being a competent pilot, flew by unnoticed, without me being affected by a sense of racial oppression. At Holloman, when I was around the other pilots (Even the military officers) nobody questioned my intelligence or right to fly airplanes. The look of astonishment on the face of the civilians informed me I had passed from being suspected of ignorance and gross incompetence to a world of intellectual freedom and acceptance as a human being. I attributed these things to an air of confidence brought to me by studying everything that was new to me.

WHILE RESEARCHING MILITARY FLIGHT TRAINING, I learned that the Air Force allowed applicants with a high school GED to qualify for the *Aviation Cadet Training Program*, provided they scored higher on the entrance exams. I didn't feel strongly about the outcome because of my near nonexistent traditional schooling, and besides that, other Black airmen I knew said that I would need a Black congress member to sponsor me. I did not know what a congress member was. Later, I found they could nominate their constituents for the service academies at *West Point* and *Annapolis*.

The Air Force's *Cadet Program* usually needed two years of college, so the GED route seemed like an excellent opportunity for me. I owed it to myself to try, but I was concerned that academic subjects on the test might trip me up, so I studied the things I had missed in school.

I applied for the program early in 1958 and in a few months received orders to report to Cannon AFB near Clovis, New Mexico for testing. The TNM&O bus carried me from Alamogordo to Clovis, and I called the base for a ride to the testing center. Cannon AFB was a fighter wing, and when we reached the base, I saw two F-86D Interceptor Jets with their vertical stabilizers (tails) painted in a black and white checkerboard pattern, taxing in our direction. They began their takeoff run immediately after pulling onto the runway, kicking in their afterburners after a quick roll. It was as if they were on a critical mission and had no time to waste. Stirred by the scene, I took it as a good sign!

Butterflies in my stomach fluttered as an African American, Airman First Class (E-4) behind the desk, looked me over as if I had strayed into the wrong place.

"I'm Airman Second Class Van B. McKellar, here to take the Aviation Cadet's entry exam," I said.

"McKellar," he responded, shuffling through some pages on his desk and then picking them up. "That test doesn't start until eleven hundred," speaking curtly, then looking at me for an answer.

This exchange was getting uncomfortable fast, so I said, "Where do you want me to wait?"

He replied succinctly! "You can wait anywhere you want to; just be back here at 1045 hours."

Since the time was only 30 minutes, I asked, "Is it alright to wait here?" pointing to a row of chairs off to the side.

"Yes, sure." Gesturing towards them.

I went over and sat down.

After about five minutes, he broke the silence, "You know, I took that test myself, but I didn't pass it. And you won't pass it either."

This time, he looked at me condescendingly, smirking as if I was a pitiful, naïve little country boy. He was getting to me, but I didn't snap back.

A few minutes later, he took me into the testing room and gave me my instructions, emphasizing which actions would cause me to fail. When the time to begin the test came, a bell or a buzzer sounded, I opened the booklet. After a few questions, I realized the test was like my old friend from elementary school, the *Reading Achievement Test.* I'll get some of them, I thought. As we progressed, many questions were about airplanes and flying. It looked as if I might have a chance. There was a break; then, the test started again. I completed another section in which I believed I did well. The rest of the examination was about average. I didn't know if I had enough right to qualify, but I wasn't troubled because I gave my best effort.

My life as an enlisted man was great. I had my second stripe and a good start earning the third one. I was confident that I would reenlist when my four years were up. As far as flying was concerned, I was happy with the General Aviation planes, but working on military aircraft kept the big ones on my mind. The most incredible opportunity for anyone in the field was mine, and I looked forward to serving as an Air Force pilot.

After a few months, paperwork began coming in. Extensive dental work and many medical exams were scheduled to prepare me for my new duties as a pilot. I opened each letter from *Air Training Command* with joyous expectations, snuggling up with them as if they were from some unseen lover. I was like a six-year-old waiting for Christmas morning. Finally, in December 1959, one came with orders to report for *Pre-Flight Training Class 61-F*, at Lackland Air Force Base. I was ready!

My race to honors had been like a competitor in a steeplechase, the track and field event where the runner must also jump hurdles and leap over water as he races for the finish. Since leaving the cotton fields two years earlier, I had overcome a severe deficit in education to get into the Air Force. I became an aircraft technician, assigned to a base with an environment where I learned to fly airplanes, and now was a candidate for the finest flight school in the world.

Chapter 9:
Cadet Days

Air Force pilots' ranking in the military pecking order corresponds to knights in the old feudal kingdoms of Europe. Knights came from either nobility or ruling class houses. They were the king's most honored warriors, highly trained in the art of combat. These refined noblemen dined at their master, the king's, table. They rode into single combat on terrible steeds, and all commoners gave them the highest respect, second only to the king himself. Such are the officers who fly the fire-belching chargers of the air. Aviation Cadets are pilots in training equal in rank to squires who are knights in training. Although squires did not sit with the king at his table, they took second meat on their own board and even first meat on celebration occasions in the Hall. Those not born into the hierarchy must eat the crumbs.

I completed three months of basic training at Lackland in 1956 as a recruit. In 1960, when I was twenty years old, I went back for another three months as a cadet in the first four phases of pilot training, called *Pre-Flight.* Preflight days were markedly different from basic training for recruits. Cadets did all the physical stuff recruits did. However, *Preflight* training included lectures, aptitude tests, movies, and comparable classroom instruction in leadership and aviation ground school. Of course, there was homework. The amount of the cadets' workload was so immense that we sacrificed our sleep, huddled under our blankets, studying by the light of a flashlight. In public school, my grades were low, and I agonized about it. My classroom grades in *Preflight* were average, but I felt better psychologically.

Pilot and Navigator candidates attended *Preflight* together. We were known as either *Red Birds* or *Blue Birds,* depending on whether we were student pilots or navigators. So, the stripes on our shoulder boards were red ones and the navigators in the class wore blue stripes. They designed the first few weeks of *Preflight* to see if a candidate could stand up to demanding challenges. By now, such training was old news to me, but it was taxing in some new ways. Cadets do everything at attention: march, walk, sit, and even eat. I won't ever forget my first partaking of the *evening dining privilege.* The upperclassmen shouted and barked orders, while the machine-like responses of other lower-class cadets eating "square meals" in the dining room looked like robots in a sci-fi movie. During a fire drill, I broke my right wrist and was given some latitude at mealtimes, but eating left-handed was also tricky.

Whenever an upperclassman caught an underclassman giving less than 100% effort, which was known as *casualing off*, It meant *gig* slips, which added up to walking punishment tours, at attention, of course. The downside was that time lost from studies when walking tours might set a cadet up for failure.

Another emphasis in *Preflight* was producing socially polished Air Force officers. They instructed us in formal etiquette and introduced us to tennis and golf. Many cadets already knew hoity-toity social manners and played both sports well. I never got the hang of driving the golf ball, but I was better than average at putting. However, I suppose they considered me to be suitable officer material. At midterm, when we advanced to upper-class status, they awarded me two red stripes, the rank of pilot cadet sergeant.

Deceit was no stranger in dealings with the guys on *The Hill*. I was always on guard in my circle of acquaintances and with others I felt were untrustworthy. Perhaps this was because of the persistent desire for material possessions. I did not sink into this line of thinking because my young ego did not measure its self-worth by the characters I knew. My desires differed from anyone I knew. I agreed with the writers in my old books that life could be better if everyone was more honest.

An uncommon side of being a cadet is rigid loyalty to an *Honor Code*. While the one we swore our oath to in *Preflight* may have been worded differently, its essence is identical to the one for the cadets at the Air Force Academy.

Honor Code Oath: "We will not lie, steal, or cheat, nor tolerate among us anyone who does. Furthermore, I resolve to do my duty and to live honorably, (so help me God)."

The *Honor Code* required shared integrity among cadets having different beliefs concerning ethics in diverse matters. It inspired me to be honorable in all areas of my life by living the code, and because I never knew of an instance of misconduct in *Preflight*, I was delighted at last to be among men of similar honor.

My sense of social standing rose in *Preflight* as I found myself around young fellows with a common interest. My old antagonist, athletics, did not factor into the equation; neither did my inability to do the things the *old gang* did before joining the service. This time, a level playing field raised the climate for personal growth, and I was comfortable with classroom activities.

Soon finals came, and with it, the anticipation of our next posting. My orders read "Report to Graham Airbase," near Marianna, Florida. Before we left, they issued our flight suits and flying helmets, which everyone knew as *Brain Buckets.* When I was home on furlough before reporting to Graham, I put on the flight suit for my family and friends. My companions were not impressed, but my mom was proud.

RIDING THE GREYHOUND BUS TO MARIANNA, FLORIDA I traveled through the troubled states of Louisiana, Mississippi, and Alabama on the way. I did not know if my bus had integrated seating as per the ICC requirements [It did not], but I was not in the mood for a hassle, so I sat in my favorite spot in the right rear as usual. No signs of the *Civil Rights Struggle* were visible from my window, but I knew it was going on. Still, I enjoyed the new scenery passing by until after midnight. We wound through tiny towns in Louisiana and then into darkness. Around daybreak, many Black men stood on the corners, apparently waiting for a ride to a job somewhere. I didn't like what I saw; I felt they were headed for field work. Not that Air force life had made me soft. I remembered the poverty in the outside world and the conditions under which they lived. I imagined their dreams were as black as the empty countryside. When dawn came, the Mississippi coastline appeared, and scenes of the Gulf held my attention.

When I arrived in Marianna, I hired a privately owned cab that belonged to a Black man to go out to the base. He told me that other Black pilots from Graham frequented the local night spots. [A few juke joints]. There were Africans that he knew. I was eager to meet them all.

Graham Air Base was home to the 3300th Pilot Training Group cadets. An Air Base is not an Air Force Base. It was a civilian contract facility that used nonmilitary instructors. However, we cadets lived military-style and under strict discipline. My class, 61-F, was just before Class 61-G, the final class of Aviation Cadets. After that, future Air Force officers would attend the new *Air Force Academy* near Colorado Springs. However, for now, Graham was my new home. At Graham, the accommodations were not the typical military barracks. Two small apartments were in a single motel-style building. Each room housed two cadets. The landscaping around the buildings gave them the look of country cottages. Ground keepers kept the curvy pathways free of loose leaves. Hedges and other shrubs lent to the idea of a summer retreat. The trees held back the rays of the southern sun, and it was quiet.

The dining room was near the sleeping area. It was the regular cafeteria-style, with Black American women preparing and serving the meals. Everyone bragged about how delicious the food was. Each time the servers received praise for the excellence of the food, they grinned and replied ever so sweetly, "*Thaaank* you."

The first few times I came in, they beamed as we exchanged knowing smiles. No doubt they had seen Black cadets come through before, but few were African Americans. The difference in class privilege between those served and the servers was apparent in their interactions. While no one spoke to me as if I were an underling in New Mexico, the old racist attitudes of the townspeople continued unchanged here in the Deep South. However, there was mutual respect and courtesy between the workers and me.

I was assigned to *Devil Flight*, and my call sign was *Devil 31*. My instructor was a gray-haired man with a German last name, which he claimed was his lineage. He introduced himself as Mr. Kessler. He had two new students besides me. He would be our instructor for both phases of primary school. During our first meeting, Mr. Kessler. explained what he expected of us. We noticed he made specific points with a small round club in his hands, not a pointer but a bludgeon.

He explained: "I had a student who crashed and broke my back when he froze at the controls while landing a T-6…."

Glancing at each of us so that we got the message, he continued, "So, if either of you…," whacking his hand with the club, "… don't release the controls when I tell you to…, well, we will not repeat that experience."

That short story broke the ice, and we were a team. I would come to feel my bonding with Mr. Kessler was genuine. In flying, he was a superb pilot, with thousands of hours in planes of all sizes, and had instructed many students.

Since the primary training planes we flew were the T-34 Mentors (My old solo planes from Holloman AFB) the stress that I usually felt before doing new things was practically nonexistent. I say almost because, after about 45 hours in the T-34, my aircraft for the next phase of Primary was the T-37 Tweet, a small twin-engine jet made by *Cessna*. This kind of stress is not anxiety but love at first sight. We were slated to complete the bulk of cadet flying hours in primary training. The syllabus called for about 45 hours flight time in the T-34, of which 25 were dual and 20 were solo. In the T-37 phase of primary, about 58 hours were spent with the instructor, and 25 were solo, for about 128 total hours. I could not have wished for a better person or set of conditions to hone my flying skills than Mr. Kessler!

I expected my first flight to be the usual check ride to familiarize a pilot with the features and characteristics of a new plane, but it was not. It was more like a lesson for a beginning student. On my first flight with Mr. Kessler, I expected him to be impressed by how well I flew a T-34. However, his behavior was more like I was a beginner. I could feel his hands on the joy stick, ready so he could take the controls quickly. I had been trained by men who were military pilots and had about 35 hours in the T-34, flying from both general aviation and military bases. I came to the Cadet Corp fully qualified to fly the plane safely. So, I believed his antics were a bit over the top, but I decided to not allow any negative thoughts to dwell in my mind

For about 5 hours of flying time, Mr. Kessler would show a maneuver, and I would perform it, to which he responded, "Good!" Then another cadet made the first solo in the class. I knew him; he was a good guy who also had prior flying time but in a smaller tail dragger. I thought the whole thing odd, but since I cared little about the honor of being first, I put it in the back of my mind. I was allowed to follow immediately after him. As was the custom, the other cadets threw me into a water-filled ditch.

Mr. Kessler. demanded perfection in all operations and recovery from abnormal attitudes and emergencies. This is standard training, but Mr. Kessler was a sadist with pulling stuff outside the box. Mr. Kessler would wait until it seemed there was no way I could make it back to the runway or there was no place to land. Then he would pull the throttle back to simulate engine failure: Without the sound of the engine and prop, the world became unnervingly silent. (The auxiliary landing fields and the surrounding areas allowed for flying close to the ground.)

"Alright," he would say, dragging out his phrase, "What are you going to do now, Mister McKellar?"

The first few times, a crash seemed inevitable, and we would break off the exercise.

He would then take the controls and begin sarcastically talking smack to me as we climbed back to altitude; "Didn't you see that little spot over there, this side of the trees?"

I would look, and sure enough, the bit of discoloration on the surface might be big enough to land. I began to think ahead of the plane, should the engine fail. In succeeding false engine out exercises, I would take the stick and drop rapidly down to a small clearing with a few forward slips to lose more airspeed.

When we were so close to the ground, I braced myself and gritted my teeth he would say, "Can you make that?"

"Yes, Sir," I'd reply convincingly and apply full throttle, the engine roaring as we climbed away.

It was the same with attitude recovery, except I would be under the hood, where I couldn't see outside the plane to orientate myself. When Mr. Kessler handed the controls back to me, I would recover to straight and normal, or whatever attitude he requested. Recovery had always been easy for me once I saw the horizon, but Mr. Kessler soon upped the game to recovery on instruments alone. These tactics were a precursor to performing aerobatics while flying by instruments only. This would come in the T-37s. The T-34 phase of flying passed. I had a check ride with an Air Force Examiner, and there were no problems.

Photo of T-37 for illustration only

The eagle soars

WE MOVED INTO THE T-37S. This time, there were no demonstrations by the instructors on the first flight. They gave us verbal instructions concerning engine operations, but we relied on our own judgment. The jet engines started more readily than the gas-powered ones, which required more engine controls. The propeller-driven planes I flew before the jets moved awkwardly on the surface, but the T-37 taxied like an automobile. The view from the high, side-by-side seating cockpit was better. During my first takeoff in the jet, I positioned the plane over the center stripe that ran down the runway. When taking off in propeller driven aircraft, gyroscopic torque pulls the airplane to the left. However, jet engine planes are not subject to such forces. This time, there was no crosswind interference, so the airplane stayed over the stripe. I lifted the nose at the proper speed, and we sprang from the ground. Sensing that we were safely up, I pulled up the gear and retracted the wing flaps used in takeoff. By then, we had passed through a hundred feet of altitude. It was like when Will Smith flew the alien craft in the motion picture

Independence Day. I felt like shouting, "I have got to get me one of these!"

After that thrilling flight, to say that it elated me does not fully convey what was going on in my mind. My thoughts differed from my deliberations after my first propeller-driven flight in the T-34 at the red-dirt Alamogordo Airfield. This time, it was not a student mulling over what it would take to be a successful pilot. The images that overshadowed my thoughts included putting the T-37 through everything in the flying sphere. My thinking processes had grown beyond an inexperienced young man finding his way in the world. From the moment the jet's wheels broke ground, there were no more moments of feeling like a student. Sure, there was plenty to be learned. But as a pilot, I wasn't a boy anymore, and my expectations now were of mastery.

On the next flight, we flew to one of the practice areas and did the stalls and other exercises to allow me to get the feel of the plane. After a couple more hours of performing takeoffs and landings, I knew I could fly the plane safely, but there were other things to learn about this new type of flying. When I had five hours, Mr. Kessler signed my logbook for a solo flight. This time I was the first in my class to solo the T-37 Tweet. I loved the feeling of being outstanding, and a trace of the competitor's attitude set itself up as a part of my makeup. As the training progressed through the T-37 phase, those who would not make it as pilots were gone, and only hard-core flyers remained. These are the people who eat, sleep, and live to fly. So, we all seemed to get along.

Now I was more than familiar with the T-37. Later, one day, before the Southern stars came out in their glory, I suited up and set out on a required practice flight. The atmosphere was so thick at sea level that the scaled-down jets responded to full takeoff power with a gusty roar. Holding the airspeed at two-hundred knots, I climbed eastward and away from the coastline until I was over the Atlantic Ocean. I was pleased at how serene I felt as I reached an altitude of about fourteen thousand feet. The engines were not as powerful in the thinner air, but the hydraulic flight controls were responsive to the slightest touch of my gloves. I knew that the ground control facilities were watching but also knew I would put on a good show. Before night fell and the visibility lessened, I wanted to cut a rug to the soulful melody in my heart, and the laws of gravity were my dance partner. First, I turned my head left, then right, to clear the area for other traffic. My chest tightened as I fell into a forty-five-degree angled dive, engines screaming, now. Then I was near the maximum speed for my plane, I rounded out of the dive and pulled up so abruptly, I felt my cheeks sag in my oxygen mask from the G-forces. Passing through the vertical plane, the attitude gauges turned over in their cages to compensate from being inverted. But I was one with the music and rolled out topside in perfect position to complete my maneuver. This wasn't free style, so I hit every step in the book. Somewhere, during the graceful loops and lightning rolling, I left my body and my machine behind. And, as in the little ghetto boy's dreams, I was flying free high over the sea.

Time and space returned, and the fuel indicators begged: "Down; down!"

"Down; down," my humanness echoed as night fell on the earth below.

Estimating my course back to Graham Air Base, I saw the horizon brighten with land lights. When I returned to my bedroom, my ears tingled because I was satiated, sleepy, and the world was right

Many of my fellow pilots came from countries other than the United States. Most of them flew the T-28 Trojan in the second phase, and their group was called Lobo Flight. During the T-34 phase, one roommate was from Vietnam. He was a quiet, reserved man. My next roommate came from Eritrea. He, I, and two other pilots from Ethiopia hung out together on base and in town. We all flew T-37s. My first experience of being up close and personal with Africans was positive. Although we had preconceived notions about the other's culture and social relationships, we got along well. My pal, Mamo Tachie, and I grew closer than I did with the boys back home. We followed different paths to get to flight training, but our experiences had groomed us to a similar level of education and social values.

Black Marianna townspeople were accustomed to seeing Mamo and Africans from other countries but spoke of only a few Black American pilots. Although they seemed surprised to learn that I was not Ethiopian, they were mildly shocked to find I was from Texas and had the same Black person's background as they did. I mention this to point out how few American Black men were admitted into the cadet corps during my tour of duty.

After living integrated on the Air Force bases, visiting downtown Marianna brought unpleasant reminders of the social hierarchy I lived under in Fort Worth a few short years ago. But now I disliked how openly racist the White population was outside the gates toward Negroes (a proper name then). The first time that I visited Marianna was on a Saturday morning. Three Ethiopian cadets and I piled into Michael's car and drove to the town square, where the shops and stores faced inward upon a little park. The sidewalks were about a half of a block long on each side. I noticed the buildings were old, not the *Old South* of bygone days, but not new. In the center of the quadrangle was a brick or concrete wall that was just high enough to sit on. The square was where the locals mingled and sat around. Presumably, the White folk talked of sugarcane crops and native pecan harvests. I don't recall whether a walkway was on top of the square, but there grew at least one massive tree. I don't know the type. Several cars were parked there.

The Africans and I wore Class-A military uniforms of our native countries. As we went through the stores, the shopkeepers were polite to us. I bought a small FM radio that day. Unexpectedly, the young White girl that waited on me was flirty; she was not just outgoing but putting out feelers, which I joked past. Race relations, being as they were, this small talk had the potential for severe consequences. I later learned why I did not see any other Black people on that visit. Because colored folk's hours were from morning until noon, they had finished shopping and hanging out on the square.

At another time, we went to a place that reminded me of Oak Street. It was at the bottom of a hill and away from the business sector, Like the *Jitterbug Inn* back home. There was a dance floor where people my age congregated. The Ethiopians went there to meet girls they knew. A lovely girl and I hit it off from the start. Whenever I came in from the base, we borrowed my new local friend Donald's car and passed the time in romantic seclusion. Not long after, we spoke the words of love and were locked in its spell.

I changed my drinking habits after I blacked out while drinking moonshine. After that, I did not drink when I went to town to be with Merle. When I was in the cadet club, shooting pool or playing table tennis, I usually drank only one to be friendly. I didn't want to be affected by alcohol when I flew.

Chapter 10:
Icarus

Cadets govern their own affairs just as a Wing of regular pilots would. There are cadet officers corresponding to all the required ranks up to a cadet full colonel. Since cadets are trainees, and not commissioned officers, they are supervised by a regular Air Force officer, usually a captain in rank, The Tactical Officer, or Tac Officer., oversees the cadet's military and moral and ethical training and their other needs. Protocol requires that the Tac Officer does not associate with cadets on a social level.

Near the completion of primary flight school, trouble developed on three fronts. First, I received a message to report to the *Tac Officer*. Upon reaching his office, I was informed that I had been accused of buzzing the *Cattle Barns*. I had no prior knowledge of the accusation. I was stunned!

(Buzzing is when a pilot flies his plane so close to a structure that it shakes because of the disturbance caused by engine sound or propeller vibrations.)

Our instructor, Mr. Kessler, spoke to us about the *Cattle Barns* at the start of training. They were several lengthy structures about five miles from the runways at Graham and were ideal for setting up the landing approach to the field. Some instructors taught their students to use the barns, but as we became more proficient at making our approach to the field, many of us did not use them. I never enjoyed using them because the area over them was congested with new students. Mr. Kessler warned us to keep the proper altitude over the barns. Stressing the point, he said, "If you get too low over the barns, the man on the ground has a good pair of binoculars and will call you in, then it will be over." [Meaning we would be washed out of school.]

They informed me at the Tac Officer's office that a formal hearing would occur. At first, I thought, this is a mistake and would be cleared up quickly enough, because I wasn't anywhere near the *Cattle barns* at any time. Because I had experience flying the traffic patterns at Holliman and Kirkland AFBs, I didn't have a problem entering the traffic pattern from any angle. Besides that, the T-34s flew the traffic pattern eight hundred feet above the ground. The T-28's and T-37's traffic pattern was two hundred feet higher, at one thousand feet above the ground. No sensible person would fly beneath airplanes in a landing pattern. A rational-thinking pilot should see that the complaint was a mistake or something else was happening.

My knowledge of legal matters was virtually zero. Still, I offered the above paragraph in defense and asked to question the person who made the complaint. Somehow, the *Cattle barn* accusation went away, and because I thought it was all an innocent misunderstanding, I did not realize what was in the air.

PHOTO BY UNSEEN HISTORIES ON UNSPLASH

IN THE WORLD OUTSIDE, THE CIVIL RIGHTS STRUGGLE WAS BOILING over. Black college students staged sit-ins at stores with Whites Only lunch counters for their customers. Many local White people felt that their right to refuse service was being violated and were as angry as Blacks that were denied those same services. *Rosa Parks*, an early civil rights champion, gave a face to the struggle when she refused to give up her seat to a White man on a Montgomery, Alabama bus in 1955. Plus, the federal Montgomery bus lawsuit *Browder v. Gayle* resulted in a November 1956 decision that bus segregation was unconstitutional, but the violent segregationists were not conceding. The protestors were peaceful even while being kicked and beaten.

The entire country took sides in the matter; the news media covered every event. Cadets stationed at Graham did not take up the issue openly. As service members, we did not involve ourselves in political matters. In addition, this was when politics and religion were touchy topics, so we did not discuss them. We all, Black and White, understood what was happening in this highly polarized and deadly fight. However, the appalling news footage shown to the world of Whites being lethal oppressors was not news to me. After I joined the Air Force, I thought I had escaped the same persecution.

It is no strain of the imagination to realize that some Whites in the Cadet Corp blamed Black people for these damaging revelations about them that went out to the world. In addition to that, it seemed every gain in Black civil rights was seen by the Southerners as an invasion of their sacred territory. I still think they singled me out as a Black man to be the object of their reprisals. On the other hand, I was irritated at African American's continued maltreatment but not wishing to portray the Militant, said nothing. Affected by these negative feelings concerning acceptance in the newly integrated Air Force, I was like the patriarch, Job in the Bible: I thought I was safe. *But, into my quiet and rest, trouble came.* In all honesty, because I was not openly under the constant barrage of bigotry myself, I had grown trusting and naïve!

When I went into the Black section of Marianna, we talked a little about what was taking place, but the small community did not burn with the fervor that flamed elsewhere in the country. That was the case in many other sections of Black America. Although those in the thick of the battle fought so hard, it appeared the entire Black race was outraged. Primarily, Black churches and a mixed crowd of college students were the vanguards of the *civil rights struggle.*

I cannot agree with but understand why the Whites took their attitude about our demands for equality. In my opinion, Whites had grown accustomed to segregation and their privileged status quo.

I don't remember when the hazing on the bus that picked us up at our quarters and carried us to the flight line began, but it echoed the civil rights issue. There may have been over twelve cadets riding on the trip. I got on first and sat up front but a few seats back to have a better forward view. As the bus filled up, I greeted everyone that got on, and most responded cheerfully. It was always a good day to fly, so the conversation was good-natured.

However, I remember that after the *Cattle barn* affair, I would have at least three cadets screaming in rhythm: "Get on the back of the bus, *Gate.* (One of my nicknames) Get on the back of the bus, Gate; Get on the back of the bus, *Gate.*" This cacophony of nonsense continued until we arrived at the flight line. Some gentlemen on the bus shouted; those not in on the shouting said nothing. At first, I would come back with clever answers. But when it became dead serious as others joined in, I broke off answering them, thinking that it would end, but it didn't. Then, I understood that this was more than joking around.

One ugly side of covert racism is that when there are more Whites than Blacks, the Whites ask asinine questions about Black people. Regardless of whether they get an answer, everybody is expected to laugh. The Blacks don't have to belly laugh. But if a smile is on their faces, and the Black person endures this nonsense; they may accept him within limits as a *good old boy.* When he does not, he is marked. Such practices are highly improper, and adherence to *The Cadet Honor Code* should have intervened. However, because the cadets in my Flight tolerated racism in their midst, The Code was as ineffective as in the past.

Note: During his entire term at West Point, the Corps refused to speak to the first Black American cadet, Henry Ossian Flipper. He graduated in 1877, was commissioned a Second lieutenant, and served in the 10th Calvary. "While serving in Texas, he was accused by a superior officer of embezzling commissary funds and conduct unbecoming of an officer and a gentleman. At his court martial, Flipper was cleared of the embezzlement charge but was found guilty of unbecoming conduct and dismissed from the Army in 1882."

[https://www.buffalosoldiersofwestpoint.org/buffalosoldiers-at-westpoint]

Again, the Corp disregarded its oath to The Code when they silenced another West Point cadet, General Benjamin O. Davis Junior. From the time he entered the academy until he graduated in 1936. Their only objection was that Cadet Davis was Black.

I do not compare my plight to that of General Davis. Instead, I am calling attention to a well-known story about the American military's double standards from the earliest times.

Black officers and cadets moved through the Corps with honor. There were high-ranking Black cadets in other flights during my term. One Wednesday at noon, as we stood in formation on the flight line, *Chappie James* made a lightning-fast fly-by in an RF-101 Voodoo. However, my experience in the cadet corps differed from some other Black members but was familiar enough.

I became more agitated over the bus chanting foolishness but thought I could bear it for the next few weeks of Primary. However, I made a grave mistake before then. I fell into a routine of going over to the Cadet Club more than usual for a drink to ease the angst that had sneaked in on me. During one of those nights, several of us cadets were singing the song,

Silhouettes, over in the corner at the Club. We were well-oiled, very loud, and irritatingly off-key as drunk men under stress sound during intoxicated four-part harmony. Ordinarily, this would not have been an issue, but the Tac Officer was in the Club. Commissioned officers, including the Tac Officer, did not socialize with cadets in the club. I saw him standing at the bar but thought nothing of it; we were simply carrying on in the club. I realize that our singing may have been annoying to some, but it could not compete with the tirade on the bus. Perhaps some of the upper-class cadets didn't want the Tac Officer to see how rowdy their underlings were. I compare the situation to parents who bring their children under control when the grandparents are in the house so that mom and pop won't think them too easygoing. We were adamant about our right to sing and kept on singing loudly. After all, it was a common occurrence in the club when we passionately sang "The Air Force Song" at roof-rattling intensity while we were highly intoxicated.

I was drunk when the Tac Officer came over. I may have been on the brink of going into an alcohol blackout because the scene was fuzzy, and I couldn't make out what they said. However, I did hear when someone in the group explained to the Tac Officer that he had no authority in the club. Once I sobered up, I realized that was incorrect, but then it seemed logical and escalated into an argument between the Tac Officer and me when I joined the conversation. I can't remember all that was said in the back and forth, but I remember that the argument became a personality clash between the Tac Officer and me. We both had become belligerent, as men can sometimes do when alcohol is a factor. Again, I couldn't remember what was said, just incoherent bits of disagreement. I don't know how I got home, but I realized I was in deep trouble the following day. It didn't take long for me to swear off drinking forever!

I continued to fly but eventually was called before a legal board for a hearing. Someone not involved suggested that I "Get some representation." I didn't have money for an attorney and knew from experience that in a disagreement between a Black man and a White man, the Black man always loses regardless of who was wrong. I saw that Black men lost absolutely in the highest courts in the land and local ones. For that reason, I believed that *Jim Crow* conditioning led White people to consider a Black man's efforts at law as laughable. As comical as the antics of *"Algonquin J. Calhoun, Esquire,"* the overreaching Negro lawyer on the famous TV show *Amos and Andy.* I also saw that Whites acted as if Black legal matters were deceptions involving the *NAACP* or some Black Militant organization. So, I presumed they would boot me out of the cadet corps without remedy. I heard no more from the

Board until after graduating from Primary Flight Training. I received my assignment to Reese Air Force Base, near Lubbock, Texas, for Basic Flight School. Then they called me back for their decision. They punished me harshly rather than dismissed me from the Corps. Besides some other actions, I received two *Commander's Awards* called CAs. These were the most severe punishments a cadet could get before being dismissed. I did not think appealing would help my situation.

At first, I was relieved that they didn't drum me out of the Corps, but after calculating the number of punishment tours that came with each CA, I realized it would take the entire time I was in Basic Flight School to walk the maximum number of tours. I wondered if I could do all that was required of Basic and still walk the tours? Perhaps, but the question became; could I get enough sleep and rest to perform the flying safely? Sadly, I understood they had spared me nothing. They set me up in such a way that when I failed, it would not appear as punishment for the incident with the Tac Officer; they needed a situation in which I, only, was at fault. Therefore, it must appear that I failed because of my own inability.

There was another reason I resigned from the Corp. It was the All of you Black people are the same line of thinking that the city used to bar us from the *Fort Worth Public Library*. They employed the narrative to disparage Black people, but this thinking has a flip side. Because the judgment of one fellow is a judgment of all, when a member of an oppressed people rises, it must follow that it is a success for all and proof of all's abilities. I knew Black officers and pilots were rare compared to Whites in *Jim Crow America.* I saw only one Black officer in person in my three years in the service. She was a Major and wore medical insignia. Whites outside the military may not readily appreciate Black people's plight because there has never been a question of their race's competence as leaders. However, I always noticed how proud other Black airmen were when they saw me in an elevated position. When I left Holloman for the corps, my Black friends felt as honored as I did about the prospect of having another Black in the higher levels of leadership. But more than military members felt that way; the civilians on the base and in town shared in my position. I knew acutely that the negative judgment of my race also rested on my shoulders. Although it was unfair, I was a poster boy for Black officer candidates. I would not allow the sight of a Black cadet walking punishment tours day after day as an example that Black people are incompetent when promoted above menial tasks. I would not be used to provide validity to the same excuse the White commanders used since the Civil War to misuse and malign Black troops. Also, I considered I was not wholly at fault and that other factors had been in play. Could this have been part of the recent racism I was dealing with? Why did the Tac Officer come to the club when I was drunk and vulnerable? I had never seen him there before.

Since the White cadets and one White officer involved in the quarrel were not charged, my black skin is the obvious answer to why they singled me out for punishment. They had tried to get me on the *Cattle barn* buzzing but failed because of a lack of hard evidence. They wanted to push me into doing something stupid by hazing me on the bus, but I held up. When I was drunk at the club was the occasion that they needed, and as an intoxicated man usually will, I helped them to do it.

Today, I am certain that the Air Force outwitted me when they imposed so much punishment on me that I had to drop out of pilot school. I still have no legal training, but how the events happened is clearer to me at eighty-five than at twenty. My interpretation of these matters is not a judicial opinion, but my assessment alone. The question stands out now: Did the Tac Officer's intervention in a cadet matter subvert my right to *Due Process?*

The incident began when some cadets in the cadet club complained about me and some other cadets singing loud and off-key. They ask the singers, not any one person, to tone it down. If our refusal to comply with the request was an infraction, it was a cadet problem, in which the cadets had the authority (a legal mechanism) to hear and dispense punishment as a remedy. If any cadet needed restraining, the cadets had the power to do that as well.

The Tac Officer was out of sequence when he interfered at the cadet club because resolving problems flowed upward in the military chain of command. Suppose the cadets could not affect a solution after exhausting their review of the problem. They would then forward the matter upward to the Tac Officer. However, when the Tac Officer officially inserted himself into the issue before the cadets had heard the case, he broke the chain of command in a downward stroke. In so doing, he deprived me of my right to Due Process. After which, the Hearing Officers became free to exact the harsher unfair discipline. In addition, if the cadets had charged me with being drunk and disorderly, the punishment would not have been as severe as the punishment imposed by the Board because our club was our place where we drank and unwound.

It was ridiculous for the Board to expect a drunken man to behave like a clear-headed one. It is even more unfair because I was in a place that allowed alcohol consumption on the premises. Alcohol impairment regularly took place without punishing the drinkers for drunken behavior. Considering the circumstances, the Hearing Officers disciplined an alcohol-impaired person because he did not act with the clarity and reason of an unimpaired one.

They had to resort to something like this to get me out of their midst. My ranking as a pilot was too high to fail me because of flying. I never had a complaint from my instructor. Indeed, it was just the opposite. My instructor always complimented me on my piloting skills. I passed my check rides, including the final check ride with military instructor pilots, without a negative mark either time. My academic standing was around the middle of the class, maybe lower, but nowhere near the bottom or wanting. I did all the training on time and did no punishment tours except the introductory one we all got in *Pre-Flight* Training. My record, before and after the *Cattle barns* accusation, was spotless. But why me? Other Black pilots moved through the Corps and received their commissions.

Was my black skin a black mark on my record? These shenanigans were racism, to be sure, and were not new to me. I knew it from the shops on Pine Street; the savage chanting on the bus, like *Masai* boys who try to bring the mighty lion to bay. Again, something sinister was rooted in their bullying; perhaps it was fear of competing with Black men fairly. I was a strong young Black man who had climbed *Mount Olympus* and acted like it. My swagger and trash talk were typical of many skilled young Blacks, usually sports stars. It is an embedding in the Black experience and should not be frowned upon by those who prefer mock humility. Although the Whites celebrate such skillful maverick officers within their ranks, they want Black ones who behave similarly to tone it down. That is sheer bigotry. However, there was another factor, a thing darker than racism. It is so reprehensible that it drives men to seek shelter within these borders. It is the exact reason for this country's existence.

The other cadets had from two years in college to bachelor's degrees. Since attending college was costly, we may infer that they came from families with ample wealth to warrant them having a degree of culture and refinement. I came from a wretched tradition that they could not imagine. I came from poverty-stricken roots at *The Bottom of Baptist Hill* in Fort Worth, Texas, which was more like a third-world country. *The Hill* was also in my mannerisms and the inflection in my speech. It seemed the corps didn't embrace Black cadets who were smack talkers. Perhaps if I had been one who knew how to take a joke about the negative aspects of Black people and not snap back with one about Whites, I would have stood in good stead. But

I no longer toyed with the idea that Blacks must be patient, which meant that racism remained the status quo. Perhaps there was still a frightening hint of the *Field Negro* about me. To some Whites, I fit the profile of an *Uppity Nigger*, who would not reform just to alleviate their fears of Black men.

As American military men, their chests should have swollen with pride at the idea of a diverse brotherhood protecting the sacred words: "*We hold these truths to be self-evident, that all men are created equal, that they are endowed by their Creator with certain unalienable Rights, that among these are Life, Liberty and the pursuit of Happiness.*" These are hallowed words upon which this country's White people separated themselves from prejudice based on social class in their former European countries. However, some Whites in exalted positions have not embraced that mantra wholeheartedly. Once the Colonists overthrew King George's tyranny and abolished old laws, which lay at the root of oppression, they should have dealt with the system that led to them in the beginning. This is the practice of classism, which often will not suffer those it considers as lower class. Sadly, this has somehow thrived in our experiment of democracy.

After reflecting on the unjust punishment imposed on me, I went to see the Tac Officer with some questions. I asked him if I self-eliminated and went back to my old unit, would it hurt my military record? He assured me it presumably would not, but he had to take it higher up. He told me when I saw him again, since I had less than two months left on my initial four-year enlistment, they could discharge me with a good record and an *Honorable Discharge*. Later, I would understand my need for counseling throughout the incident.

Nevertheless, I was still ignorant of taking care of myself in legal matters, aside from my high rise through the system. However, it seemed the right thing to do then, so I took the deal. Throughout the time my release was going on, I remember how eager to help the officers were. Usually, that would have been a dead giveaway. It did not because I knew outside the military, a Black man usually got the maximum punishment for any involvement with White higher-ups. I would not fight and make things worse. Still willing to "lend me a helping hand," they rushed all the paperwork, gave me my Certificate of Completion of *Primary Flight Training*, and discharged me on the spot. Without the sad farewells that usually accompanied cadets who left the Corps, I went to Marianna and drowned myself numb on moonshine.

ONCE I LEFT THE AIR FORCE, I RENTED A HOUSE IN MARIANNA. Merle would often join me when I wasn't working or helping Donald with house painting projects. Cadet class 61-G graduated, and Graham Air Base shut down, leaving many civilian employees unemployed. The line at the unemployment office stretched out to the parking lot. One day, as I came out of the office, I practically walked within touching distance of Mr. Kessler, who was in a line full of White people going into a door on the other side of the small building. We recognized each other.

I was truly glad to see him, I walked toward him, grinning and saying his name. "Hey, Mr. Kessler, how are you (I was eager to chat about anything)?"

He turned his head upward and stepped stiffly away from me with an expression of revulsion on his face.

He said nothing, and I spoke no further, feeling disgusted as he appeared to be. His look was the same as White guys on the base had when Black airmen ran into them off base and downtown. This two-faced behavior was a big thing then.

When we spoke to the White guys back at the base, their inevitable retort was, "Man, I didn't recognize you in your civvies."

Of course, they recognized us, but they, too, "knew how Whites should act" in society at large. Mr. Kessler had always seemed friendly to me before. His attitude toward me now revealed he had one-sided, intimate knowledge of my problem, which should not have been discussed in public. It was no big deal since we didn't move in the same social circles. Besides that, with Mr. Kessler sitting next to me in the right seat punctuating any variance of my performance with his club, I honed my flying skills to perfection. I would not throw away our treasured hours together just to retaliate in the form of bigotry.

I was happy to be with the Black people my age in Marianna who accepted me into their fold. I lived as they did, hunting, going to juke joints deep in the woods in Georgia and Alabama, and local spots tucked away in places I could never seem to find again. We drank moonshine, which Black folks knew as *Splo, Ram, and Bust head.* My *blackouts* increased, but somehow, I stayed out of trouble. Merle and several other girls went with us, which was terrific for a while. As fall approached, Donald and I made money, gathering pecans for halves with the owners. When that played out, I moved home to Texas, and Merle and Dot, her three or four-year-old baby daughter, went with me.

Embarrassed over how events in the service had turned out when I came back to *The Hill,* I made up an explanation why I wasn't in the Air Force anymore. My friends didn't care. They just wanted me to drink cheap wine with them. By then, my family had moved into a larger house on East Lancaster Street. It sat back off the street in the trees and had an air of privacy. I practically deserted Merle, leaving her home with Mama and hanging out with the old gang that drank every day. Eventually, I reenlisted in the Air Force just before the cops threw me in the drunk tank at the Fort Worth City Jail. (A horror story for another time). After I got out, I reported to Walker Air Force Base near Roswell, New Mexico, as an Airman Second Class. I returned to my old job on the flight line as a hydraulic technician on B-52s. I rented a house and sent for Merle and Dot to come to Roswell.

When a good man stumbles, there must be an account of why it took place. In my case, those dear to me sought answers to the tragedy. Perhaps, "I could stop before it was unstoppable." I liken my fall to when I was a child and fell from the top of the hill across from I.M. Terrell. As I walked along the edge, cocky and not looking where I stepped, the ground gave way, and I rolled down the steep, rough part of the slope. Fearful thoughts ran haphazardly through my mind as I failed to grasp the clusters of vegetation, bump after bump. I uprooted clumps of weeds as I grabbed to get a hold. "With each painful wallop, I wondered, when will I ever stop? Am I going to die?" When I fell to the bottle, I disregarded a known peril and began the same uncontrolled downward tumble. This time, my loved ones also endured each blow as my drunken condition demolished what was good in each of us.

As in my fall from the hill, my descent didn't take long. Similarly, I was often brought home in a lifeless heap. Alcoholism affects us differently, but the common thread is the destruction of something beautiful. For many alcoholics, death is gradual, lasting decades; for high-flying types like me, it reverses their skyrocket rise, then they tumble into an Underworld of sotted souls.

Things went well on the flight line; however, I drank more with my Air Force buddies during my off-duty hours. I didn't have *blackouts,* but I got sloppy drunk, and Merle and I argued about the least of things. Many of the fights had to do with accusations about fulfilling marital roles. The ones that began with, "Things would be better if you did your duty as wife/husband should do."

Sometimes the other wives attended the gatherings, but we men didn't include them in a way that satisfied their social needs. Now that years have passed, I understand Merle's predicament; I simply dumped a young woman into unfamiliar surroundings. She didn't bond with people with whom she shared the things people usually do with devoted friends. We men got drunk and talked loudly about sports and stuff on the job. So as her participation in the dream died, the marriage increasingly became unglued. Perhaps there may have been a chance to salvage our family, but in retrospect, I don't know if I was mature enough to see that I was at fault. I turned into a man whose nature changed into something demonic. I became irrational and screamed and yelled at her when I was drinking. Oh, I was quick with apologies and promises when I was not drunk. We were in a death spiral! While stationed at Walker AFB, Mama died in 1962 of a stroke at forty years old. I went home on emergency leave in time to be there. It was a terrible blow to us, but Pop held the family, my two younger brothers, and two sisters, together. We older boys, two Air Force and one Army, went on with our lives.

After about a year, I was transferred to Ramey Air Force Base in Puerto Rico. There was no complication involved, just a routine transfer. Merle and I returned to Marianna and moved the furniture we bought in New Mexico into the same house we had before in Florida. I left for Charleston AFB to catch my flight to Ramey. We said soft goodbyes and kissed without tears. I never saw her again. We lost all contact. After returning from the island, I talked briefly with Merle by phone. There were no hard feelings, yet I am apologetic for the sorrow I caused her with my alcoholism. I didn't blame her for giving up because our relationship was unworkable.

Photo for illustration only

RAMEY AFB SAT HIGH ON THE ISLAND TO AVOID OBSTRUCTIONS to the giant planes taking off and landing. There also were civilian houses nestled high near the city of Aguadilla. On one end of the Base, a steep trail went down through a shady coconut palm forest to the sea. Young trees of varying height grew off from the sides of the sloping passage beneath the canopy of the giants. These clumps of green and brown undergrowth spread here and there. It was eerily quiet the first time I descended. Had I trespassed into some forbidden forest kingdom? If so, mine was not the first intrusion. The pathway was popular for those who took long hikes. However, the route was narrow and didn't spoil its appearance of untouched nature. The trail ended at the edge of the trees and opened onto a beach with a fire pit off to the right, where we loosened up and whooped it up Hawaiian luau style. To the left, along the shoreline, there was an outcropping of flat rocks and a place to fish. I hooked an odd-looking, wide-bodied fish that none of the base personnel could identify. This tranquil area had a charming name, but it escapes my memory. Regrettably, I didn't get to know it well enough.

Ramey had the makings of a plumb assignment. Many earth-toned buildings on the base harmonized with tropical colors and themes of the Caribbean islands. The warm and sultry weather spoke of nights in the isles. After work, we dressed like island tourists. It was beautiful, not pristine, but the big nasty cities of the mainland were far from my mind!

The native *Castilian Spanish* gave meaning to the phrase *Romance Language*. It devastated me that Merle was not with me. I did not fully enjoy this piece of paradise because each time I saw something fascinating; I thought of seeing it with my first love. Before her, whenever I heard of some interesting place, I would be off with the guys. Now I didn't see or hear with the same sense of wonderment because I could not bring her back to the setting and make the world ours. I could not finish any thought without guilt and self-pity. In my misery, I could not understand why I did foolish things or said hurtful ones that I didn't mean. Something gloomier than solitude and regret drove me to drink unrestrained. Still, in this either, I didn't have the will to "meet the rigid issues of life" as I did so long ago in the fields.

My drinking became severe enough to have me visit a psychologist on base. After interviewing me, he said nothing that addressed my mental distress, just that I drank too much. The counselor called me mister. "Mister McKellar, these behaviors are typical of heavy drinkers." As he continued, he expressed disapproval while explaining that the Air Force lacked a remedy for heavy drinkers. The Air Force simply discharged them.

One night, I ran around, in, and outside my barracks in an intoxicated state, and the *First Sergeant* became involved. This led to a non-judicial punishment, an Article 15 hearing, and a *General Discharge Under Honorable Conditions* on April 12, 1963. I flew to Charleston AFB and was discharged there. The terms of my discharge meant that I was still eligible for all benefits except re-enlistment. So, I left to seek treatment for my alcoholism outside of the service.

Section III: Addictions

Chapter 11:
Caught up in Alcoholism

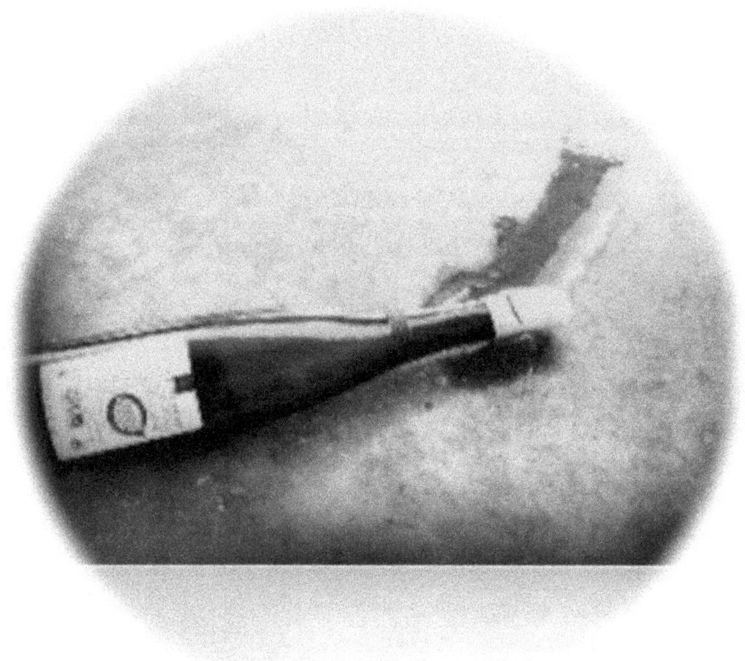

A few months after my discharge, my routine on *The Hill* became monotonous. Again, no one cared about my downfall in the Air Force. Failure was so commonplace here that I don't think they saw my situation as something terrible. After a few toothy grins and tight embraces, ties with the guys picked up again.

I learned good jobs opened up as the *Civil Rights Struggle* gathered momentum. The word around The Hill was that the *Bomber Plant*, now *General Dynamics*, accepted applications from Black workers seeking unskilled work. So did the other aircraft manufacturers, *Bell Helicopter*, and *LTV*. The *General Motors "Buick Olds and Pontiac"* plant in Arlington, Texas also hired Black employees. However, these well-paying mid-level jobs were less than a plum position needed to restore my bruised ego to its higher sense of self-worth. Now that I was back home, my failure to complete Air Force pilot training weighed heavily, as if a death sentence had been passed on me. I aspired to be somewhere else in an optimistic scenario where my inner fears of the real me weren't pointed out as a failure before the world. Threads of depression clutched at me because of some unnamed guilt. I knew I had done nothing wrong, but I was not strong enough to bear any accusation without becoming annoyed. *The Cadet Corp* had drummed the message: If you can't make it here, you won't be able to make it anywhere. I know now that it was only an attempt to burn bridges behind us to keep us hyper-motivated, but it fell on me with deadly effect. Although I said very little, I knew unspoken guilt when I was around *bougie* people. They had succeeded under the same type of circumstances in which I had failed. Intellectually, I was equal to the *bougies*, but I didn't want to relate my story to them.

So, I hung out on the street corner and smoked cigarettes, trying to fit in. It wasn't long before my Air Force cash ran out, and I adjusted to my new lower environment. Routine labor jobs for Blacks were available in some sections of the housing construction boom that went with the rise in White middle-class economics. This job shuffling does not mean the old system collapsed. The low-level Whites rose, and we moved up into some vacant positions. But becoming small businesspeople and getting contracts from the public was still the domain of the Whites. Skilled Black men were angered by the unfair wages they received for building houses, while White contractors made most of the profit from administrative tasks. Living paycheck to paycheck, as we did, they had so little cash liquidity that we couldn't get paid until they received a check from the major builders.

I started working pick-and-shovel jobs with a childhood friend who had mastered cement finishing. We worked hard and had enough money to almost last the week. The neighborhood girls fairly clung to me, and traces of my shyness ebbed away.

One Friday morning, our White boss, Earnest, appointed my friend Melvin Graves to oversee the work and left to pick up the paycheck. Melvin preferred to be called *Bozo*, but he was no clown when setting up the foundations for new houses and buildings. The contractors never said he was a supervisor; instead, they said that a Black man in such a position "looked after things 'till they got back."

When four o'clock came, we threw the tools in the truck. We loitered around the back of the old work-worn green Dodge and became so impatient we could not sit still. We kept staring down the street. But Earnest's personal red pickup didn't appear.

Fed up with this kind of treatment, we decided upon a dicey solution because it was the only practical one open to us. We had an idea where Earnest might be because we had been with him before when he had stopped by a well-known *hillbilly bar* on East Berry Street frequented by the sub-contractors.

Likely, our little boss had cashed the check from the builder, was tossing beers down in his favorite waterhole, and lost track of time. Traditionally, Black workers caught up in this kind of abuse by White employers had to wait until the boss returned or try to catch him the next day. Eager to get paid and do our own drinking on *The Hill*, we piled into the truck with *Bozo* at the wheel and headed out to the bar to find the boss, barge in, and get our money.

The risky plan grew from an afternoon of frustrating mumblings and improbable threats of busting into the joint and taking no crap from the occupants inside. I smirked and was careful to appear ready to brawl. As we rode, I envisioned a crowd screaming and yelling as blue uniformed police wielding Billy clubs came toward me. I didn't have the protection of the Air Force anymore. As bad as the cadet experience was, my realistic fears of physical harm came from seeing bloody police and Black people's encounters before. When sober-minded, I addressed problems other than this direct confrontation that could lead to a physical fight. Call it the mercurial nature of a Gemini, but besides the apprehension caused by the impending conflict, something else stirred in my thoughts. It was rising resentment! After all, White men came into Black drinking and eating establishments whenever they wanted to. They received the best service in the house without a negative word being spoken. The *good old boys* in the bar probably had us outnumbered and weren't going to back down, and surprisingly, neither was I. Fortunately, it was all just emotional agitation because, before long, we were there.

Bozo and I entered the door, puncturing an atmosphere of cooler air, colored lights, and blaring country music. Two White guys in multicolored cowboy shirts with mother-of-pearl buttons came toward us from the table in the center of the room. They looked stunned as they approached us, waving (not brandishing) pool cues.

About six voices chorused louder than the jukebox music, *"Hold it! … Hold it! … Y'all can't come in here!"*

We had profaned the Holy of Holies!

Then they all walked toward us. I remember a slim character that, except for his pockmarked face, reminded me of the *coat hanger incident* on Lancaster Street when I was a boy. We were adamant and stood firm. Irate faces glowered at each other, but no one got close enough to take a swing. *Bozo* pointed toward Earnest, sitting on a high stool, and draped over the bar wearing a blue jean shirt and pants.

"We come to see our boss about something." *Bozo* emphatically declared, not moving from the doorway.

Our little boss was close to putting away a few too many. He rose slowly and looked baffled as he took deliberate steps toward us.

He gestured with both hands while saying, "Now everybody, just settle down."

Needing a voice of reason, a spirit of relief punctuated the tension as we all stepped back mentally.

Earnest steadied himself as he embraced *Bozo* and me as we went back through the door. No one from the bar followed us. Outside, he pulled the big checkbook from his red pickup, leaned on the hood, wrote one for each of us, and went back inside. My first foot in the door of forbidden territory was minuscule and a nonevent in the *Civil Rights Struggle.* However, for me, it was a long-awaited act of rebellion against a suffocating unwritten rule, and it was absolutely magnificent.

Because some Black people were earning slightly higher incomes at that time, the departure of White residents (known as *White Flight*) opened up more upscale homes for us on the upper south side. Pop's social security retirement income allowed him to rent a White-trimmed gray, three-bedroom home in the *Morningside Edition.* It was on Maddox Street, just across from the section of *Hillside Park,* that fell gently toward other houses at the north end of the park. It was the roomiest place the family had ever lived in. Both porches were large, and the screened back brought the gracious southern style to mind. It overlooked a lower yard with an enormous paper shell pecan tree off to the right side, which provided shade in the summer and money from the nuts in the fall. A tomato patch in the back garden and a flourishing array of colorful Azaleas on each side of the front walk bloomed under Pop's green thumb. One bedroom was for him, one for my two younger sisters, and another for whichever of us boys was in good favor with him financially. I wish Mama could have been with us, but that was all in the past.

Chapter 12:
When the Wine ran Red

Near 7:00 PM, in mid-August 1963, as the stars were coming out, Pop's house on Maddox Street rolled beneath the eastern horizon as the western sun dipped out of sight. This plunged the ugliness of The Alley behind East Lancaster Street into the shadows so that the flickering of the neon signs of the juke joint beckoned bewitchingly to passersby. Although I was not on The Hill, the memory of their blinking flashed for a moment in the back of my mind.

In the early darkness, I set out for the evening. I didn't have a car, but the two or three miles to Lancaster Street passed quickly. Like everything these days, I had mixed feelings about meeting the guys because of my earlier bad experiences with drinking. However, the events on Berry Street persuaded me that a little get-together with my old friends might be the ticket to slipping into a better mood about life. I felt I had the willpower to have one or two beers, get some barbeque, and come back home and read.

I was not a honky-tonk man or preferred to hang out in dives and the like, but my crowd on *The Hill* didn't have the economic base needed to own the country clubs, supper clubs, nightclubs, and other upscale drinking establishments that I felt would better suit my more refined nature. Of course, Blacks did have nicer places than the juke joint in *The Alley* where I was headed, but they, too, were frequented by another class of customers with whom I didn't regularly interact.

As I walked briskly through the night, better feelings came to the forefront of my meditations. By the time I reached East Lancaster Street, no ominous thoughts played upon my reverie. I skipped across the four lanes and turned into the alley from Cypress Street.

The filthy alleyway was now more inviting in the failed light. Trash cans and more objectionable elements lay so innocently in the darkness. Still, danger from the unseen shards of broken glass and other razor-sharp items lurked just out of sight, waiting for a slight misstep. I had explored the alley when I was a boy, rummaging through the enormous bins behind the leather company and the other shops seeking discards that were a prize for me. Now, eager to relieve my craving, my mind put aside just how dangerous the denizens of the beer taverns could be. Like the old *Jitterbug Inn* of my youth, *The Alley* had been the site of killings now and then. I wasn't naïve, but I had been away for seven years and had returned an able-bodied man. My mind didn't recoil in fear from the prospect of horrible events such as those I saw as a child.

It is easy now to understand how the cunningness of my addictive nature used my need for fellowship to seduce me into a drinking environment. The co-workers I went to hook up with worked as laborers on all manner of construction and road building jobs for the customary $1.25 per hour. Although hustling was on the decline, a drinking person still needed to be wary of those few who still engaged in robbery, clipping drunks, and the like. Had I been able to admit to myself that I was in the grip of a greater compulsion than the need for socialization, I would have seen things more clearly. Now, oblivious to the hidden physical dangers laying just out of sight in the alley, my conscious thoughts, too, were distracted by the neon lights just ahead.

The silhouettes of figures near the broken fence across the driveway became recognizable as three people I knew slightly. I spoke to them; they murmured and nodded as I opened the door and stepped into the noisy room. The ice instantly broke as someone called out my name. It came from two tables to my right, where several of the guys were gathered. *Joe Boy* beckoned for the server to take my order for a beer as I sat down to an exchange of greetings. It only took one beer to loosen me up. A short while later, we went outside, where a bottle of cheap wine was passed around. The happy times sped by and soon I was so drunk that I had a difficult time keeping up with the various conversations. Amidst the sound of the jukebox and the uproar of voices, there seemed to be a roaring in the background.

Realizing I had gotten hungry, I finally said, "I've had enough for the night!" Some of us piled into a car that *Joe Boy* drove and whisked me and my rib basket back to Pop's house, where I went around to the back porch.

I was positively giddy as I went over the parts of the night's events in *The Alley*. My mood had less to do with the effects of the alcohol I consumed than the feeling of having fitted in with the crowd on *The Hill.* Through my mental cogitations, I never once considered that I was under the cunning sway of my fledgling alcoholism. I only felt the acceptance my tortured soul had needed. It didn't meet the standards for the fellowship I deeply longed for, but it surpassed expectations that wonderful night. The warmth of the Texas late summer, early morning darkness lulled me into a peaceful slumber on Pop's back porch. No matter, I envisioned scenes of the next visit with the Old Gang.

Almost everyone has heard the stories of those trapped by alcohol and other forms of addiction. No need to describe the well-known drunkalogues that speak of shattered lives and broken dreams. The epoch that followed my night in *The Alley* was, nevertheless, a troubled one, which virtually destroyed my familial and social environments. For the sake of brevity, I will deal primarily with one of the most nightmarish aspects of wanton drunkenness. The tragic tale is often misdiagnosed by non-medical bystanders as a split personality.

My experiences with drinking after the first night in *The Alley* were disastrous. My original reservations had been about social acceptance within an unfamiliar setting more than my drunken conduct, which was all too common among my old friends. Indeed, acting out while under the influence of some powerful substance was expected of one of the old crowd.

The problem was that my drunken antics soon became excessive, as *blackouts* occurred each time I drank. As in a dark dream, nothing was impossible in the living nightmares of my *blackouts.* My reactions to alcohol were unlike anything or anybody else that I ever met. There seemed to be no predictable response that my thoughts or behavior would take once I swallowed my first drink of alcohol, regardless of the type or concoction. From what I was told and partially remembered, I had to be rescued from all manner of impending calamities, including fights that I was too drunk to engage in. Of course, there is no shortage of people willing to rob and beat up a smaller guy who is too impaired to defend himself properly. But I internalized the guilt because somehow, I felt I was the instigator, although my reasons why I wanted to fight made no sense to me.

Tim W., an unsmiling, creepy looking man, who habitually wore a gray windbreaker jacket and fedora hat, was a *serial killer* that lived on *The Hill.* That he was a murderer was no secret to the honky-tonk crowd. Undoubtedly, he was a darling to the legal system that had allowed him to go free after paying the required fee for six known *Misdemeanor Murders.* He knifed a *working girl,* who was a good friend of our family, to death when I was a boy. I had no reason to like him and always gave him a wide berth.

One night I was practicing pool shots on the table in The Alley when he walked up to me with his hand in his right pocket. This was a signal that he was ready to pull out his knife for a fight. He had the drop on me. Since he was so close to me, any move, and he could whip out his blade before I could mount a defense.

I was caught off guard as he spoke softly, "Hey Sporty, the other night when I was having it with *Jr. Adams*, it looked like you were trying to get behind my back."

I was startled and said to him: "I don't know what you are talking about."

He sneered and replied dourly as I kept my distance from him, "Well, I got my eyes on you too."

After that, I kept my eyes on him from then on. After talking with the guys, I learned that during a drunken *blackout*, I had indeed made moves to interfere in somebody else's deadly affair. All this had a horrifying effect on me, but I continued to put myself in harm's way during the *blackouts.*

Several times I had come out of a *blackout* in a strange place only seconds before the fight. Sometimes, I was conscious of a crowd clamoring for my eager assailant to give me a beating. One lucky time, a razor was involved, but a fellow I hardly knew broke up the scrap with his gun. Other times, I lost the fight. In the ensuing two and a half years of constant *blackout*s, my face showed the effects of lost battles. Losing fights, though objectionable, was a small tragedy compared to my embarrassing attempts at having a smooth hand with the ladies when I was only being bothersome. Gradually, I came to believe that something inside me was trying to punish me severely, even if it cost me my life in the process.

The alcohol addiction continued to beguile me to the extent that I didn't suspect I was in the grip of a spiritual impairment. Because I had shut out church and religion, I only considered the physical and mental aspects of my predicament. Those of my family and friends that suspected my problem was spiritual tried to help. They saw the demonic behavior, but, having no intimate understanding of the forces at work, couldn't explain the aspects of addiction in such a way that didn't offend me. After a while, my family began dropping hints that it would be better if I wasn't around at all, no matter how my absence came about. I believed as painful as the prospect might be; they would accept my death as one such solution.

Confused and bewildered, such logic as I could bring to bear eventually defaulted on me being *crazy*. This unwelcome diagnosis was reinforced by everyone who knew of my *blackouts* when drinking. However, throughout the periods of soberness following my drinking sprees, I endeavored to keep the very model of human decency. As a result, those who had not seen me during one of the many misadventures never failed to greet me with glad enthusiasm and warm affection. But the healthy good guy image grew smaller on account of the diabolical behavior that characterized my increasing episodes of *blackout*s while drinking alcohol. Although I still managed to work as much as any of those who hung out on the corner behind *Brandon's Grocery Store*, my reputation reached rock bottom along with my loss of dignity as I grew more helpless to stop my hapless drinking cycle. My usual sunny disposition became dark and moody for long periods of time. I felt the need for solitude and reflection over the unjust things that had befallen me. Increasingly, it seemed that the dreadful things of the world sought me out for mishaps of life. I could not make sense of my predicament.

Yet, occasionally, I seemed to have remarkable good luck, as tragedies were averted. These miraculous events I saw as an unknown aspect of my intelligence. But the sciences and logic that had lifted me out of these gutters offered nothing that kept me above self-loathing. Also, lacking knowledge of the forces involved, I, and those close to me, continued to suffer.

Especially troubling to me was the painful realization that I was a *dead-beat dad* to my first child, Vanessa. Her mother, Frankie, deserved much more support than my constant drunkenness and the occasional few dollars I managed to scrape up. We had parted just after Vanessa was born. So, ultimately, it wasn't the fights and other self-destructive behavior that brought me to rock bottom. It was the shame of what I had become. Had I not risen to the exalted ranks of those who have mastered the airplane, I would not have appreciated just how far I had fallen.

In the latter days of darkness came a moment of clarity, and I acknowledged the depth of my depravity. Briefly, I mulled over taking my life but hopes of being on top again never let suicide become a practical choice for me. Since other people could drink without falling into the kind of *blackout*s that bedeviled me, clearly, it was not the alcohol itself that brought out the 180-degree changes of personality that overcame me. As terrifying as the prospect was, I at last concluded that the secret to understanding the elusive mystifying dark *blackouts* was hidden somewhere within my mind. With that, I completely accepted that I was insane and needed professional mental therapy of some kind. The last resort idea I toyed with carried unknown risks. Then, I saw only the smallest glimmer of hope within my reasoning, but since I could no longer live in misery, I had no other choice.

Chapter 13:

The Road to Recovery

When evening came on August 11th, 1965, I retreated to the couch on the screened-in back porch at Pop's house. I rearranged the somewhat lumpy old love seat, so that I was just another shadow in the fading light. Then I took a sip of the fifth of *Thunderbird* wine and began my nightly pity party. I don't say this lightly because, in my estimation, I was a miserable example of a father for my year and a half old daughter. Slowly, the sneaky alcohol effects caused me to feel better about my life.

After a while, I made the drunken decision to walk the few miles to Vanessa's mom's apartment in the new addition to *The Projects* to see my baby girl. It was about 9:00 PM when I reached *The Hill.*
The adults were not at home; however, the older children knew me well and greeted me cheerfully.

"Hi, Van Jr., did you come to see Vanessa?" "She's upstairs."

Then, promptly, they returned to the TV. I knew the way!

My little daughter lay asleep on the bed. I looked down at the *tiny mouse-looking face.* It was indistinguishable from that of the other McKellar babies I had seen through the years. Pain engulfed me! Family recognition tugged at my heart. She was all the faces that grinned at the happy little boy who lifted his siblings from their cribs to play baby games and care for them. At that moment, I had nothing left, but I needed to give and be necessary again. Then came the realization that I had a greater purpose now. I must overcome my self-interest and take care of my child. People who understand addiction will say you can't sober up for someone else. You can only beat the bottle for yourself but love for my helpless baby compelled me to fight my demons when love for myself would not.

I said goodbye to the kids, reminding them to lock the back door as I left. I had stashed the half-full bottle of wine behind the red brick retainer wall, but when I picked it up, instead of making the usual promise to myself of starting a new routine after I finished this last one, I smashed it against the wall. Though not religious, I raised my hands and moaned, "Lord, have mercy on me!" I returned to my father's house and fell asleep until morning.

The following morning, I trudged the mile and a half to *John Peter Smith Hospital*, seeking medical help for my drinking. The unusual idea about breaking my drinking habit had developed from my conviction that I was experiencing some baffling psychological issue. The pattern of a supposedly rational man who drank and did insane things was sad enough, but when connected with the experience of returning to the bottle repeatedly for no understandable reason, was reason enough to seek psychiatric help. I hadn't hastily chosen to change, no matter the consequences. I had mulled it over in my mind several times. It was an uncertain strategy, but I was determined. I realized I would seem foolish to those who knew me, but I was past caring about their ridicule. In those days, many in the Black culture did not publicly admit that they or their family members suffered from alcoholism or mental illnesses. I knew that people on *The Hill* did not concede that either disease was a treatable medical condition. We felt so much phony stigma attached to being Black that we did not need another damnable disorder hiding in the family's closet. For our family to acknowledge mental illness in its bloodline was to cast a shadow on every member. Although I accepted, I had problems with using alcohol. I also felt that true alcoholics were decrepit old White transients and a few equally unkempt Black men I knew. Thinking that I was not such an alcoholic, the sole reason for my affliction must be mental. However, my present course only alienated me from my family.

After lying to the receptionist, I sat in the back of the overcrowded hospital emergency room. I told her I felt like I was having a nervous breakdown. After a brief time, someone escorted me into the hallway behind the desk. The impatient person who interviewed me listened as I explained my situation. I told him I had come to the public clinic because no rehabilitation centers were available for me. I told him I didn't know where else to go for the required psychiatric sessions.

Midway into the session, the man shook his head dubiously and said, "Your dilemma is not psychiatric because you have the presence of mind to seek help."

He rotated his big red hands as he spoke to provide visual evidence of his simplistic circular reasoning. We both grinned as he rose to end the session. Notwithstanding his refusal to treat me, I learned my father could get me admitted through the night clinic if he told them I showed signs of mental distress.

After a lengthy back-and-forth argument, Pop took me to the night clinic just after sunset and signed me in for observation. Bringing me in under these conditions distressed him, but he felt compassion for his boy. He endured the humiliation because he knew I needed help that he could not give. I had *hit rock bottom.* There seemed to be nothing else. When we reached the check-in desk, the orderlies became confused because Pop and I had the same name. It was further complicated because Pop, the older man, had alcohol on his breath, which gave the appearance that I, the younger, sober person, brought him in. I chuckled softly as I explained that it was me who had mental problems.

The murmuring in the waiting area became distinguishable after the orderlies closed the big door behind Pop. Surprisingly, the atmosphere was stress-free. Providers in White uniforms walked about as if this was a typical waiting room rather than a special one catering to patients suffering from mental impairments. I overheard patients calmly requesting information about getting released, but no one was being belligerent or otherwise violent. Some men and a woman sitting in the chairs along the room's walls sat quietly, as if they were relaxing at home. It seemed that I wasn't the only one that wanted to stay. Behind this side of the locked doors, my mind began to settle down; I was in no rush to be outside, where I could get drunk again. Taking stock of my asylum, I wondered when I would have my first session with the doctors.

After a long while, I heard my name called from somewhere and replied, "McKellar?" "I'm Here!" I lifted my head just in time to catch sight of an orderly moving off with a pile of clothing. I stepped fast to catch up and noticed we were going down a hallway lined with cells with people in them and past rooms with one-foot barred windows on each side. We stopped several doors down, and I went in first. There were two beds in the room, nothing more. As my guide left, he said, "Take everything off and change into these." Pointing to the gray clothing on the bed. The same orderly returned to collect all my old clothes and muttered something as he left.

A moment after that, I gathered my thoughts. Curiously, I wasn't gloomy. I assessed my situation and my surroundings. The bare whiteness of the walls was comforting. It was as if I had at last found Sanctuary. Not that I was safe from society, the feeling was that; there locked away, I could do no further harm to myself or anyone else. The rapid racing thoughts I had since I entered the clinic ceased completely now as peace set in. Although I didn't have any idea what my next steps were going to be, I wasn't anxious, because it was out of my hands now. *The Wildman* had at last been caged and I could rest. Pleasant thoughts seeped into my consciousness. I was doing something practical now. I accepted my predicament as the beginning of a new adventure, and I was mildly excited to be getting underway.

About two hours later, two men knocked on the door and entered in one smooth moment. The more muscular of the two attendants was the quiet one and had the authoritative demeanor of a cop. The straitjacket, the smaller, talkative one carried, wasn't a complete surprise, but it came earlier than I thought it would. "This is for everybody's safety," he said as they grasped me and began working it on me. As I twisted with their pressured manipulations, I thought they weren't sure how it hooked up. I wanted to offer suggestions like maybe it goes this way or that, but I did not. Then, in a momentary shift of mood, I almost wanted to cry but held my tears and my balance as the White straps tightened snuggly on my arms. A verse from one of my old poems that didn't fit the occasion transited my musing,
"Dear lord, have I gone too far to gain Thy grace again?"

"Now," a voice murmured, as if answering my thoughts, "We're taking you to see the doctor."

As I thanked the men softly, an imposing voice in my mind whispered, *"Everybody knew it would come to this!"*

Amazingly, despite the short burst of sadness, I still wasn't ashamed I had come. One man walked in front while holding my left arm in his right hand; the other walked behind as we threaded the corridors. The hallway ended in an area with a waiting room and office doors.

A knock on one door: "Come in," I was seated across from a middle-aged White man who asked me questions that were more akin to administration than psychiatry. On the return to my cell, despite my arms being bound, my balance was nearly perfect as I matched their steps. After they left, a million thoughts ran through my mind, but I never questioned my decision to take the path I had.

Later, that night, the aides brought a Black man into the cell. He was about my age and body type. The aide went over a monotonous dressing routine with him. The new man repeatedly asked if I had seen his family. As I tried to talk with him, I recognized he was under some compulsion. Before morning, I received a big shot of Thorazine, the drug of choice for treating alcoholics suffering from schizophrenic disorders. It made me feel drugged and like the world was slower. I didn't anticipate shots or oral medications; I thought my treatment would be on the couch. But. I stuck it out, hoping that the meds were beneficial to me.

In due course, I discovered that the state institution was in Wichita Falls, a smaller city than Fort Worth, located 117 miles Northwest. Getting sent to Wichita Falls was not as straightforward as making a request. The clinic didn't send patients to the state hospital without a court sentence. My first hurdle was to persuade the judge that he should send a rational person to a mental institution because he wanted to go. When I put my mind in motion, I saw that the solution was simple. Everyone knew that if you missed your court date, the judge would automatically sentence you to at least 90 days for the first offense. I didn't go to court, and the judge sentenced me to Wichita Falls for treatment.

ABOUT TWELVE PEOPLE WENT TO THE COURT, but the morning we left for Wichita Falls, only four of us rode in the large van. They shackled my hands to an eight-inch brown leather strap that fastened tight around my midriff, and we were off. *The Texas State Hospital for Mental Health and Substance Abuse* is currently a sprawling, diverse complex. However, in 1965, *The North Texas State Hospital at Wichita Falls* was an extensive campus of big multi-story, red-bricked buildings with heavy metal screens over the doors and windows. These structures typified other state institutions elsewhere. I *felt a way* about them as we arrived.

The van stopped at a smaller one-story building about two hundred feet from one of the large ones. I was uneasy as I stared at the institutional structures, wondering which one I would be taken into. I relaxed when I learned that the small building we stopped at was my dorm building. It housed alcoholics on one end and TB patients on the other. The usual check-in routine followed. Confirming my earlier racist assessment of who alcoholics were the open bay ward was filled with *case-hardened* old White men wearing tan-colored uniforms. They stopped what they were doing as I came in behind the attendant.

Their stubble bearded faces grinned and made snarky statements such as "Hey, Slick!" and "New meat, fellas!" This wasn't the *Huntsville State Penitentiary,* so I didn't get upset. But I snapped back a word before relaxing on my bunk. I had spent six years living with hard-drinking White guys in the Air Force, plus I was thick-skinned too; after all, we had a drinking problem in common. To be sure, no regulations forbid these men to utter bigoted name-calling, so *nigger* flowed unbridled from their insolent lips. No matter, I had other things on my mind than wasting my breath, giving them my rendition of racial sensitivity lessons.

These old White men were so laid-back that they exhibited an air of entitlement when speaking with the attendants, complaining about one thing or another. It seemed the place operated more like a retirement home than a hospital. After long hours of playing dominoes and forty-two with them, I got to know them better, and I became convinced that the state hospital had become their residence rather than a treatment facility for them.

While my new dorm setting was peaceful after bedtime, noises from the main building across from us went on all night. Banging, howling, shouting, screaming, and unique puzzling sounds came from the building. It was even more unsettling because I had housekeeping duties on that ward at dawn. I was 26 years old, young, strong, and one of the few men assigned work outside the dorm.

My duty ward, MH-1 (The designation may be off), was a medium-sized housing unit. It was the size of a three-story motel, except it was red brick and trimmed in White. It had a locked screened day porch about 1/3 of its length, centered at ground level. Immediately inside the front entrance was a large round dayroom that may have been about thirty feet in diameter. I could not identify some items in it, which I assumed were for eerie purposes. A dozen patients wandered around aimlessly, others muttering incoherently, while others sat quietly on benches or wheelchairs. They, too, turned and stared at me as I stepped across the area to the nurses' station to report in.

Other patients down the halls kept up frightening cries. It took a few days for me to stop watching everyone fearfully and settle down. I realized the staff would not have dangerous patients walking around unrestrained.

Practically, all but one of the patients on my work floor were White and, despite their infirmity, were conscious of our racial differences. Not knowing why, I felt a deep desire to deal with these men kindly, regardless of the unkind words they spoke to me. I now realize I needed to be more humane if only to deny the resentment I had suffered from the world.

My work turned out to be a more extensive learning experience than just meaningful work. Besides cleaning the floors, I was happy to give a helping hand to whatever the nurses needed. But most of all, I got to know the patients well, bonding with some in a few short weeks. I learned from the nurses and other staff that some didn't have mental impairments but were brought to the hospital by their families. At home, I was a *royal pain* to my underprivileged family with my drinking, but they all tried to prevent me from being put away. I chose to come to Wichita Falls and would leave after ninety days. Yet here, shut away in this asylum for an undetermined time, were helpless people of both races who cried for their families constantly. I came to believe that beyond the unfeeling rejection of one's fellowman through the lie of racial inferiority, sacrificing the powerless extended to abandoning family members. It was then that I concluded that besides Black Americans, many individuals were denied compassion for selfish reasons. However, I didn't know the complete history of these households, although I imagined their plights, I understood that my harsh thinking might be unfair to families whose way of life I had not experienced.

I met with a psychiatrist who spoke with a heavy accent twice during the first two months. Our sessions were little more than formal interviews. He told me nothing about my condition or future treatment plans but wanted to know if I experienced alcohol withdrawal problems and noted my answers on a pad. Each session called for medication changes. The nurses in the ward where I worked reluctantly gave me some information about the meds. Then, I stopped taking my daily yellow pill that drugged me so heavily that I lost my curiosity and zest for life. I believe that initially, Thorazine prevented my withdrawal from being an awful experience, but later it caused me to languish in a zombie-like state.

Near the end of my ninety days sentence, I saw an alcohol counselor for the first time. He was an extremely likable *Native American* named Henry Walker.

He listened courteously to me and said, "Hell, Van, you're not crazy; you sound just like you're a damned old alcoholic, like me."

As he related his drinking history, which was like mine, I had reason to be hopeful because I had met somebody who had recovered from my sickness. Henry told me that a well-known group of recovering alcoholics was having a meeting at the hospital soon. This alcoholics group adhered to a *Twelve Step recovery program*, which he also followed. He strongly urged me to attend, so I did.

Except for Henry, who worked openly as an alcoholic counselor, I will not show a group member's full name to protect their anonymity.

At the meeting, I met a huge dark-haired White guy from Mississippi, whose gruff voice and roughened round face did not hide the hint of a smile. I liked him immediately. When he finished extolling the program's virtues, he looked me in the eye, slammed the podium forcefully, and said abruptly, "But I'm still the same S.O.B. that I ever was."

Until then, I thought their way of achieving sobriety might be like joining a religious group. In the back of my mind, I feared a person entered a flock and then forced himself to adopt new unhappy ways of behaving. The big man's frank statement broke ground with me because it suggested you don't have to turn into a *Sad Sack* to stay sober, and I needed to hear that.

His and the others' stories seemed miraculous enough, even though I still wasn't sure what *snake oil* they were peddling. While we were mingling after the meeting, a cheerful, auburn-haired woman whom I judged to be in her fifties came over. She, too, was a member of the group. She clasped my hand tightly and offered me a business card and told me to call them when I returned to town. I promised the big man and the woman that I would call them next week when I made a state-required trip back to town to see if I could adjust to living in society. I put the card away but thought no more about the group since I heard nothing that offered an easy fix. □

Wichita Falls, Texas, lies in "Tornado Alley," an area in the U.S. known for producing thunderstorms that rise to altitudes over 66,000 feet (about twice the cruising altitude of a commercial jet). One night before I left the institution for two weeks' leave, a massive storm flexed its muscles. We awakened and lay silent as the wind whipped against the building, peppering it with rain and hail and shaking everything. As the lightning flashed and the thunder rolled, we sat meekly as if a big bar room bully was cursing and threatening to raise Hell if he heard one peep out of anybody. I knew thunderstorms. For a good reason, every pilot fears the power of a cumulonimbus; they are usually destructive, so we fly away from them. I had weathered countless storms on the ground safely, but this time I was afraid.

I had often flirted with death when I was drunk. I had few things of material value, but living was precious to me now that I was sober. I had said I was an agnostic because I wasn't an atheist. I loosely considered God might be around, although He never communicated with me directly. But fear caused me to offer prayers to someone whose existence I questioned! The storm passed without further event, and I was my old, agnostic self again, yet I had prayed as if I had to explain to God that I was trying. There had been moments, usually in church, when my internal struggles subsided, and I felt safe. I could not account for the comforting spirit, but I knew it was something other than the choir singing. However, I reassured myself that these incidents weren't equivocal evidence of God's presence, even though something mysterious occurred that night.

I rode the Greyhound bus back to Fort Worth a few days later. Pop had moved back to *The Hill* into the *New Projects*, so I *holed* up with him temporarily. The next day, I strolled over to a friend's bar on East Lancaster Street. I felt no compulsion to drink; however, my friends teased me about being locked up in the sanatorium. While they joked that I was crazy, they would not allow any straightforward discussion of something that also tainted them. After all, we had so much in common. Instead, they created stories of how I was stoned and *talking my usual smack* to the cops. "Yeah, man, they loaded this drunk *mother-so-and-so* into the wagon and hauled him off to the nuthouse."

I was troubled that they refused to accept that I had taken extreme measures to break away from the drinking life we had in common and that my way of life in the streets had ended. Once the two weeks at home were over, I returned to the hospital. Although the state would not chase me down if I did not come back, I returned to ensure my record would be clear.

The Alcoholic Recovery Groups

AFTER SERVING NINETY DAYS TOTAL, I RETURNED TO FORT WORTH and sought work but found none. Soon, I started hanging out on Lancaster Street again. I was standing outside the bar when the smell of the place caused me to feel anxious and had cravings laced with defeatist thoughts of What's the use, anyhow?

In the first grip of a panic attack, I went to a phone booth across the street and called the number on the card I got at the meeting in Wichita Falls.

An eager male voice on the phone ordered me to "Stay where you are; we're coming."

In about twenty minutes, a compact car drew up to the booth. I saw the beaming face of the friendly big man, whose name was Wally. By the time we reached the house, I was relaxed, and my cravings were gone. The woman that gave me the card was named Billie. We all talked until nightfall and headed to a group meeting on the other side of town.

I became anxious as we entered a crowded building of noisy White people in small groups, cigarettes, and coffee mugs in hand. The atmosphere was electrified! Various people came up and introduced themselves, but I forgot their names almost immediately. I looked around for Wally and noticed that he and two other friends I had just met were highly agitated about something. I inquired and learned that several men "did not want to meet with a *nigger*." Billie's face flushed as she became livid, rushed across the room, and was so animated it looked like she was dancing as a crowd formed around her. It didn't take long to settle the dispute. We found seats, and then someone called the meeting to order.

Disclaimer: I do not find fault with or accuse any twelve-step groups or organizations of racial prejudice or of tolerating racist ideologies and practices. I have written about racist experiences because they were overriding. Although I express my own imperfections concerning racism and my responses to it, that racism exists is not the aim of this memoir, which is enduring adversity and overcoming addiction. To my knowledge, it has "never been group policy to practice or condone racism, but it is understood: that, guidelines are few because members must not be tied by rules, or they may discover their interests have been sidetracked to purposes other than overcoming alcohol addiction."

The Twelve Steps offer necessary nourishment for physically, mentally, and spiritually weakened alcoholics. In addition, the steps can be food for the soul of any famished addict. Race was never included as an ingredient in the original recipe. Individual prejudice brought exclusion to the table via social status, a standard component of a segregated society. It is a mechanism by which some resentful members oppose the right of all people to sit erect with the dominant culture.

Except for the meeting at the big group, I had no more outright racist encounters for a while. Sometimes, there were those few who grumbled in the background. This kind of complaining did not discourage me. I held my ground because the groups said they were open to anyone who claimed to be an alcoholic, so I wasn't invading someone else's domain. Nevertheless, the race-baiting group members had opened an old defensive wound that had not gone away. Plus, I was still affected by the local White men outside the groups who made the same wisecracks and told the same insensitive jokes. At first, my ignorant racist viewpoint that White men rather than Black men were hopeless alcoholics tried to resurface. But when I listened intently, I was encouraged by their life-changing experiences working the program. I would not pass up a chance at permanent sobriety by becoming a victim of my own biased views. Neither was I going to quit because *diehards* wanted to make me feel Black People didn't belong. Also, while listening to the group's Customs, I learned, that all that was necessary to join was a desire to stop drinking, and if you claim membership in the group, you are accepted."

Finally, a point upon which to legitimize my tenacity! Soon, I was around the *twelve steppers* enough to recognize their differences in looks, behavior, and other qualities. I saw these people distinctly and accepted them as suffering alcoholics like me. It was likely true that those offended by my presence as the only Black man did not view me as an individual, but rather as a Black outsider. So, they persisted in their bigotry. A small accusing voice in me whispered, *These White people paid for these meetings, and you have no right to be here.*

I didn't know where that came from. Perhaps I had some misgivings because I was short on money. However, I hung in, choosing to remain as long as there wouldn't be a physical battle.

As we continued, I believe disturbing comments were being made to my sponsors. It seemed they wanted to shield me not only from alcoholism but from some unknown, unexpressed fear. Billie was as tough as anyone I knew, but prejudice was too popular to defeat.

So, we started new meetings at Billie's home. She had had a few sessions there, but now six to eight of us came once a week. Her large open dining area seated about that many people around the table with room for four more nearby. We hung up the flashy little signs found in every meeting room. *They would keep me on course as I healed.* A sizeable *Serenity Prayer* plaque was placed conspicuously on the wall opposite the entryway to the hall.

We all wore neat casual attire on meeting nights. I was excited, but more than that, I genuinely felt redeemed. We all did. Nowhere was there a hint of the stereotypical, near tacky, battle worn social rejects struggling to hold on to their humanity. Our meetings were like any group engaged in important business. It was great to be free from the grip of the destroyer. The sincerity of the cheerful greetings we gave each other as the crowd gathered on meeting nights was marvelous. There was a magical presence in the house as we hugged affectionately, genuinely pleased to see our friends. Even with the coffee and cigarettes, it was heaven! I recognized various points in the others' talk as each person shared. It was all good, but I had to refrain consciously from muttering an Amen, as Black people do when we agree with what is being said in such a sublime atmosphere. It was the custom to only smile and give a slight nod to show our agreement when another spoke.

As our trio visited other recovery groups, Wally and Billie were eager for me to meet three other recovering Black alcoholics who lived in Fort Worth. They popped up in different meeting places, but no one knew them well enough to find them. Billie worried I needed to know that other Black people were in the program to avoid becoming disheartened by the little tidbits of negativity masquerading as gags and the lot. But I knew there was little chance of that happening! I had heard the wisecracks and the old "I just think you'd be happier with your own kind" segregationist speech so many times I knew it by heart. Remarkably, in 1965, the city's population was about 373,000 people, yet finding only 3 Black alcoholic members in the group proved impossible. There have been increases in the percentages of Black members in the group since then, but not significantly.

Chapter 14:

Beginning the 12 Steps

I was a passionate advocate for the *12 Steps* to every Black person I thought could benefit from them. The people I spoke to about the recovery program were not interested in trying it. To a man, they were polite but did not make any commitments to attend meetings with Wally and me. At first, I wondered if the program was unattractive because it was a lifetime commitment and not the quick fix people in pain desperately desire. Then, considering the overt rejection attitudes I experienced, I thought my Black

Brothers might be reluctant to subject themselves to abuse. However, their lack of enthusiasm may have been because of the program's longevity.

When I first glanced over the twelve steps, I felt dispirited by them. I now understand my hesitancy because I approached them as the sick person I had grown into while drinking. I was courageous when I was sober. Where I was not, a little drink would enhance that want for a societal backbone. My early thoughts were, Man, I can't do this crap. It'll never work for a scientifically minded person, anyway.!

I sensed that engaging in all that religious-sounding stuff in the steps would force me to wear a false public image. However, a bit of need from within me nudged me forward. Hoping I might become that better man I had sacrificed to the bottle, I gave the *12 Steps* an earnest attempt with a small but willing heart. I was new to being completely honest with myself concerning my shortcomings. Still, I wasn't condemned as I progressed through the steps, nor was I affected by any other person who looked to judge me.

I didn't list work on the steps in the progressive order listed in the program because the events mentioned in this memoir occurred in various periods as I advanced through them. I began at Step 1. which, for me, was a confession of guilt or proof of my qualification to be in the ranks of alcoholics, more so than a wholehearted admission of being one. I found mine was an old story I had heard around the table more than a few times.

Step 1. (Powerlessness)

Step 1: "We admitted we were powerless over alcohol—that our lives had become unmanageable.

At our sessions, long-timers pursued various steps. However, when new members were present, group sharing often began with the first steps. *The First Step* is a recognition of hitting rock bottom. Many long-term alcoholics thought being at their lowest point was necessary for recovery. They, too, tried everything to stop our destructive fall on the way to the bottom, but ultimately failed. A broken alcoholic is ready to face the demands of the quest for sobriety. I was at rock bottom and willing to take on anything rather than be drunk again. Still, it would not be easy for me because so many elements of the program were contrary to how I achieved the little strength I had.

One night, as the group members around the table told their stories, I could no longer deny their sad histories were mine, too. When my turn came to introduce myself, I stood before my peers, full of emotion. I said, *"My name is Van, I'm an alcoholic, and I am powerless over alcohol."* The last part of the statement escaped in a muted choking voice. Everyone clapped and mumbled upbeat sounds, and I was officially in the group. I enjoyed being the new guy at the meetings and the fuss they made over me as I passed weekly increments without taking a drink. Everybody was glad for me, and I was so proud of myself and puffed up that I had not considered the wording of the *First Step* from all angles.

Step 2. (Considerations of Greater Powers)

Step 2. Came to believe that a power greater than ourselves could restore us to sanity.

The further consideration of a power greater than myself brought forth mixed feelings. Ever since I could remember, others had implied that I was *crazy*. I worried there was some truth to the insanity issue. I suspected it was because my dreams and aspirations were inconsistent with what was available to me. As I contemplated what powers might be superior to me, I recognized a problem in my line of thinking. Such powers suggested a supernatural being. I thought, "I can work with sensible steps but not an unclimbable abstract stairway." Belief in something tangible is why I sought therapy for my irrational behavior when drinking. So, when I was told at the state hospital that I was "Just a damned old alcoholic," my belief that I was somehow insane diminished some. I assumed that with help with my thinking processes, I could conduct myself without religious hocus pocus. The little tidbits of God and religion I knew had neither logic in what I thought I knew nor rationality in what I had heard. It was all incoherent gibberish. However, before I dismissed the spiritual part of the second step, I needed to see what may be amiss in my thinking. I rigorously examined aspects of my spiritual knowledge in the light of such common sense as I could bring to bear. But I couldn't explain all my unusual experiences away.

However, I was still at an impasse with God if He existed. It was not if He could, but whether He would. The God that I heard about was also quick to exact retribution. While I might not have crossed the final line, I broke so many little rules that I knew there was a disagreeable streak in me that got loose sometimes. Such a God would ultimately take me to task about my dirty little secrets. Although not one to admit it openly, I was envious of those who asserted a close relationship with God because God, as spoken of by others, rejected me. I dared not speak aloud of my negative feelings toward God lest the insanity question rear its head anew.

Many former drinkers at the gatherings told of having submitted themselves to a spiritual authority, which they called their *higher power*. From their conviction, I perceived that something had created a change in them. I listened attentively to the stories concerning the reforms in various members' lives. I came to believe that something was at work and had changed them from weak drunks to hopeful men and women. The group didn't specify what such a power might be like. The long-time members said, "Your *higher power* can be a fencepost as long as it prevents you from drinking." I assumed they didn't want to encourage theological controversies or allow such exchanges to intrude upon finding one's own conception of God. But this freedom of thought did not help me then, because knowing God only by hearsay proved inadequate for developing a coherent interpretation of who and what He was. I saw it but didn't understand it. However, I admitted to myself that greater powers existed but took no further steps.

I see now I lacked sufficient *faith* to believe that God would rescue me, personally, from drinking. Despite the vexation of dealing with the pros and cons involved, it came to this: "I will not *trust* an unseen and personally unknown deity with my life." Many White men in the group apparently felt as I did. That may have been why some of them felt no qualms about antagonizing God, as He is rumored to be. For example, when speaking about God at the podium stand, even Wally would say regularly, "Well, He never did a damn thing for me!" Oddly enough, I still hear that view from men at sessions some fifty-six years later.

I continued to wrestle with the God question but eventually became satisfied with this outcome: I trusted in things unknown when I lowered my defenses to ask for the love of another human. And I eagerly embraced the novel changes that came with that relationship. This was when I opened my soul to Merle in anticipation of the joyful experience of new love. It mattered not that Merle was human and capable of being physically embraced in my arms. At the same time, God, to my knowledge, was unseen, untouchable, and unproved. The thing that made the relationship workable was my willingness to become exposed to rejection and to trust in the unknown. I did not work these things out in my mind before lowering my defenses to things unseen. I still had reservations about doing something that had no guarantees. However, the rewarding experience of breaking through my shyness was now a part of how I approached life. And like the love between unfamiliar persons, gaining the love of God needed only a tiny *leap of faith.*

I took the leap by accepting the positive developments in my way of life and not dwelling on former interpretations of God or justifications and reasons for my fortunate turn of life. I was the same broken man that had just been through Hell, but now, just as perplexing, things had taken a significant turn for the better. I had abstained from alcohol for over six months. I worked for a group member and rented a small apartment over a furniture store. I had a new girlfriend, and I dressed sharper those days. However, because I had failed so miserably before now, I had to acknowledge that something more significant than my willpower kept me from taking that first drink. I admitted to an *unknown power's* workings and no longer spoke about it with an undertone. My stated concept of God for public consumption was that He was the *Spiritual Anonymity* behind the mysterious power that facilitated all aspects of my recovery. As I continued along this path, the lack of communication with God caused no significant impediment while working the steps.

As time passed, I noticed some White men had a more difficult time accepting that they were powerless over alcohol than I had first did. These ordinary men were descendants of a race that had treaded the *Black land* down with the gun and threat of military force. Indeed, many White nations of the world continued to share dominion over nonwhite peoples as they did in the *Scramble for Africa.* After publicly claiming to have abolished Black slavery in most of the world, certain European countries met in Berlin in 1884 to decide how to divide Africa's peoples and resources among themselves. Already having oversite in the doings of newly freed slaves in Liberia, the United States did not join in with them.

The irony is the colonizers didn't feel the need for the input of one Black person during the partitioning of my ancestral home. They didn't care about traditional boundaries; they carved up the country for convenience. This vast world power flowed down through White lives. Beyond military and political control over nonwhite peoples, a privileged hierarchy of family wealth and religious, social, and civil organizations safeguarded their concerns. Local and federal police departments protected and served their interests. Any White person held complete authority over the wretched races living among them. As White people, the men around our group table did not know what it meant to be entirely dominated by anything. Most of these guys were full of swagger when they spoke of being *the greatest nation in the world.* They may have felt nothing was beyond their control. But, it seemed, as sick alcoholics, these men struggled to cope with the concept of being powerless.

I was born into a culture on the wrong side of the treading, even though my maternal great-grandfather had a significant foot in it. It meant nothing to this great nation that the slave, Robert (Bob) Hopkins, shook off his chains and volunteered for *Company A, 1st U.S. Colored Infantry*, at Washington DC, on May 19, 1863. To stabilize this nation, he overcame the demands of the battlefield on foot and later (July 18, 1867) as a member of *Company I, 10th U.S. Calvary.*

As a *Buffalo Soldier* mounted on a Bay horse, my great-grandfather fought terrible battles with indigenous peoples. His outfit protected exposed White settlements, and the Kansas Pacific, and Union Pacific Railroads. After a second enlistment with the *Buffalo Soldiers*, he fought battles with the Comanches in Southwest Texas. On May 27, 1900, he was finally awarded a $13.00 a month Civil War pension for injuries. It was not the blue-plate special befitting one who suffered to bring about this country's *Manifest Destiny.* Even so, to his surviving daughter, my grandmother, and the rest of our family, it was equivalent to bringing home a hefty doggie bag once a month.

In the distant past, I had prayed to God occasionally for relief that, to my mind, did not come. I came of age, living under conditions I could not control. To recognize that I was powerless in minor matters didn't shame me as much as it did them. Despite my drinking problem, I went to work daily. I kept up my responsibilities, so I believed I managed my life well when sober. Unspoken in this defense of my conditional periods of powerlessness was the hope that, somehow, I could drink like the average person. I did not give in entirely.

My group sponsor, Wally, was one of the White men who struggled with superiority issues that were exemplified by his brusque mannerisms. He would come around the hangouts on *The Hill* asking for me as a friend would, but his aura of personal power inevitably caused my Black friends to say my boss was looking for me. When he and Pop first met, they hit it off with mutual respect. W drove the pickup into the driveway as Pop came out on the porch, hurriedly putting on a casual jacket. Wally piled out of the Datsun, grinning as if meeting a long-lost relative. They approached respectfully. Wally spoke his full name first.

"G. Wally, extending his hand for the clasp. Not his regular extra firm squeeze, but gently.

By this time, Pop was on the ground. His jacket was on, but loose.

He too, was respectful as he said pleasingly, "Van McKellar."

I had wondered how the two older men from, I thought, different worlds would react to each other. Whatever anxiety I had about their meeting disappeared as they grasped each other and continued speaking as if they were old relatives.

There was something unspoken, something that could not be spoken of, not tragic, but it recalled past friendships that had crossed racial fences. I saw it, but my limited knowledge of bygone racial relationships would not let me comprehend it. Sensing the need to let them get acquainted alone, I walked over to the low porch and sat down within earshot but heard nothing as they walked back to the truck. Pop had worked for very wealthy men of power before as a handyperson and sometimes as a driver. So, he knew their character and was used to talking to them more casually than others did with the boss man types. Perhaps this was what was going on, but it wasn't conclusive. Afterward Wally remarked with feeling that Pop was a "Good old man." Pop knew that Wally had no more money than we did; still, he asserted with affection that Wally was a powerful *"Son-uv-a-gun."*

This impression, and other little snippets of Wally's life story, revealed that he had known power for reasons akin to the ones I mentioned earlier. We talked about these things by the weak yellowish glow of the old electric lantern while relaxing on our all-night fishing getaways on the Brazos River. He carried an army forty-five automatic pistol to dissuade mischief makers. I had a thirty-eight revolver and a sturdy pole for snakes just in case he missed his vaunted headshot. Moments such as these helped me form the basis of my theory about why White men could not see why they found it difficult to shake off the power they were born into.

Although I had less material wealth to lose, I did not get away completely free. The concern was where *Rock Bottom* lay. Just as my White fellows couldn't tolerate the thought of living as a second-class citizen, as one in a continuous fight with the power structure, I could not accept that I must surrender. In each situation, we were troubled by a lack of essential humility.

Also, in the *First Step*, my failure to effectively manage my life differed from the White alcoholic's missteps. The dissimilarity lay in the term's meaning, "our lives." A growing familiarity with how Whites lived showed me they were entwined with the things that supported their culture. They literally owned estates, homes, and investments and had careers and inheritances. Many had leadership responsibilities in the family and community. Conceivably, their very culture could topple from the weight of a blunder. The slave masters released Black families from enslavement without substance or legacy from their work. I came into this life and continued without owning a single feature I spoke of as part of the White's life. So, I saw my lack of self-control concerning alcohol while drunk as the entire manageability issue. I now realize alcohol was not the only unmanageability problem; it was merely a symptom of my darker, unresolved matters. Failure to manage my life properly occurred because of mental defects in my personality lurking in the background. However, the question of being powerless, though an error, did not prevent me from profiting from the step. I admitted I was powerless concerning the consumption of alcohol. Yet, I was slow in finding that measure of humility, which was the first step in being open to the healing power of the program.

However, I am not a psychological specialist. I speak about these matters to emphasize that alcohol is an impartial oppressor and impairs regardless of race or social status, but uses these factors to create Resentment, which is the mental crippler.

Step 3. (Will vs willpower)

Step 3: Made a decision to turn our will and our lives over to the care of God as we understood Him.

Instead of putting the workings of my will under the microscope, I promptly pounced on *willpower*, which I said I had in abundance. But my boasting was about hardheaded stubbornness. When things went my way, I saw my stick-to-it approach to living as *faith* in myself. Still, I knew I was on shaky ground, and though I didn't come right out and say it, I needed something more.

The phrase of the day among alcoholics was that their willpower collapsed after the first drink. I knew the old falling down story well. However, in my case, self-control failed me before joining the boys for the first round. *Those days' fearful memories are always in my mind to haunt me.* I recall going to a place where the crowd was drinking, intending to remain sober, but somehow, the glass was in my hand, and having just one little snort, seemed sensible. Soon after, I *blacked out,* and the next day couldn't remember how many drinks I had or in what condition I had finished. Now that I was sobering up, I looked to recapture the good name I had before the days of drinking myself into a stupor. However, I realized even those moments were not true happiness, only the enjoyment of seeming to fit in. I was slow to catch on, but I finally realized the *3rd Step* wasn't solely about a lack of sufficient willpower in my drinking. It was about my weakness of will in choosing how to live.

Nearing a year of sobriety, my youngest brother and I moved from the two-room apartment above the furniture store. I had a 1965 Chevrolet Impala and had begun buying the trappings I felt a young bachelor should have. I attended a one-year machinist school sponsored by the *Manpower Development Training Authority* (MDTA) and stayed upright and dignified. These changes in lifestyle, though meagre, were buying me respect in the right social circles. I had been on an uphill tick before, so nothing in my recovery was genuinely remarkable. There weren't enough factors in these things alone to decide about the will unconditionally, but I looked deeper.

The White communities in America had long profited politically through collective wills such as the *Declaration of Independence*, *The Constitution*, local laws, and other shared aspirations. I could sense this will when they pledged allegiances and recognized their religious zeal and body language when standing for the *National Anthem*. Giving one's will over to *Higher Powers* for individual betterment was business as usual with many of these members. However, such documents hadn't been written with Black people's advantage in mind, so the feeling of inclusion in those shared wills was missing in my lifestyle.

On the other hand, devout people in *The Black Church* congregations lived with the same strength of will as the White community. Traditionally, our church was the spiritual backbone that had borne us through subjugation and *Reconstruction* as we faithfully served the Lord. I didn't know which gathering to follow because *The Will of the Lord* had many meanings among the various denominations within the church. The spirit which inspired them was also alien to me. Thankfully, I didn't need to perform the actions said at that moment. A big part of my dilemma remained that I didn't know enough about *Higher Powers* to commit to them.

The self-analysis poem "The Man in The Glass" was a favorite at the meetings. My sponsor regularly recited it from the podium with feeling, again while looking directly at me. Afterward, it became a topic for our exchanges about our own self-worth. Reciting the poem led to me writing bits of my own verse in response, for reflection, to release pent-up passions, and for enjoyment. I realized the inspiration for my poems came from a place separate from my intellectual processes. It was as if I was feeling the influence of a superior consciousness, which worked out the rhyming schemes. Of course, this wasn't proof of God's existence. Nonetheless, it made me aware that a source of greater intelligence was available inside me. *A Higher Power?*

Since I had been in the group, I perceived that something not readily seen was at the core of others' recovery. However, my reluctance to see spiritual things blinded me to them. Then I considered the similarity in the patterns of the long timers' first three steps. My story was virtually the same, except for turning my will and life over to something other than myself. The equation was simple; if I wanted to be genuinely sober, I would have to turn my will and life over to the care of a previously unknown *Higher Power.* As in the *Second Step,* I took another *leap of faith* to trust the unknown force people said was God. This time, it was easier to take it. Although, I still felt that the object of their belief was something other than the Actual God Himself. But it was easier to continue seeking, because The *Twelfth Step* spoke of a *spiritual awakening* as the result of working the other steps. It was enticing enough for me to commit to them with newfound enthusiasm. Seeking something greater than abstinence alone, I moved toward the next *Step.*

Step 4. (The Moral Inventory)

Step 4: Made a searching and fearless moral inventory.

The first three steps, which were primarily spiritual in tone, and, to me, were more about attitude than down to Earth practicality. The *4th Step* would prove to be more like the psychological analysis I wanted from the state hospital, but didn't get. Although I wasn't afraid of an immediate backslide into drinking, the need for more mental therapy was still important at this time in my quest for complete sobriety. The everyday pressure of working and living in the Whites' segregated system, with its unequal practices and privileges, agitated me more and more. There was no relief when I hung out on *The Hill,* because I felt I was expected to conform to the reckless ways of my Black associates, which further bottled up my need for unrestricted freedom.

A mechanic's perspective: To treat damage from such a thorn in the flesh, I must first drain and clear away the infected tissue to create the best possible conditions for healthy, fresh growth. Afterward, I would introduce new material and then bandage the area to protect it from contamination. A *searching and fearless moral inventory* seemed the first step in cutting away the abscessed way of thinking that lay at the root of my resentments and irrational behaviors.

Despite my preaching the necessity of a complete moral inventory, I tiptoed around one for many months after beginning the *4th Step*. Instead of delving deeply into all aspects of the issue, I looked only into my conscious thoughts. As a substitute for the depth needed, I also made a written list with my liabilities on one side and my assets on the other. Then I worked on the shortcomings revealed. Needing something positive for the moment, I took comfort in my virtues. Still, I felt pangs of guilt about not performing the actual inventory. These jabs at my consciousness came from a place similar to my rule of not passing things I didn't understand when I studied.

I was physically robust and psychologically fit, but there was trouble. I graduated from the MDTA school and found a job as the first Black machinist at *Landers Mill Manufacturing Co.*, a prominent local factory on South Main Street. However, regardless of my other advances in personal rehabilitation, I was two characters to White people with whom I mixed. Many in my recovery group saw me as their fair-haired boy, but I was an intruder to a small minority of my white co-workers. The Landers family were fine upright people. You would expect the *good ol' boys* in the shop to be overjoyed a Black man had "reached out and found a good job and gotten off their tax money." After all, it was one of their main grumbling points, but they were not satisfied. Neither did they let up with the smart-mouthing and inconsiderate racial gags, which brought hollers from the bystanders. Plus, White agitators contended that being a machinist was beyond the capability of a so-called *colored man* (This was the boys in the Pine Street shops mentality).

Undoubtedly, the knowledge of the countless accomplishments and inventions of Black people in this society had not trickled down to these hardliners who conveniently ignored the truth. I was aware a mistake of two-thousandth of an inch might wipe out a very costly part, which was sure to produce cries of, I told you, about Black people and machines. In this environment, I feared my work might get sabotaged by sneaky employees, so trust issues overshadowed on-the-job relationships. Again, bringing forth hasty generalizations and stirring up resentment in me.

Since I was a boy on *The Hill*, I had filed away canned responses to every imagined slight or insensitive question as a defense mechanism for my bruised personality. Behind the quick replies, which I fired back like a gunslinger when I was disrespected by anyone, was invective, leaving me feeling like a bully. I despise bullies because there is an ugly sickness in false heroism. Sadly, I still did not recognize what drove me! At about this time, I saw some value in claiming to be "thick-skinned" and keeping my composure when under attack. But it, too, was a sham and survival mechanism because I still bore resentment toward my antagonists. More than a bully, these give-and-take exchanges on the job made me a bigot. Fortunately, I was at the *4th Step*, hoping to unravel this psychological mess.

Because of the adverse influences of these issues, I became more serious about writing my inventory. Feeling the guilty, eager beaver, I tore right into myself to explore the reasons for the complete alcoholic train wreck. This time it was a step-by-step written analysis, and no flaws would remain obscured.

After the *blackouts*, the fights, and the drinking bouts that ended with me being locked away in the state institution, I wasn't too afraid of learning new, humiliating things about myself. I still felt some consolation that my usual calm disposition when sober was the opposite of my improper conduct when drunk. Yet, I hoped there could be no truly horrible surprises for me. With the inventory, I would fearlessly go where the clues led me. Although I still didn't know if God existed, the prospect that He lived became an extra incentive for me to be thorough and honest in my inventory assessment.

The four sections of the inventory I used then were:

1. Resentment,
2. Fear,
3. Sex Conduct, and,
4. Harm done to others.

Each inventory framework was on a standard 11 x 8 ½ sheet. Below the instructions were vertical divisions that divided the subheadings inscribed horizontally across the guide.

The four categories in the Resentment section were:

I am resentful at _____.
The cause _____.
Affects my_____; and
Where was I to blame?

Note: The Inventory Guide Form I used is an old one. More inclusive ones are available for free download from *12-Step Groups* dealing with many addiction types.

Resentment:

As I began the inventory, I could not think of one of my companions whom I resented bitterly. Likewise, no women I knew engaged in what I perceived as attacks on me. However, there was one matter from long ago that still occasionally stung me. It needed evaluating, so I placed it first in my resentments. I had never forgotten when a popular buddy and I were chatting on the campus at *Carver Junior High.* A young teen girl abruptly interrupted us to invite him to her party. She minced about and praised him as she talked and casually withdrew without speaking to me. Besides being incapable of dancing, singing, or being otherwise fabulous, I assumed she didn't invite me because I was nobody who raised her social status. That one incident festered in my sense of self-importance. Years later, I turned to alcohol for support at social gatherings. A few sips and I was the life of the party until I became smashed. Afterward, I blamed any social boo-boo on the booze.

In the first column of the guide, under Object of my Resentment, I wrote I resented overly self-important social climbers.

In the second column, under the cause, I explained how being slighted was the reason for my resentment towards them.

Beneath the third group, I noted how it all affected my self-esteem.

Last, in the how I believed I was to blame column, I said their rude attitudes probably came from a place of insecurity, much like mine. So, my timid behavior may have given their egos the come-ahead sign. I concluded I wasn't physically harmed by people who looked down on me; they, too, were trying to cover their insecurities and wouldn't change for anyone. I decided to not take it personally anymore and moved on.

I didn't know anyone on *The Hill* who caused me to resent them significantly. However, I was furious at those unseen faces who hid behind laws and policies that were unfair to me as a human being. That I was saddled with cynical anger at having been treated unreasonably during primary flight training ranked high on my list of resentments. The officers and cadets who rejected me as unsuitable because I was, in their estimation, a *Cocky Negro*, came next in my resentments' column. I was also tempted to jot them down as snobs, but their rejection carried a particular sort of grief. I had lived closely with the cadets involved in the bus hazing and shared the common dream. They should have known me better than that. For years after my flight school troubles, I turned the whole sorted mess over in my mind, looking for my mistakes. Still, I unearthed no errors that called for marking me for repudiation. My Air Force career had been fine until my trouble in flight school with the Tac Officer. Afterward, I resented the entire Air Force because I couldn't get justice from them when I was hurt in Florida and the subsequent troubles, including the drinking. Although I was drunk often, I guessed what fairness looked like and how they should have achieved it. I had given my best; anything else would have been less of me. Afterward, I realized the military differed when dealing with discrimination, but not considerably from the general population.

There were regulations in both places to prevent or overturn racist wrongdoing. However, there also were those who adhered to the old traditions quietly. These two-faced types eluded detection from higher-ups who wished to stamp out bias. Where prejudice was concerned, immorality and deceit were set up too deeply then and are still secreted in the military hierarchy. My last remark is likewise the point of view of some Black American service members in 2024, including four-star officers, speaking on TV news specials and on social media platforms. Sadly, the good guys' hands are still tied. But like the naive girl that embarrassed me, my adversaries in the Air Force probably were attempting to raise their low self-esteem by accepting some people and rejecting others. I suspected I could do nothing to change things, so for the time, I also dropped this packet of poison.

Oddly enough, I had become so conditioned through the years that I accepted racial persecution outside the Air Force as the norm. I didn't think to include the elephant in the room! Racism still ran rampant in the southern states. The senseless bombing murderers of four little girls in the *16th Street Baptist Church* in Birmingham, Alabama, on September 15, 1963, were, as the entire country expected, all but dismissed by local authorities. I was in anguish because the federal agencies were also dragging their feet. In April that year, *Martin Luther King Jr.* said, "Justice too long delayed is justice denied," which sums up my feelings about the country's sense of fairness. Next, in my resentment column, I wrote, Racists who get away with everything. Because I had listed only the outspoken figures, I wrongly presumed I had dealt with all my resentments. These were only racist individuals, groups, and institutions that affected me openly. However, I discovered afterward that I neglected to acknowledge I resented the friendly, quiet White people who insisted they weren't racist. Yet, they profited from the lopsided economy and the shelter of segregation. They irked me as much as those who outwardly relished their biased doings. Since these good citizens had self-serving pretexts to shield them from guilt, their complacent attitudes could be annoying. I was digging deep to avoid being a slave to my faults, and I expected of these so-called good White people, no less.

After jotting down the last item in my Resentments column, I was satisfied I didn't bear a burning grudge toward my other concerns. However, I still felt something was left unaddressed. At length, it came to me! When members of the dominant culture were abused by anyone, laws, courts, and other means existed to get revenge (AKA Justice) or to make them whole in other ways. No reason for resentment was left to trouble them. When I, a Black man, suffered an injury at the hands of White people, there was no place of justice for me, so the lack of satisfaction ate at me. I could only endure the pain of resentment, which prolonged my fight against addiction. With no way to escape racial persecution, I could only deal further with resentment of this type on a per-incident basis.

Referring to my mechanic's approach at the beginning of *Step 4*, the moral inventory continued to be the best diagnostic strategy to solve my elusive issues. But before systematically implementing the repairs, I needed to put together a long list of loose information about the impacted system, in this case, my ego's sense of self-worth.

Next, what were the abnormal behaviors of the device [me]?

I hardly ever reacted to serious differences of opinion without resorting to a fight-or-flight response (Bad temper).

I recognized I had all the physical and cerebral skills my detractors had.

I noted their failures and the other outcomes.

I responded to touchy comments differently than others did.

Since I was the one who usually got emotional, I wondered if it must be how I dealt with disagreements.

Mood swings began.

I used to get up and try again after falling. Now, where social disasters were concerned, I had lost my resilience.

I countered by emphasizing that I was as good as anybody and becoming flustered.

I didn't fear bodily harm from the people I contended with, but I was offended when they boasted they were better. Even though they could do some things easier than me, "I am smarter," I brooded.

I was outraged because they obviously didn't appreciate those instances in which I was superior, and no one took my side. My dilemma was not one of cowardice. Being looked down upon caused an emotional reaction. And I would sooner blame others than have it brought to light that I also had human flaws.

Analyzing my notes, I recognized not all my fears were in lockstep with my resentments.

Finally, I had something to put into the inventory, as I did in the Resentments section. Faltering along, with all the inappropriate grace of one emotionally impaired, I took up "Fear" next.

Fear:

King Solomon of antiquity once told those who deal with delicate matters to:

"Catch the little foxes that spoil the vines, for blossoming vines have tender grapes." (Song of Solomon 2:15)

Now that I was on the rise in the material world, my financial and social development was in flower, but fear, nibbling like a snoop of cunning foxes, continued to threaten my recovery from alcohol addiction through unidentified stresses. Vague, petty annoyances in the background gnawed at my thoughts, making me afraid of something nameless, and becoming easily irritated. Surely, it was memory of the mysterious *blackouts* that were the backdrop of such fears, but they were only voices and not the terrible creatures that desired me. As for the foxes, they would sneak into my unconscious moments from time to time to continue their villainous forays.

In former days, when I drank, liquid courage cloaked my dread of rejection; however, I couldn't use it to eradicate my anxiety now. Still, I stayed sober, although minutia I never fully came to grips with contributed to me regularly feeling something was amiss. Where White people were concerned, it sometimes seemed I carried a chip on my shoulder. Yet, as I wrote earlier, my obscure fear was not embedded in resentment, but came from things I thought had died when the alcohol abuse ended. Instead, along with the vivid dreams I had while sleeping, occasionally, I woke from a nightmare, badly hurting because I dreamed I had been drinking again. Not a vision of disorderly intoxication, but simply that I had one glass of wine, and my sobriety was shattered. The nightmares were so convincing that remorse touched me, as if drinking had actually taken place. Shuffling the actual state of my corrupted thought processes with the false image of an up-and-coming, polished young man recalled timeworn poetry. *"I'm burning the candle at both ends. Oh, where can I set it down, my friends?"*

It seemed even those who knew me closely could not see the kaleidoscope beauty of the facets of my style of living as merely a facade. I was bedeviled by trouble as I altered my behavior again and again. I didn't have answers that made sense, so I would respond by asserting that I was a Gemini, and we are born conflicted. But all was not lost. Two years passed, and I was at a turning point in my story.

My success working through the resentments encouraged me tremendously with my relationships, especially with young women on *The Hill,* whom I tantalized with the idea of long-term affairs with the sharpest guy around. I hand-wrote poems for my girlfriends on parchment paper with silver ink. Being popular with the girls boosted my sense of being home anew. Perhaps having more than one sweetheart at the same time is best taken up in the *Sex Inventory.* It wasn't the most high-minded way to live, but to a late bloomer, it was exhilarating, and I had it all for the moment. I leased a neat three-bedroom house at the south end of *The Hill.* It was on the last street before the brickyards and sheltered in a thicket of trees. An attached carport kept the leaves and tree sap from landing on my highly polished, two-year-old dark red Chevy Impala. I bought a 1957 Chevy from the boss's son for my younger brother, Laddy Boy. We never lacked company or people dropping by. Class B General Machinist's pay was still good then. I could afford good furniture, a kicking component hi-fi system, and a console color TV. I was having some small influence on my companions, so when we hung out, we did things I could live with.

Beginning with the first column of my Fears Inventory sheet, I wrote: I am afraid because… And then I was stunned because I couldn't put a name to my fears. I jotted down each thing I felt addicts might reasonably fear during their rehabilitation but came up with only five I felt applied to me.

Written on my list of these five things were the following:

First: The fear of failure. The notion I would fail in my quest for sobriety had fallen aside over a year ago at my first year of abstinence party. Admittedly, I was still ashamed because I had committed shocking things during drunkenness that my tender ego had to deal with while sober. However, something that appalled me about drunkenness could not lure me back into Hell, so I took up the next item.

Second: The fear of success was only a little thought that popped up now and then. My drinking personality had boasted so much that I hoped others had overlooked those fantasies that no one could live up to, but this was nothing to fret about. I was solidly entrenched in my new career with a good reputation.

Third: Sobriety as a fear factor fell away when I committed myself to the state institution over two years before. With that pledge was the prospect of a better life through my recovery efforts.

Fourth: The **fear of losing my former reputation** was not a valid reason to be nervous. True, there were the miserable friends that missed the company of their old boozing crony, as were the few rivals that enjoyed watching me fall. This was purely wishful speculation if it even took place, and there was no reason to fear rejection.

Fifth: I don't recall when the **fear of dreaming** and the accompanying nightmares started, but they never stopped until well after I performed the *Fourth Step*. Because I didn't understand what they were about, I often went to bed uneasy, hoping I could sleep peacefully until morning. Fortunately, a catalyst that sets these scary events in motion had been spoken of eons ago. In a well-known legend of severe human struggles, the biblical patriarch, Job, meekly protests to his *Higher Power*. "When I take to my bed for comfort, you scare me with dreams and terrify me with visions." I didn't know the whole Job story or how he evaded his predicament, but the prospect of God being behind these dreams stirred my passion for understanding them. Because of how I saw the world's condition, I hadn't embraced the *Higher Power* concept at that level. In my estimation, if there ever was a God, he was long gone by 1967. But figuring out my dreams was too important to dismiss this tip.

I believed there was no reason to go beyond the first column of the inventory sheet. My fears didn't involve people or conditions that could affect my life or otherwise harm me. I considered I might suffer from inner condemnation. Yet, the consistency with which good results followed my feeble attempts to believe in a *Higher Power* was encouraging. So, while still working on the inventory, I embarked on my journey to learn the interpretation of dreams, and from whence they came.

As I kept the ideas written in the introduction of this chapter in mind, I reclaimed more of my self-esteem and increased my personal and spiritual power. My social life was more enjoyable, and I was moderately happy with my overall progress. Still, the moral inventory did cause some sad reflections as I unearthed painful memories of those regretful days. But by the time I reached the end of the fears section of the inventory, my calloused heart was becoming fertile ground. I was ready to investigate my former Sex Conduct.

Sex Conduct:

After I had been in the Air Force for a while, I saw I was in a community that valued science and reason. It was all I hoped it would be, and more. I was too busy learning it all, so my early sexual conduct had no role in my intimate relations beyond wishful thoughts. But Mother Nature put an end to my shillyshallying and brought me along the expected path, albeit at a slower pace than my peers.

Some old-school vets in the squadron boasted of being fighting, hard-drinking, hell-raising womanizers. The telling of such tales was like waving a red cape in front of a susceptible newcomer. Once out of basic training, we younger airmen went with the more experienced types into the various camp-following institutions off-base for our initiation into the mysteries. At first, I drank to keep up my courage, but eventually, sex and alcohol became intertwined, and I was no longer wet behind the ears.

Now that the genie had escaped the bottle, it never failed to perform its smoke and mirrors tricks whenever I was under the spell of the booze. I remember doing many embarrassing things while drunk that I would never have contemplated when I was sober. It was an attempt to gain recognition for those social shortcomings such as dancing, singing, fighting, and lying about doing larger-than-life actions. What I don't recall is what I did during the *blackouts*. It is reasonable to assume that if I raised the bar on my abilities while mildly inebriated, I would go overboard during a *blackout*. So, I must acknowledge that I probably committed things I can't remember when I was drinking heavily.

No other person was attached to me intimately during my drunken shenanigans. Other than clumsy attempts at flirting, my sex misbehaviors were better handled in my inventory's Harm Done to Others section.

Harm Done to Others:

The four categories in the Harm Done to Others section of my inventory were:

Who did I hurt?
What did I do?
Why did I do it? And,
What were my true feelings about it all?

There were many occasions when I was a victim in my interactions with others. However, there also were times when I acted from motives other than self-defense or knee-jerk responses. I hoped all that could be overlooked now that I was changing. The problem was a nagging fear had also crept into this harm's committed category since I had been sober. Yet, this was not all tragic. Something good was coming to the forefront these days. Although I didn't feel I could salvage my life I had in aviation before the drinking nightmare, I hoped to build on the new foundation.

As to the things that needed reconciling, I experienced only a slight pang of guilt over the sinful side of myself since I had been tackling the inventory. Still, I needed to make amends for those I had hurt directly or let down in some other way. Thankfully, the direct action to be taken would begin later in the *8th Step* when I would list such people and then, in the *9th Step*, make the apologies and restitution. All I needed to do now in the Harms category was to consider and list my offenses, which were less intense for me than confronting people I had harmed. I began the list with those who had invested themselves in me.

Mama and Pop headed up the list because I felt I had disappointed them the most. It wasn't the Air Force kerfuffle that caused their grief. Failure was all too common in my neighborhood. In fact, for a Black boy to succeed at anything that involved the White world was a rarity. They had been optimistic, believing I would become one of the rare ones to make it out of the slums. It must have been excruciating when I became an insane alcoholic with all the trimmings. I had nothing to put in the "Why did I do it" box because my alcoholism was not a crime that I committed against them. Although, I thought of it as a tragedy brought upon my whole family.

Merle was next on the list because she was the person who suffered the most from my *Dr. Jekyll–Mr. Hyde* antics when I was in my drinking years. My sober side enticed a hopeful young woman into a dream that became a nightmare when I turned to drink as the solution to everything. In my self-centeredness, I assumed I had the right approach to nearly every issue and felt aggrieved whenever I was opposed. Now that I could see it better, I was even more devastated over losing her. These mournful feelings caused me to list my name after Merle's name. Although the entire mess was my fault, I had suffered along with her. And, no, I hadn't forgotten that two imperfect people were in the relationship, yet I was the one who couldn't let go of the bottle.

After listing my name, I couldn't think of anyone else I had harmed. This was the end of the section of the *12 Steps* that dealt with introspection. As I advanced through the rest of the *12 Steps*, I collaborated with others, including God (as I understood Him).

After completing the written portion of my personal inventory, I felt mentally stronger and invigorated. I had faced the aspects of my personality that had stunted my growth and tripped me up through abusing alcohol. I was still hungry for life and as a matter of course and sought the food (Fellowship) that still eluded me in the groups. But addiction is also a spiritual disease and since I was still spiritually poor at that point in working the *12 Steps*, I had not considered the well know saying that "*man does not live by bread alone* but every word that comes from his *Higher Power* (God as he understands Him.) In truth, I went forward existing on crumbs of the *Bread of Life*.

Chapter 15:

Crumbs from the Children's Table

I didn't see a lot of Wally, my sponsor, and friend, after two years had passed. In the beginning, we saw each other almost daily, sometimes working together or at the same place. Our connection remained intact even as my new career as a machinist consumed a lot of my time. Wally had moved out of Billie's house and was the live-in manager at a motel in Dallas, that catered to White guests. I visited him once, and we went through hearty, good-natured kidding, and I told him I had smoked a little marijuana with the boys on *The Hill*. He didn't disapprove and told me the group's founder had experimented with pot use, so, it was not frowned upon by the group [Then].

During our visit, I perceived nothing amiss in his life. I was too wrapped up in my social and economic upturn. I was stunned when Billie told me that Wally had begun drinking alcohol again. It was our mutual embarrassment, not disappointment, that led to our separation. I hope Wally wasn't negatively affected because he felt his slip may hinder my sobriety and progress. I was determined to succeed. I don't know if Wally continued with the recovery group when he was off the wagon because I also missed meetings during those days. Of course, we stayed friends, but our sponsor/sponsee bond was difficult to maintain. Such relationships do not have inflexible laws that define them. Without a verifiable course of action for our peculiar circumstances, we lost touch.

We knew we needed to get along if we were to give the program a serious shot. At one time, when he lived in Mississippi, some unknown racial dissatisfaction had driven Wally to investigate the *Ku Klux Klan* for membership. And I had mulled over Black militancy when I first learned about it. From our honest talks, we each knew that our negative attitudes about the other's race hindered our ultimate freedom. We never explained the specifics of our dissatisfaction with our opposites to the degree that it would demean the other. However, we understood the value of accepting each other with all our real or imagined shortcomings if we were to heal. I didn't understand then, yet we shared the same realization that inspired writers of old to inscribe meaningful sayings that are relevant today. My years in pursuit of discernment have convinced me that successful truths enlighten those who strive to be morally right for their own sake. Though unspoken, some members' actions were governed by a famous but often unheeded admonition:

"But I say unto you, love your enemies, bless them that curse you, do good to them that hate you, and pray for them which despitefully use you, and persecute you."

Early on, when he, Billie, and I hung together like the *Three Musketeers*, Wally began referring to me as reverend after a weird event happened. It was on August, the 11th 1966, at my first anniversary of sobriety meeting with the big group. The hall was crowded that night and included a group of nurses, one of whom was a beautiful young Black person who beamed as she signed my Alcoholics Recovery *Big Book*. I trembled when my turn came to speak, although I seemed very composed. I began with my drunkalogue (A short recounting of my troubled days). Near the end, I was compelled to speak about my *Higher Power*. I remember saying that God (As I understood Him) speaks to me through my consciousness and several other things. I didn't mean to assert the Creator of the universe talked to me but simply referenced a source of my moral guidance. I thanked everyone for coming. At the start of the meeting, the crowd had been recommended to hold their applause and comments until all the speakers had finished. A silver-haired White nurse was touched by my words and smiled at me throughout my talk. At the conclusion of the program, she was the last person in line to congratulate me. As she clasped my hands she said, "Help your people Reverend!" Billie and Wally smiled approvingly at me as Wally's expression morphed into a knowing grin and an I *gotcha* wink of his big right eye. Then other audience members added similar comments.

A few days afterward, Wally started addressing me as Reverend playfully, with a pretend scowl of disapproval that quickly transfigured his big beaming face. After that, on any pretext, he would accuse me of preaching, although it was he who danced all four hundred pounds of himself around. He showed unusual religious knowledge and mimicked an unknown tongue while rolling his eyes around. Although I denied any spiritual affection, I liked the accusations. The vivid days and night fishing jaunts eventually faded to memories as his and Billie's relationship grew unsteady. To make matters worse, I had already slacked off meetings with the recovery group and started smoking marijuana when Billie told me that Wally had been killed in a car accident involving a larger vehicle. Wally's unexpected demise deeply saddened me. I didn't attend the funeral services. We had said it all before we drifted apart. Besides that, I didn't know friends and family who were there and didn't feel that any sharing of grief would be a genuine common loss. At that, I distanced myself from the group. But through it all, I still didn't drink alcohol again! However, Wally's slip caused a significant problem for me.

What follows is my reasoning and not that of any experts in Alcoholism treatment that I know of or have heard about.

True Fellowship was one cornerstone of recovery when I was with the groups. According to their literature, fellowship could replace that unknown persistent nagging in the back of my mind of not fitting in.

That peculiar sense of belonging fosters well-rounded members who share much in common. The chief among those qualities is sobriety. But the *Jim Crow* society made it impossible for Whites to embrace a Black man as a genuine friend without being persecuted. Blacks were labeled as *Uncle Tom* if they were seen to be too close to Whites.

Wally and I were unique because we stepped out of the well-established boundaries. During the period that both Wally and I missed the group sessions, the lack of fellowship wore on me. We had our occasional get-togethers, but they proved to be inadequate. I can't say for sure with Wally, but I suspect he was having problems with the Whites like the ones I had with the fellows on *The Hill*. In my case, we all talked about our drinking experiences. However, the still practicing hell raisers glorified the ones I needed to avoid. There were non-drinking friends I could have hung with, but they were dull and locked in the life laid out for them by some convention.

To be effective for a recovering addict, fellowship must provide a unique sense of sharing the same aspirations. Things had worked for Wally and me because we each perceived that the other was a loner and didn't have a niche in his own racial group. Even though we could not provide each other with a sense of common purpose and belonging, we still had a connection that allowed us to provide support. For the moment that had sufficed, now I was back to a similar form of rejection that I experienced at my first meeting. True, the original overt dismissal softened when I became better known among the group members. However, the "impenetrable veil" of racism still barred me from the fellowship of brotherly love among the remaining Whites. It was only a little better among my Black neighbors on *The Hill*, who accepted me as somewhat of a loner. So, although I could partake of the general fare at both the Black and the White tables, I was not part of the privileged group with access to much needed fine delicacies. I know now that I succumbed to the fellowship substitutes that marijuana provided for my still slightly hurting, addictive personality.

Some individuals in alcohol group frequently express, after a relapse, the sentiment of "I wasn't done yet," indicating that they believe a longer struggle with their issues would have led to better recovery. I was doing well in staying off the alcohol then. But I didn't fully understand my addictive nature, so it was my unresolved character defects and not the substances alone that beguiled me. The truth was, *I stumbled because "I wasn't done yet!"*

Chapter 16:

A Fellowship of the Weed

The *Gold Dot* was once an infamous, well-known juke joint on *Baptist Hill* in the 1940s and 50s. It had a reputation for shootings and knife fighting, being more common than the East Lancaster Street honkytonks. Despite its evil reputation, the *Gold Dot* was among my childhood neighborhood's most popular public houses. It was the principal place where the hustlers and girls from my street went to ply their trades and socialize. I wouldn't have ever frequented such an establishment.

When I returned from the Air Force in the early 1960s, the owner had demolished the *old killing floor,* as such joints were usually called. Not far from the ruins, he built a larger brick nightspot near the west end of *The Hill,* just East of the downtown railroad tracks. The new hangout for Greater Fort Worth/Dallas hipsters was called *The Glass Key.*

Somewhat removed from a haunt for rowdy carousers and common drunks, *The Key* catered to a more socially polished Black trade. But not the *Negro upper crust,* who had no exclusive public places in Fort Worth to go for evening libations. However, the occasional educator or famous band member stopped by for a nightcap after a downtown concert. Inside, the restaurant section wasn't muted but had a pleasant aura. The inevitable jukebox could only be heard outside when the door was opened, but not so loud as to need excessively raised voices as in a honky-tonk. The round tables were draped in fresh White tablecloths. They held ketchup, hot sauce, and other condiments to complement their excellent fried chicken and catfish sandwiches. You could also find a far better hamburger than was sold in the new and popular fast-food places.

Head-in parking spaces were available in front and on the sides of the light green building and in the shadows of the trees across the unpaved street alongside an undeveloped area. There, hustlers hawked cheap whiskey by the ½ pint, marijuana, and the less reputable means to satisfy an addict's cravings. Cop cars crept past on rare occasions, but the Cops only glared intensely unless specifically called for. Although it was not fin-tailed and had a diamond in the back, after I left the *12-Step Group*, my pretty red Chevrolet Impala could be found near the front entrance. It was a beacon for the pot-smoking crowd. Exploiting my own addictive consciousness and behaviors gave me insight into the world of the street people and the elegance of one born to it. I had nothing to sell, still I was there, as much a fixture as the rest of the outside throng. I didn't have to do anything to earn my right to be there. I was a late blooming, reluctant son of *The Hill,* taking his rightful place in the hierarchy of hustlers. Without fanfare, it was accepted that I was somebody to get to know. Mine was a name that was greeted with emphasis whenever I appeared.

Since I wasn't a real *inside* hustler, I don't know how they actually felt about my status among them, only what they said to my face, and that was workable. Although I dared fancy myself as an imposing edifice like *The Key's* glaring neon sign, like all farces, I was only smoke and mirrors. I suppose pseudo-hipsters like me were the Black version of the Drug-store cowboys who hung out in the honkytonks on East Lancaster Street so long ago.

How had I changed so much since I began my recovery from alcohol addiction and fallen so easily into a similar rut?

My reversal didn't stem from a lack of essential fellowship alone; I had never truly felt togetherness among equals in the White group. Yet I refrained from drinking. I believe my requirement for socialization was satisfied because my sponsor and I worked and hung out together. If possible, I needed to be at the top of what was attainable to satisfy my addiction's constant thirst for peerage among the so-called greats. The first joint I smoked with Joe Boy and Sixty led to returning to the *Glass key* to get more.

I enjoyed indulging in my marijuana-induced fantasies while getting lost in science fiction novels and jazz music. Before long. My need for real world companionship exerted a greater force. Eventually, I hosted pot parties for old-school classmates, who hung out at *The Key*, in my secluded house near the south edge of *The Hill.* We didn't experience the depth of fellowship I needed, merely a mutual back-patting acceptance of our self-importance.

Relating the details of the high times here now would only repeat a less violent version of the emptiness I found in my alcoholism.

I endured each hour with an empty heart as cliques of people with whom I only had marijuana smoking in common enjoyed the comfort of my home. I was more of a *Maître D* than a confidant to these intimate strangers who only stopped by to get high. Eventually, a paranoia-type feeling I got when smoking grass forced me to see the precariousness of my situation. It intensified when my classmates began bringing unfamiliar people along despite me telling them not to. I should have insisted, but I gained more recognition as the unwanted visitors spread the news that I was somebody important. Still, I couldn't shake the feeling that my home would be raided by cops or robbed by gangsters. About that time, I had a streak of bad luck. A guy passing a car in an intersection ran into me and destroyed my red Impala. I wasn't hurt, but I got laid off because the company's contract with a customer ran out. Working occasional gig jobs, I still couldn't come up with the $1,000.00 deductible and had trouble making ends meet. From there, it was all downhill. I realized I had once again lost control of my affairs. Although, faithfully living my *12 Step* routine through it all, no matter how much I wished it, reciting the *First Step*, "I am powerless over my situation, and my life is unmanageable," was unsuccessful in turning around my situation.

Note: It is believed by many in the field that when an alcoholic who has been sober for a significant length of time returns to drinking, something unexpected occurs. Soon the disease impairs their body and mind to the same degree as if the person had been drinking all along. The reasoning is that alcoholism is a progressive disease whether or not drinking continues. I would argue that it is not only the substance that is the culprit but also the work of the addiction itself. Now, I had succumbed to such a sad situation. But for some reason unknown to me then, I did not despair as I did with alcoholism.

Seeds of Faith

My Pot smoking fears so inhibited me I believed any White man who came near my street might be the police in disguise. These fears spelled the end to my parties at the house. However, the mind-tripping moods also made me dream of a high-paying job in California. Soon I became determined to leave my home and go to the *West Coast.* It came down to the risk of being caught or the lure of living in Los Angeles. My uneasiness intensified, but through the lens of my Pot fantasies, I confidently affirmed that life in California was my destiny. Indeed, life had prepared me for just this moment, I said. The way I put it; it was foolproof. I knew people who lived somewhere in L.A., so I'd find them, and the machinist job opportunities would open. I even visualized returning to town for a visit and sitting in my fabulous new ride, spinning tales of my success. I also was convinced my family, seeing I was out of control again, feared I would sink into something akin to drinking life, didn't want me back in town.

Of course, all this made no sense to my family, but what could anyone do about it? Besides that, my move wasn't as suicidal as it seemed. I reasoned if the finding friends plan didn't pan out, I would have enough money to get a room at the YMCA and take any job I could find, including day labor. The YMCA gambit would be far more difficult than the "finding friends to live with idea." Beyond that, when I was drinking heavily, I learned how to sleep outside with those who had no other shelter than *Mother Nature.* But that was such a drop in status and any move would carry the taint of failure if there wasn't a better change of circumstances. So, I hid it unspoken, deep in the back of my mind. I so desperately hungered for a successful makeover that, to my thinking, the California plan was rational. It was the ideal geographical cure to satisfy my addiction's desire for a clean start. After all, I reasoned, I had made considerable progress working on myself thus far. My earlier economic and societal successes showed me I was going in the right direction. The deception convinced me I had changed myself but couldn't do anything about others stuck in the backward southern mentality.

To my mind, the new effort promised better surroundings and better people. All that was left was to buy a bus ticket to L.A. and raise $100.00 in travel money. So, I scraped up $150.00 before leaving the house and a blue 1957 Chevy for my younger brother Laddy, and my sister Jackie, who was also younger than me but older than Laddy.

Pilgrimage to the City of Angels

LADDY, AND HIS FRIEND SIXTY HUNG AROUND THE WAITING AREA of the bus terminal after I boarded at about 6:00 PM and found a window seat. They stood outside the building waving as we got underway. Stir full of bluster, I gave the thumbs-up sign as we passed them on the right side.

The vision of Laddy and Sixty faded into the background as the *Greyhound Scenic Cruiser* raced westward through the tired old streets of Fort Worth. Speeding through town was a jerky affair, as the passengers' weight shifted forward at each red light and then back as the diesel howled and lurched forward when the signal turned green. At last, I was on my way! The driver sped on as if hastening me to my destiny.

As we careened down West Lancaster Street, my misgivings about the scheme became undeniable. I could now see the foolhardiness of my undertaking. Too much of the plan hung on the presumption that people would behave as I had predicted. I was usually right in guessing how things would turn out in small, inconsequential matters, but now my life was on the line. However, I consoled myself by reasoning I was strong enough to pull through should adverse circumstances occur. How I deduced I would not fall into ruination was not based on logic alone. Something intangible was also at work. Each time fear raised the thought of impending downfall, a small but straightforward affirmation came attached to the uncertainty that "I would be alright." Like a child consoling a poor and needy parent, this teensy inner voice had no more substance than pennies when dollars were needed. It wasn't like the *leaps of faith* I had taken to win the love of a girl or to believe in powers greater than myself. At the root of these prior things was the belief that my virtuous inclinations pleased the objects of my desire.

On the bus traveling toward the unknown, I knew of no external assurances I could point to, just a brief occasional feeling, "I would be alright." But that nearly imperceptible thought was enough to ward off a complete panic attack. This back-and-forth wool gathering would go on for the entire two-and-a-half-day trip. Soon, we were on the interstate part of Highway 80 where the flat featureless West Texas landscape draped in darkness was as unobtrusive to my drowsy eyelids as elevator music was to idle thought. In the loneliness of the coming evening, I fell into an uneasy sleep.

I woke several times through the night to the voice of the driver interacting with people coming aboard; sometimes he was gone for a moment, but it was the door's opening and closing that punctuated these stops. Morning found me hungry and looking out into the bleakness just East of El Paso, the big breakfast stopover. I often went to El Paso on the weekends while I was stationed at Holloman Air Force Base. Sometimes I flew one of the club's planes over the city, so the lay of the land thereabouts wasn't totally unfamiliar. I hoped the prices at the lunch counter wouldn't be unreasonably high. When we arrived, I shifted into a more alert mode.

El Paso was large enough for street hustlers to be in and around the station. It was also a border town where prostitution was a way of life for many. Even though the significant trade in human beings occurred on the other side of The Rio Grande, the hustlers still looked around transportation terminals for runaway young people to steer astray. Although I didn't see anyone who appeared to be a hustler or recognized any untoward activity, I wondered if the children fleeing their homes felt the agony of uncertainty I did. Perhaps not because of their innocence, but I knew firsthand the dangers of such undertakings. Surprisingly, a sausage and egg plate inside cost the same as at a regular cafe. Thirty minutes fairly flew by; now refreshed, I sat in the back on the right side of a new bus taking in the sights.

The New Mexico state line came quickly. Then the small communities of Las Cruces and Lordsburg. After that, the monotony of the Arizona desert where I nodded off to sleep now and then. During these intermittent periods of drowsiness, I had a half-asleep thought of my Los Angeles friend, Johnny, speaking to me. He wore a slightly tattered wife beater undershirt and asked me without expression, *"What are you going to do now?"*

The scene had no background to interpret, yet I inferred he wanted me to leave his house. It was my first time having this kind of thought while I was awake, and it made me anxious, but I eventually pushed it away as the evening fell. Two days riding and sleeping in the narrow bus seats left much to be desired, but it would be over tomorrow, so the last night was tolerable.

Morning came, and we were cruising through the fantastic land of California, and I was once again encouraged a bit. It was still desert topography outside the cool windowpane, but its *Death Valley* facade became exotic as we approached places named *The Joshua Tree Forest* and *Twenty-Nine Palms*. The mythical places had become a reality by the time we pulled into the city itself.

Los Angeles

The interior and exterior of the bus terminal in L.A. were nearly the same as the one at Fort Worth, despite the variance in the size of the cities. However, there was considerable activity in this major metropolis. I noticed the difference in the body language of those meeting or dropping off familiars. There were obvious strangers engaged in a salesman-like conversation with people who didn't fit the scene. The hustlers had a confident aura, and the outsiders had a clueless look. I hoped I exuded that "nothing to get here look" to the tricksters, but you never know because some will always try to con an old con. Besides, I had my bags in hand and appeared as out of place as the recent arrivals.

Once outside, I had a flash of good luck, which allowed me to lose my apprehension. I recognized Floyd standing on the sidewalk about 30 feet ahead of me just as he caught sight of my face. What a relief! We sauntered toward each other and gripped hands as casually as if we had seen each other the night before.

"Floyd Jr." I slid his name out long and softly, "My man," giving deference to show respect.

He was about three years younger, but just as mature as I was in the ways of life, if not more.

Knowing this, he pronounced my name faster and louder, "Van Jr." came forth from his crooked smile, "What're you *doin'* in L.A., *Mane* [Man]?

His use of the street jargon belied his overwhelming intelligence." In two minutes, I gave him the same story that had taken me two months to explain to my family in Fort Worth.

Floyd had been a hustler since we were children. He didn't know about the work situation, but he said Johnny did, and he lived relatively close to where we were. So, we climbed into his "*Short*," as his car was known in those days, and left downtown. I was relieved enough to enjoy my new surroundings more as we rode.

The outside of Johnny's apartment looked much like the ones we lived in back home. I suppose I thought his pad would be grander since L.A. was touted as almost paradise. He answered the doorbell, and we embraced fervently with thunderous salutations and powerful hand dapping. We all were tight, but Floyd was never one to waste time with social lollygagging and soon left me with Johnny. I had supper with Johnny and his family, whom I had never met before, and slumbered on the sofa in my clothes that night. I was awake when Johnny and his wife began stirring in the morning as he prepared to leave for work.

When he came in, he gave me the exact look I saw in my thoughts earlier on the bus and asked, *"What are you going to do now?"*

A somewhat incoherent conversation followed, and then he agreed to drop me off at the produce market where Floyd hung out.

We found Floyd near a small clump of trees at the edge of the truck parking area, where a noisy dice game was in full bloom. Once Floyd knew how much money I had, he took me to *Clark's Hotel* at Central and Washington near downtown. The bus going South on Central stopped in front of the hotel and one also ran on the cross street. So, transportation was less of a problem. After paying two weeks in advance, I had enough for food and bus fare.

My foot was in the door!

Section IV: Spiritual Awakening

Chapter 17:

A seat at the Children's Table

After I was in comparative safety, and survival was not my highest priority, my prevailing negative mindset re-emerged, and the anxiety that caused me to leave returned. Job searches proved fruitless in the first week. As if that wasn't enough, I was slowly beset by an illness that caused me sleeplessness and made me extremely weak. I had only seen Floyd once, about two days after I moved in, but I learned of a free clinic and went there to seek medical treatment for my condition.

While sitting in the waiting area, I spoke with an amicable Black woman who appeared to be several years older than me, so I called her ma'am and gave her the required respect. We swapped stories about why we were in the clinic. During our talk, she told me, "Read the 23rd Psalm while drinking seven sips of water and you will be okay." I stayed polite while the conversation faded away, as it grew more frustrating than helpful. A few minutes more and I was being examined by the doctor, a refined Black man who seemed to be in his forties. He asked me about drinking and drug use. I emphatically denied the alcohol which he suspected me of using and rejected the drug use. I omitted the recent marijuana use because it was not considered a hard drug, and I had not smoked any since I left Fort Worth.

When I returned to my room, I was even sicker than I had been before I went down to the clinic. My anxiety was high as I drew a glass of water from the sink and placed the wooden chair in the middle of the room. Next, I took the hotel's copy of the *Gideons Bible* from the desk drawer. I removed my shoes and knelt beside the chair and laid the book on the seat. Using the Index, I found the correct passage easily.

Wanting to stir up a reverent mood, I clasped my hands together, looked up and mumbled "Help me," and then dropped my eyes upon the page.

I began: "God, I don't know if you are there, but I'm in trouble and need help."

I acknowledged I hadn't been a true believer because religion was a non-issue for me.

I said something like, "I don't know how to be sincere, and if I wasn't in trouble, I probably wouldn't be praying."

(I remember apologizing through the prayer, trying to show whoever might be listening just how penitent I truly was. Yet God, unwilling to lose His wayward child, overlooked this confession of insincerity.)

I repented, "Please forgive me and teach me the right way so that I can turn my life around."

I meant every word I had spoken, but by the time I finished reading and drinking water, nothing happened. A bold thought came, *"You knew that this wasn't going to work."*

I read more, hoping that I might sound impressive, but to whom?

I was so like a desperate false lover now that the 23rd Psalm ritual had borne no fruit.

I read the 24th Psalm, which spoke of God's majesty but could discern no help. Determined to hold on as if my reading of the Bible would grab the attention of a *Higher Power*, I turned next to Psalm 22, which was on the left side of the open book with Psalms 23. As I began at number 22, I saw the writer was in a similar predicament. Now that I had something to identify with, I became deeply engrossed in the prayer.

Now I know the prophet also spoke of Jesus' coming suffering on the cross hundreds of years later. And not only Jesus' and David's ordeals, but many of God's servants have undergone strikingly similar predicaments.

When I came to verse 11, (Be not far from me; for trouble is near; for there is none to help.) I wept as the words worked their effect upon my tormented soul. Sorrow gripped my chest so tightly my breath came in short gasps. Still, I wasn't sure anything would happen because I remember saying after the verse, as I saw myself as the sinner I was, *"Lord, I did this to myself. I can't blame you."* I continued sobbing as the psalmist's predicament mirrored mine. However, during this time, I became more hopeful as I saw with the writer that I was appealing to God's compassion. I also felt my prayers were now sincere, and it pleased me I had the right spirit. When I came to the 22nd verse of the 22nd Psalms, I read:

"I will declare thy name unto my brethren: in the midst of the congregation will I praise thee."

Then, something extraordinarily amazing happened. I envisioned myself standing in a brownish suit surrounded by a congregation of people. My hands were raised upwards in praise and speaking aloud. Just as I realized preaching was my true calling, a wall appeared several feet before me. Then a White cloud billowed twice from the wall toward my face. Nothing was uttered either aloud or in thought. I felt no physical contact either way, but I experienced *Friendship* coming from the vision.

Astonished and overcome with joy and emotion, I shouted,

"Oh, God, you are alive, here in the twentieth century!"

Just as quickly as it began, the cloud receded back into the wall. I felt Glorious; it took a moment to realize I wasn't sick anymore. "I am alright now," I spoke audibly, "Everything is alright now!" I had no fear of anything, no need for approval from anyone. In the moment I knew that the spirit of God accepted me as a *friend*, the pains of personal, cultural, and racial rejection instantly fell away. With it went loneliness and the need for fellowship with the traditions of the world. My soul felt only joy.

There is no doubt that after my *Spiritual Awakening*, with regular group meetings, I could have lived a very fulfilling life as a machinist or in any career I chose. The alcoholism recovery group had not provided the intimate fellowship I previously looked for. But now the sickness of the spiritual side of my addiction had been resolved through my reconciliation with my *Higher Power*. Seeing God in a visual representation made me realize that God had seen me as a *friend*. This inspired me to share this message beyond my experiences with alcohol addiction.

In the following days, God (As I knew Him anew) embraced me in that personal love that opened my eyes to just how special His children are to Him. This embrace of my personal Savior was so captivating and complete in the early years that I felt our relationship was exclusive. I went over the past events in my life when I had momentarily achieved a connection to a calling higher than myself only to dismiss it in the face of reality. Then. it dawned on me that God was my *Old Friend* from childhood! He had been watching over me all the time. I realized there was no such thing as good luck, all along it was the working of my *Higher Power* in my life. Despite my former worldly braggadocio to the contrary, God's approval was all I had ever wanted for as long as I can remember. I was ecstatic for weeks as I tore into the Bible. I focused on reading popular biblical heroes, dreams and dreamers, and things of historical interest. One day soon after the vision, in innocent ignorance, I said to *My Friend, God*, *"You'll have to teach me about Jesus; I don't know much about Jesus."*

I said this because of the many conflicting things among the people at large that are part of the Christian narrative. I began with The Gospel According to Matthew.

I spent lots of time reading in my room but did not shut myself off from the rest of the world. Indeed, wherever I went, I engaged whoever would listen in a conversation that began with, "Did you know God is real?"

After the cloud experience, I became convinced that *The Living God* actually did speak to me through my consciousness, as I said at my first year of sobriety meeting. I remained alertly aware that my mind also held many profane thoughts as well.

In a zealous effort to please God (As I felt I understood Him), I became fascinated with the idea of fasting. I found verses in the Bible telling the correct way to behave while undergoing a fast, but I could find no instructions about the length of days. Based on biblical evidence, superstitions, and guesswork, I believed that going without food or liquids for three days and three nights would be noticed in the spiritual realm. I also read I should keep my fasting a secret, so I pretended everything was normal.

As I traveled during these days, the *Street Preachers* at the bus stops and street corners in L.A. held me spellbound. When the bus stopped, the doors opened, and the evangelist's voices and bible-slapping echoed inside. I was moved. It seemed they either preached about the rightness of their institution's beliefs or the imminent destruction of unrepenting mankind. Two days into my first fast, I was riding the bus, but going without sustenance was too trying for me, so I thought to end it with a satisfying meal and a cold drink when I returned home. To take my mind off my suffering, I was talking to two church sisters when a disheveled Black man got on. He might have been in his fifties, and he was slightly intoxicated. As the bus pulled off, he lost his balance and suddenly sat near us. Almost immediately, he began speaking to the women about a religion that was offensive to them. I admonished him for his unchristian beliefs with religious fervor, but he rudely cut me off. He had a understanding smile on his bewhiskered, deep brown face as he made a circular motion around his stomach. He winked his eyes and said twice,

"I know what you are going through. God sees you too, and He's *gonna* bless you if you keep it up."

I was shocked that he knew I was fasting. I nodded appreciatively and thanked him. His message encouraged me to complete the three days and nights I had planned initially. Much more than that, it deepened my belief that God was my constant companion. That same day, I found a good-paying job at *U.S. Electric Motors,* a manufacturing company within easy walking distance of the bus stop. My new position was a 2nd Shift tracer lathe operator, which meant my hours were from 3:00 PM to 11:30 PM.

It was two weeks before my first check, but I worked the rent payment out with the hotel owner. I still had enough money for food, so it never became a problem. I was intensely devoted to my new spiritual quest (Which I now say was a new addiction) that I overlooked eating regularly. My life as a new believer in God transformed into an all-consuming adventure. Now that I was awake, I saw evidence of my *Higher Power's* influence everywhere and in everything. It was/is a feeling of oneness that causes some to claim they know the center of the universe. The odd behavior I facetiously labeled the *God Madness* on others was now on me, and I reveled in it! Life was good for me again. I was building a new guilt free life that threatened no one's boundaries.

That year, Southern California was hit with unusual, heavy rains. I miraculously escaped being soaked as I traveled to and from work. In my exultant state of mind, I saw this as further proof that I was on the right track spiritually. After about a week of avoiding getting soaking wet from the capricious cloud bursts, I was standing at a South-Central bus stop around midnight when a few drops signaled the start of a downpour. For a moment, I believed my blessings had run out, but a powerful emotion came over me as a car swerved and stopped in front of me.

A friendly voice asked, "Do you need a ride?"

"Thanks," I responded as we both opened the door together.

After the first greetings and mentioning the weather, I told the young Black man who looked to be about my age, "Man, I sure have been lucky avoiding these rains."

I began explaining the recent good luck with the weather when he asked softly,

"Do you think it might be the Lord, Brother?"

Spontaneously, we both began praising God. My newfound acquaintance burst into the *unknown tongue* that I at once recalled as characteristic of Pentecostal religions. With my delighted acceptance of the familiar expression, a friendship was born. When we reached my hotel, we talked about the goodness of God a few minutes. But before I left the car, we agreed I should attend his church the following Sunday.

Note: I felt glorious as I lay in bed thinking about the recent events with the *Spirit.* The vision of the cloud had been so vivid that in the instant it occurred, I believed it to have been a real occurrence. Many years later, due to the juxtaposition of the furniture I saw in the vision and the actual placement of the chairs in the room, I came to know it as a vision.

WHEN ADMONISHING THE CANAANITE WOMAN WHO SOUGHT HEALING for her *demon possessed* daughter (Matthew 15:26), Jesus called such blessings from God as "*The children's bread* (Sustenance)." Now, for the first time since my tween years at, *Mt. Pisgah Baptist Church* on *Baptist Hill*, I was going to church to feed my hungry soul. Perhaps, in those childhood days, I returned for the much needed "You are a good boy" compliments. But I also liked the idea that I was doing the right thing, even though I did not fully appreciate how it was so. This time, I wanted to experience more about serving God. Recalling past times when I heard adult church members say that the Lord told them something or the other grew into an air of unknown expectancy as the days crawled slowly by. But, make no mistake, since the spiritual manifestation in the hotel room, I wasn't only going to become a church member, I was looking for more of God Himself.

Sunday rolled around. As we pulled into the parking lot, I noticed that the White, medium-sized church sign read *"West Adams Foursquare Church,"* a denomination I had never heard of. I was still excited to be there. At *West Adams Church*, I was welcomed with hugs and warm introductions, unlike my first meeting at the big alcoholic group in Fort Worth. About seven or eight young adults eager to invite a potential member into their ranks made me feel much better. When I stepped down into the peaceful atmosphere of the building, my emotions became active again. *I had the feeling of coming home.* The inside resembled church buildings I had been in before. My friend and I sat on the far side beyond the prominent seating, next to one of the long aisles that ran lengthwise through the sanctuary. But soon he left to take his place in the choir. I didn't feel I was home free as far as Christianity was concerned, but I was overcome by happiness at being in the right place. I sobbed so much that the children were staring.

The congregation was abuzz with excitement because a famous member, *Hazel Scott,* the world-renowned gospel artist, was going to sing that day. Since I was about to burst, I fought to keep myself together when she stood and sang. Her singing moved me deeply, but, miraculously, my composure held, and I remained seated. When the time came for visitors to introduce themselves and have a few words, I waited until the others had finished. After giving my name and where I was from, I told the congregation about the intricacies of my trip to the coast.

Then, wishing to imply God was behind my irrational journey, I made an open hand gesture and said, "But I really don't know why I came to L.A."

There arose a minor uproar as the pastor, a middle-aged Black man, yelled out, "We know why you came." (It seemed everybody, including me, believed God had brought me to L.A. to save my soul.)

When the associate ministers finished their announcements, they formally introduced the pastor, Elder Smith, who would bring the message after the choir's singing. As I looked beyond the pulpit into the choir stand, they prayed aloud. I heard a high angelic voice trilling in an unknown tongue coming from among them. I was so captivated by the voice and the feeling that came with it, I regained control and enjoyed the musical presentation. Before his sermon, Pastor Smith welcomed the new people and mentioned, "Loving to have the new as members." I leaped from my seat but noticed the roaring laughter and the pastor said, "Not now, but we want you." I was so full of something I wanted to shout!

Elder Smith's message centered on Moses being a general in God's army. He went on about how God needed generals in His army [The Church] today. When I saw the cloud vision in my hotel room and knew that God saw me in *Friendship*, my burden was lightened because God forgave my transgressions. Soon I was before the altar repeating after Elder Smith my acceptance of Jesus as my Personal Savior. That was my commitment to follow His teachings always. This time no vision came, but in that instant, as

I felt the weight of the world lift from my back, I shouted *Hallelujah* at the top of my voice.

After the service, the young people engulfed me, and we were off to two different churches the same day, where we met others like us. It was a fantastic experience! The next few days were days of sanctification. During this period of spiritual atonement, I went through intense prayer and meditation and a cleaning up of how I interfaced with the secular world. Inevitably, these time-honored initiation rites found me seeking the *Holy Ghost.*

Note: The Belief in the relationship between the *Holy Spirit* and the church can vary significantly within its many denominations. How and when the *Holy Spirit* was given to contemporary believers is not an aim of this memoir. Neither is the evidence of the Spirit or its administration in the believers or church bodies suggested beyond what is scripturally reasonable.

The modern Charismatic/Holiness movement was in its sixty-first year when I sought my spiritual revelation in 1967. All the background was unknown to me, so I was unaffected by preconceived notions that might have misled or beguiled me. So, I couldn't say for certain whether The Holy Ghost would come down from Heaven or was awakened in me. Such mentioning of The Holy Ghost is only what I believed or did not believe at the time of my experience.

Although I make references to the Holiness movement within the churches in the United States of America from a Black perspective, they were not at that time exclusively so. A few years after my experience, I learned there have been great outpourings of the Spirit throughout Christian history. Sometimes It was manifested in individuals and other times a group of worshipers. I garnered from a prevalent story circulating among the Black Holiness ministers in the Faith of a more recent Filling of the Spirit. They said, the modern movement began in earnest when "The Holy Ghost Fell" in the city of Los Angeles on April 9th, 1906. That night, the Black American preacher, William J. Seymour, who led the meetings at the Azusa Street Revivals and seven other men were expecting a move from God. They were suddenly knocked to the floor by, it is said, a force of lightning bolt intensity. The eight men began to praise God and spoke in tongues, as did the believers on the Day of Pentecost described in Acts 2:38 in the New Testament.

The Pentecostal movement that ensued stretched across racial and denominational lines. This latter-day spiritual awakening flourished in many Protestant religions for several years after the Azusa Street visitation and filling of the Spirit. The more conservative worship style of White Pentecostal churches came to be accepted by the public as an orthodox religion called by the name Charismatic.

In 1923, a White female evangelist, Aimee Semple McPherson, founded the first Foursquare Church along these holiness principles after seeing four beasts in a vision. She interpreted the four faces of the beasts as the four aspects of Jesus Christ. However, the membership of West Adams Foursquare Church was predominantly Black, and the services were Black in tone. I didn't realize it then, but although not overtly so, a taint of racial segregation was present in these supposedly preferential places of worship. Most of the Black churches that came from large White denominations were biased in this way. Today, in mega-churches, money is the successful integrator.

A few days later, we left the church around 1:00 AM, long past the 9:00 PM closing of mid-week services. Several young adults had tried to help me get filled with *The Holy Ghost.* Despite their diligent efforts, I hesitated to accept the *Holy Ghost* for my reconciliation because of my earlier lack of understanding. I felt I needed to learn more about those things. But my fellow members were persistent. They laid hands on my back and shoulders, telling me to praise God so He would send the Spirit into me. The last try was in the staging area beneath the scaffolding of the choir stand near the rear exit. My tongue felt so heavy I could scarcely articulate clearly. Someone said the Spirit was on the verge of coming through because I was slurring my continuous repetitions of "Thank You, Jesus."

My friend and I waited in the parking lot until the pastor's daughter and another sister locked the door and drove off before we left. A wave of euphoria washed over us as we sang at the top of our lungs during the car ride, knowing that I would undoubtedly excel at the next ceremony. I have an awful singing voice, but the Spirit in the car was all over us that night. We were belting out a joyous rendition of Jesus Lifted Me when approaching headlights flared in front of us. As my friend swerved out of the way,

I screamed, "THANK YOU, JESUS!"

Instantly, *The Holy Ghost* came upon me! All reluctance abandoned me as I immediately spoke in tongues and was so filled with an overpowering force, I tried to escape our moving car. I let up some when I realized why my friend was trying to hold me back. When we stopped, he ran around the front and opened the door. I tumbled onto the grass, praising God, and shouting what Gospel I knew. For several days, whenever I tried to talk about anything spiritual or religious, it came out of my mouth in tongues. I could verbalize regularly when I had to but would steal away as often as possible to speak in tongues under the anointing. Over time, my spiritual outlook aligned with

Pentecostal doctrines, and things I once thought to be abnormal, became normal. I embraced the whole narrative, the customary sayings like, "I am saved, sanctified, and filled with *The Holy Ghost* and fire."

However, I never actually saw any evidence of cloven tongues of fire or their resemblance at any time. Nor did I recognize the staccato vocalizations as any rational earthly or heavenly language, but a powerful specific spiritual understanding flooded my thoughts when the tongues were vocalized. This I saw as the prophetic interpretation that went with the tongues. Frequently, others in the congregation agreed with what I felt spiritually. It wasn't a perfect fit because of my *12-Step* roots but being an active church member supplied the human fellowship I had once longed for. The church and my alcoholic recovery group had different views on the ultimate deity. Still, I grasped that what I had undergone had been known through time by those for whom the gift of salvation is only the beginning. Those who, like Moses of old, wandered capriciously until eventually climbing figurative mountains and meeting their own burning bushes. Ultimately, I realized being filled with *The Holy Ghost* was the *12th Step spiritual experience* I had longed for. After all, in both cases, I could satisfy my need to carry a vital message to those still suffering.

Opinion: Addicts relentlessly chase the feeling they first found in the remedy that eases their pain. While under the spell of their addiction, the meek can become as cunning as street hustlers. Once they have learned of its existence, they will sacrifice everything to obtain the highest of the highest. Again, I found myself locked in an endless pursuit of the perfect moment, now labeled as religious fanaticism.

My relationship with God grew exponentially through the indwelling presence of the Spirit of Jesus Christ. I read every credible religious text I could find and almost any work that claimed a connection to a *Higher Power.* I also developed a more significant insight into *Our Father's Love* for humanity from others, who were not of my Faith, but whom I believed were living in harmony with God (as I understood Him). The most significant gift was solidifying my relation to God, my *Higher Power*, through an improved prayer life. My conscious mind grew so entwined with the spirit within me that I could scarcely wait to enter a private place to pray. Usually, it was at the altar in a church or my hotel room bed. As I sank to my knees, the anointing came upon me as it melded with Praise and Thanksgiving. I burst into tongues and tears of joy and communed with the Spirit through the worship of my questing heart. Yet, the presence of *The Holy Ghost* as my constant companion didn't automatically alleviate all fights with the spirit of unbelief that preceded my earlier "Leaps of faith." Even after meditating, I sometimes became offended or wanted to react defensively to minor insults. *I was still being tempted by Satan.* He didn't have enough power to win these struggles with me outright, but so far, I had only endured these attacks.

However, one night as we were leaving after the service, I heard a loud, firm voice off to the right, and below the stairs, say, "I rebuke you!"

Even as I turned, I thought, "Someone is fighting the Devil."

In the subdued light I saw Elder Smith pointing toward an elderly church sister and repeating the phrase threateningly. Instinctively, I knew that he wasn't speaking directly to the woman. A sensation unknown until then came over me. It was like a miracle occurring as my internal temperature dropped and the hairs on my arm rose. The woman, with both hands above her head cried "Amen" each time Elder Smith shouted.

As I moved out the door, I felt much stronger knowing there was a better way to defend against these mental attacks. I didn't know enough about the *Deliverance Ministry* then, but I was satisfied that I would learn to combat this worrisome foe.

In those days, my dreams were still peculiar and unlike those of my friends. But, since my pledge at the end of *The Moral Inventory* to learn more, I didn't dismiss these confusing and often terrifying dark visions as meaningless nightmares to be unspoken of and forgotten. Although there was sometimes an unresolvable pattern to them, certain ones seemed to have an element of clairvoyance.

Since my open vision, several times each night, I have had dreams of all kinds. Before my in-depth bible study, the scary ones left me feeling guilty and uneasy because I thought I was missing something important. Now, I saw that the dreams in the bible, like those Daniel and Joseph interpreted as messages from God, were nightmares to the people who dreamed them but not to those who had the spirit of interpretation. Nevertheless, I was hopeful I was on a spiritual path, but I was also impatient because the dreams were still puzzling.

In the non-spiritual world, things were also going well. I discovered a sunbathing area on the hotel rooftop that no one else seemed to use. It was only about forty feet above street level but didn't have the thrash and crash atmosphere that plagued the throng below.

I had saved over six hundred dollars over the last few months. The work at the plant was suitable for someone who could be satisfied with a permanent job as a tracer lathe operator, but ultimately, it was not a good career move for me. There was so much more to learn. My prior stint as a general machinist was not enough to qualify me as a top-Class A Machinist in the Trade. Besides that, those apprehensive inclinations that led to me coming to California were primarily in response to things in my imagination and were not a necessary career move. When I became aware of God's Spirit in the hotel room, my emotional and physical problems ceased to exist.

In a moment of desperation, I had called on the *Name of the Lord* with the smallest of faith, saying, "God, I don't know if you are there," and He answered me in a vision of *Friendship*. From that moment, all my fears of being alone in a world as chaotic as the dust it was formed from, fell away. And, with it the pain of poverty, which from then on, has only been occasions of inconvenience to be circumvented.

Following my understanding that all I ever wanted was to know that someone in power watched over the world and would someday make things right. I was no longer dissatisfied with my life.

Chapter 18:
Carrying the Message

Photo by Sixteen Miles Out on Unsplash

After a few months of prosperity in Los Angelas, I received word that a friend in Fort Worth, who, although in his early twenties, had passed away of a heart condition. As I reflected on this, explicit thoughts came to mind as remarks at his upcoming funeral. *Eugene "Sonny" Mitchel* was a good and trustworthy person who swiftly passed through our lives. Though not an avid churchgoer, he always exemplified outstanding traits many religious people can never seem to grasp. I considered whether to continue my fresh start in California or return to Texas to fix my old life. If it had been only a matter of career and the fellowship of my new role in Christianity. I would have chosen California. But I had missed the laid-back country life of Texas for a long while. Relaxing besides fishing spots on the lakes and rivers near home was far superior to lounging on my rooftop retreat at the hotel, but most of all, I missed prowling around in my car like a jungle beast patrolling his territory. And, with a last sigh, I conceded that I hated the harsh clutter of a big city, so I planned to get out of town. Before leaving, I apologized to my supervisor for not giving the customary two weeks' notice, but he understood, given the urgent nature of my request.

LAX was noisy but less bustling about than I had expected for a midday flight. My luggage consisted of a medium-sized suitcase for baggage checking.

I hand carried a briefcase containing personal items while paying my fare at the counter. Oddly, my space-available airline ticket only cost about $45.00 for a 2 1/2-hour flight, which was the same amount I spent on a 2 ½ day overland trip traveling from Texas to California by bus.

Walking to my boarding gate, I suppressed an exaggerated feeling of self-importance I sometimes fell into when engaging in things that were above my normal financial means. But I didn't have that out-of-place look I had at Love Field when I first left home to join the Air Force an eternity ago. Yet, I was not so seasoned a traveler that I didn't want to run around the waiting area like a bright-eyed toddler exploring each unfamiliar object for all the new knowledge it held.

The call came, and just before we entered the boarding gateway, I asked the attendant in a mild voice, "What are we flying in today?"

"This is a DC-9, Sir." was her reply as she gently ushered me forward. "Thank you," I said and stepped onto the plane.

I had held off imagining what the actual flight would be like. Like an epicurean about to taste a near-forgotten delicacy, I was busy savoring the moment. My view at the wing's leading edge was perfect for sightseeing while we were in flight. I had expected a fast rate of climb but was startled as the twin-engine mid-size passenger plane reared up into the heavens like a silver Pegasus. There lingered only a slight pinch to my sensitive memory of times when I also was pilot in command of jet engine machines that vaulted into the sky. So much had changed in aviation in the short eleven years that had flown by since my flying days. So many questions to answer when time allows. I had a new dream to pursue in Christianity now and brought the thought of the business ahead to the forefront of my mind. I was unsure if there were Black *Foursquare Churches* in Fort Worth and didn't know where to find a church home. While I was gone, my brother Laddy Boy and Jackie, my sister, had moved from the house near the brickyard to the *New Projects* on *The Hill.* I wasn't overly stressed about a place to live because I had enough to rent a new apartment. In fact, I wasn't worried about anything. God watched over me! I would be alright if I didn't step out of His Will (As I understood things). There was no unpleasant turbulence because of significant cloud formations or weather. Before long, a tailwind from the prevailing westerly currents brought us home to DFW.

My brother, Louis, and his friend, Sixty, met me in the baggage area wide-eyed and amazed at how big and confusing the terminal was. We went to Chambers Street in the *New Projects*, where Jackie and her kids lived. I don't remember that anyone was glad to see my return, considering the mixed-up condition I left in such a short (to them) time ago. My seemingly uncertain situation became more tolerable when I explained that I returned for *Yogi's* (Another AKA for Eugene) funeral and had enough money to secure my own place in a few days.

The next day I strolled through the old familiar sidewalks to the upper end of *The Projects* to visit Sonny's mother, Bernice, a long-time family friend, and my daughter Vanessa's aunt. These were the years I walked most places without a second thought about the difficulty.

Setting the table

I was still giddy from being in town once again and filled with expectations of living life to its fullest on my terms. Notwithstanding how I saw myself then, I must have been a pain in the neck to friends and acquaintances, especially those blindsided by my new condescending attitude and preachy approach to ordinary conversations. But it wasn't only my recent experiences in the Church that drove me forward; the path I walked now had not been a 100% change of direction. Finding God in Christianity continued the journey I began on August 11, 1965, when I vowed to stop drinking and broke the wine bottle behind my baby daughter's house. In pursuing a higher quest, I found the alcoholism recovery groups and began working the *12 Steps*, through which I had risen from the sortied mess. Although the remnants of my alcohol addiction blinded me then, now I see like the sheep in the 23rd Psalm, I was systematically shepherded away from the banks of a raging river.

The Mysterious Power that permeates the universe reveals itself in myriad and unique expressions. My journey through the *12 Steps* may not be the method others would choose to overcome their addiction. Nevertheless, because of the commonality of our afflictions, it may well be the path to finding your *Higher Power* and purpose in life.

Following the first three of the *Twelve Steps* calmed the tumultuous strivings of my heart.

The *4th Step* revitalized and prepared me for reconciliation with my *Higher Power.*

I began *Step 5* with the doctor in the clinic and the woman in the waiting area. I completed it in the hotel room, where I confessed to God about my wrongdoings while taking *Steps 6 and 7.*

I worked on *Steps 8 and 9* with the help of the *Holy Spirit*, acknowledging my responsibility and making things right with others.

Steps 10 through 12 were direct actions in my addiction recovery regimen.

The *12 Step* suggested:

"Having had a spiritual awakening as the result of these Steps, we tried to carry this message to alcoholics, and to practice these principles in all our affairs."

I saw the friendly cloud experience in my hotel room in L.A. as the long-awaited *spiritual awakening* in the *12 Step*. But after being filled with *The Holy Ghost* as a church member, I understood the *12th Step* expanded beyond alcoholics to include all those who suffered spiritually.

A Fresh Crumb from the Table

Sonny's funeral services were held the following Saturday. I sat midway next to the center aisle with his other close friends and running buddies. I rarely wore suits and dressy clothes, except high-dollar shirts, so I wore slacks and a nice shirt. The other guys were similarly attired. When I stood to give my remarks, I suddenly became less aware I was standing by my chair, but it also seemed as if I could see and hear myself from a point higher and to the left of where I stood. My voice was strong as I spoke of things I had previously mulled over in my mind. New thoughts about how it all fit together, along with a mild admonition for those present, came quickly to my tongue. At once, I realized that the anointing to preach was upon me. I was both pleased and amazed that it was happening. As I spoke, I could hear people in the background saying Amen and voicing approval rhythmically. Just as quickly as it had begun, I prayed for God's blessing on the family and those who were present and then sat down somewhat embarrassed but felt good about it as I realized it had gone well.

From that moment on, everyone, especially me, knew I had been called to carry the *Word of God* to this suffering world. As if to verify this, the preacher, a slender middle-aged man with whom I had made eye contact with several times stood and drawled something to the effect of, "I didn't know Mr. Eugene Mitchell, but this young man (Pointing at me) has given me something to preach about." Then he made a funny gruff face, like the one Wally, my sponsor, used to make, and said, *"Young man, God's got something for you to do."* Amens and mumblings of agreement came from the gathering. After that, he went on to officiate the services. People congratulated me for the remarks after the service. There was no mention of my former despicable conduct or my drinking days. I felt a range of good emotions while thanking them softly and nodding my head. Afterward, I went back to Jackie's apartment. I spent a pleasant evening with my little nieces and nephew.

The following day, I called the only *Foursquare Church* I found in the phone book. I told the White pastor who answered the phone everything and, before hanging up, mentioned that I might drop around sometime. Honestly, it would have been a last resort. I didn't consider it then, but underneath our parting words lay racism, but the traditional acceptance of segregation made it appear so innocent. Like the pastor I had spoken to, I, too, believed "I would probably be more comfortable in a Black congregation." The real reason was only implied by him in so many words but readily inferred as wisdom by me. I would hear and accept this bigotry repeatedly, unable to see that the poison lay in my willingness to *"Be more comfortable with my own people"* regarding religious fellowship. Actual practice in social situations elsewhere had shown that I could be at home around anyone, but now that I was back where the race card was played often, I fell into the mindset of the so-called *natural order of things* from a Black perspective. It is still ironic to me how easily prejudice and spirituality can exist in a false harmony when societal norms must be appeased. I had not learned it then, but Paul, the chief apostle, had put his foot down as The Serpent reared his head in the formative years of The Church: *"There is neither Jew nor Greek, there is neither bond nor free, there is neither male nor female: for ye are all one in Christ Jesus." (Ephesians 3:28)*

I missed church that Sunday but vowed to find somewhere by the next one. It seemed many in religion were indeed a spiritual work in progress.

Chapter 19:

Contaminated Bread

Having always been an unconventional soul that affected a countercultural stance in life, I suppose it was only natural that my entry into the ministry began in an unconventional way. About three days after missing church on Sunday, I was out riding with my younger brother. We passed an old movie theater on Riverside Drive that had been converted into a church. The marquee read, *King E. E. Allen, The Greatest Prophet in the World Today*. Below, in smaller but still discernible letters, was a printed sign inscribed with the words: *The Temple of the Holy Ghost.* Although this converted building had a literal sanctuary inside, many would still consider it a *Storefront Church.* Although not spoken publicly, such renegade churches exploited superstitious minded worshippers. Like those unwary seekers, I was fascinated by the wording and returned alone later in Laddy Boy's car to meet the pastor. He was different from the suave, nattily dressed, easy-going Pastor Smith of *West Adams Church.*

King E. E. Allen was a corpulent Black man. He appeared well into his fifties and had medium-brown eyes that bulged. He wore an old dark-colored suit and smiled as he spoke. The prophet sized me up as I talked and interrupted me near the end of my Los Angeles story. Despite my initial impression of him as a street hustler, I accepted his offer to work as a junior minister because he provided rooms upstairs for me to sleep in.

Upstairs there were two bedrooms, among several empty ones. Apartment renovation removed most evidence that this area had once been a projection room. The largest room was now a combination kitchen and meeting/dining room. There were various containers of home-cooked food brought in for the pastor from last Sunday. They covered the long table. Chairs surrounded the table, but my impression was no meetings had taken place here in a long time.

Without speaking of money, rent, or wages, I was relieved that I had a place to live. He gave me the keys, and I left to get my things from Jackie's place in *The New Projects.* Thanking God for this blessing, I moved in.

Prophet Allen's primary office was on the second floor. A black guitar case leaned against the wall in one corner. He also had a smaller office downstairs. I didn't know much else except that he lived somewhere else with one of his followers. Since I lived on the property, I also answered the phone and kept the sanctuary clean and in order. I liked the idea of living in *The House of God.* When alone, I spoke into the air, confident my words fell upon God's eager ears. The resumption of my studies brought back the same spirit of understanding I enjoyed before leaving L.A. for Fort Worth. It was as if He (God), was a *Person* in another room that could hear me clearly. It would have been Heaven, but certain mysterious doings captivated me. In the days before the following Sunday's services, people came by for counseling with the Prophet in the small office. I learned from him they were not all members of his congregation. I didn't know what they came to see him about, but although Christian, some were not of the Pentecostal faith. These things remained mysterious me until the main service on Sunday evening.

The original theater seating orientation and stage remained unaltered in the sanctuary. However, the rows of individual chairs were replaced with mahogany-colored church pews. A large wooden double door, which was the main entrance, opened at the back of the benches on each side of the center aisle of the downward-sloping floor. Everywhere, there was adequate viewing of the stage area below. There was about twenty feet of space between the front row and the stage. This area held a wooden stand-alone pulpit and several chairs for guest ministers on each side. Some tables were further off to the sides. A large amplifier and speakers were also among the furnishings and equipment. These things were placed near the stage to leave room enough for worshipers to gather in front of the pulpit. The whole area was not brightly lit but not theater dark. I greeted the attendees at the double doors. Since I was a newcomer, it was more of an introduction than a welcome. Each person seemed to joyfully anticipate tonight's events.

I didn't know how things would proceed from minute to minute because the prophet had given me no instructions. Perhaps he thought I knew the routine.

Shortly, the group grew to approximately twenty-five individuals, yet despite the increasing number of members, I was astounded by the lack of personal acquaintanceship among them. They occupied their own space or sat with their companions, and there was an absence of conversation between them. However, the mood of expectation continued until a man opened with a song from the podium. The congregation joined in the singing; the Prophet came out from the stage's dark side, strumming his guitar loudly and vocalizing unfamiliar sounds while tambourines jingled vigorously to the cadence. He was strange as he danced about the empty space in the shadowy light.

At the song's end, the Prophet began shouting "*Yes…Yess…Yesss*" in a rhythmic, slurring voice that grew longer with each repetition, accompanied by a resounding refrain from the group that brought forth a rise in spirit with each intonation.

Now that we were on one accord, he began speaking in that poetic, religious, rising and falling-voice style peculiar to many Black preachers. I saw everybody was feeling the spirit much more than I was. At first, I panicked, wondering if I had done something wrong by being there and God had left me. But my anxiety subsided as I realized their rise in spirit was caused by their participation in the shared euphoric routine more so than the *Holy Spirit* because the excitement had fallen away as the music ended.

Prophet Allen had someone from the gathering read a particular scripture and told of his love for Jesus and the gift of *The Holy Ghost* to a chorus of "Amen" from us. Later, as the personal story of his experiences with brotherly love became ominous, he spoke of the *Jericho Rose*, a flower the flock seemed to know about. It was also something in the back of my memory.

He explained: "My enemies have no power in my home because I keep the *Jericho Rose* nailed above the front door of my house." I sat astonished as he said that he not only had the *Jericho Rose* for sale that night but also named several other items that he would pray over for those who bought them. I was too surprised to remember the prices, as I realized something was amiss. Then, the sermon was over, and the people came down to congratulate him on the message and to buy assorted items. I didn't take much longer to make sense of these things.

There have always been bits of profane doctrine that have attached itself to orthodox Christianity. I had known of these things when I was a boy. Mama wouldn't hear of it, but it was no secret to Grandma and Pop that other White and Black people turned to unorthodox *Hoodoo* (A combination of *Black Magic* and Christianity) practices when they felt they needed methods they couldn't get from their religions.

Slowly, I realized I had ignored what I should have seen as red flags in my rush to find a church home and secure lodgings. I didn't let on then that I highly disapproved of what was happening.

I was to learn that, throughout the South, adherents of this alternative religion were quietly woven like the proverbial tares among the wheat into regular Christianity. I would be dishonest if I did not say I wanted God to share the blame for my ignorance because He didn't warn me beforehand. But, in those days before I knew His ways, I dared not entertain the thought. Through my years in the *deliverance ministry,* I have gained insight into the silent struggles of fence-sitting church members.

It was an old custom among people I knew to find a comforting scripture when opening the Bible randomly. So, after everyone left, I locked myself inside and went to my room. I dropped to my knees beside the bed and opened my Bible with a short prayer, asking God to speak as I thrust my finger into an unknown page. It was more superstitious wishful hoping than logical communication, but the words of Revelation 2:2, stood out as I read:

"I know thy works, and thy labour, and thy patience, and how thou canst not bear them which are evil: and thou hast tried them which say they are apostles, and are not, and hast found them liars."

I was sure my prayer had been answered, and my guilt over being a part of this charade faded to Innocence. Still, I knew I must leave, but how? No matter, it was enough for then that I had mentally declared I would take steps to go as soon as I could without getting trapped in something worse.

Midweek, I saw a rat in the main upstairs room. It was undoubtedly attracted to all the loose food. I had never lived with rats before and was horrified at the knowledge that one was on the premises. However, the appearance of the rat, while disconcerting, shed some light on the fearful occurrences and noises I heard when I was alone in the upstairs rooms.

About two nights after Sunday services, I was alone in my bedroom praying. It was an uneasy moment because the devil in my mind had convinced me that evil spirits attached to the ministry were living in the building. As I kneeled in prayer, my eyes closed to prove my bravery and my faith, I not only heard rustling sounds, but also felt movements of air around my head. Clutching my biggest Bible, I climbed into bed with the book on my chest and my head beneath the covers.

I always believed that using any object as a shield instead of faith alone as a symbol of God's protection is idolatry.

But I was overcome by fear because I had convinced myself that evil spirits were running amuck. Another noise, unlike the others, caused me to flinch. I felt cold and with goosebumps rising. At that, my courage failed, and I left the building. I hurried across Riverside Drive to an old railroad track that ran northward about two miles before joining the westbound Texas and Pacific tracks near my former house by the brickyard on El Paso Street. From there, it was only about a mile to my sister's house in *The New Projects.* When Jackie answered the door, I *lied* and said I needed to spend the night on her sofa because I was locked outside the church.

After everyone had retired to bed, I was again alone with my fears. It had required enormous effort during the conversation to hide how unsettled I was. All my efforts to live a better life would be lost because evil thoughts would bully me with guilt until I could no longer lift my head. With the word, I realized these frightening tactics were just that: I was being bullied. A scene came to my thoughts, not a vision but conspicuous. In the scene, I was in a courtroom-like setting where a judge and two others were watching me and the devil on a lower floor from the other side of a wooden railing. The devil, in his traditional long tail and horns, was lunging at me and making other threatening gestures. I grew ashamed as I cowed before him. But I, the one watching the scene, realized this was what was actually happening, and that it was all a test of my faith. So, with hesitation, I left and went back to the church. I was still somewhat afraid of the rats as I kneeled beside the bed to pray again. I opened the Bible and put my finger on a random scripture. This time, the verse that my finger landed on was one in the 34th Psalms, which was not particularly relevant, but as I continued reading, the 7th verse stood out:

"The angel of the LORD encampeth round about them that fear him, and delivereth them."

In that moment, I saw that others (In the Bible) had had to face their fears and trust in God only. I have never feared spiritual evil since those experiences, period.

Seeing that I was in no discernable danger of bodily harm, I decided to do my best as a minister, and there was a certain normality in my relationship with everyone. In the ensuing days, I learned three people were close to the prophet. Two men and a younger, brown-skinned woman who walked with a slight limp came around during the week. Their visits were lengthy, and sometimes they would leave together. The woman habitually spoke to me in an intimate, close, face-to-face fashion. It was as if she was interested in me, but I wanted no part of that stuff, and besides, her breath was nasty from secretly smoking cigarettes. So, I remained distant and courteous.

Late one evening, Elder Allen told me to come with him to pray for a man dying of cancer. We went with the regular visitors in two cars to a lovely house on the outskirts of town. Inside, introductions were made. He said, as he always did, that I was a guest minister from California, which made his ministry seem more impressive. We crowded into a small room where a frail man lay unmoving with his eyes closed. We joined hands before the bed as Allen barked out a loud and long prayer.

Then, the others went into a larger room and could be heard talking about other things. As I sat beside the sick man, I felt the urge to pray and began stumbling audibly through the prayer that came to my mind. It was short, and I would not have wanted to pray in public. When I opened my eyes, I saw he was awake and looking at me, puzzled. I at once felt I had done something wrong, but quickly realized the man was conscious and alert.

I suppose it was youthful pride, but I asked him (Thinking to show that I was the real minister as opposed to the bishop), "You know who did this for you, don't you?" He looked at me and said very clearly, "Yes, Jesus!"

Immediately embarrassed before the Spirit, I agreed with the man as we talked affectionately about the goodness of God.

When the others came back into the room. They noticed the man was no longer unconscious but was looking around, so they began talking about how he seemed much better. After that, King Allen often bragged to the congregation about how he had healed a man of cancer. That moment of inner rebuke at the man's bedside should have been the thing to help me toward humility, which is so needed in intercessory prayer. However, it did not, but grew as I ministered on the prayer line, and those I prayed for testified, they were healed. I associated my fasting and other forms of consecration as being essential to the effectiveness of my prayers. Of course, my works had little to do with God fulfilling His promises of healing His people, but it was fashionable among ministers to think so.

A few weeks later, I decided on the final night of my fasting I would sleep near the altar. Still wary of the rats that ran amuck, I didn't lie down directly before the altar but chose one of the long pews about five rows back.

While in a deep sleep, I heard my name called softly, twice: "Van… Van."

I could see the vision of me waking up. Jesus, was dressed in a robe like the ones in the many pictures, called to the awakening Van, who sat upon the pew. As the scene shifted, I saw everything from off to the left side. From there, I could see the Lord and dream Van talking as friends do. I remember that the Van laying on the bench understood Jesus perfectly as He clasped Van's hands in His and rubbed them in a rolling motion. As I witnessed the thrilling scene, I also heard Jesus perfectly. Both men in the dream smiled and agreed as they talked for several minutes. Then the vision went away, and with it went the memory of what Jesus told me on the bench.

Although I have never recalled the exact words Jesus said, I am still inspired by that dream that I agreed to follow His instructions. These, I find in His teachings in the Bible and the indwelling *Holy Spirit* that was sent as a *companion and helper* to those who follow Him. Thereafter, I took no vows of allegiance to any organization and am confident his words are available in me and empower me.

After that, I settled without undue unease into my position as the junior minister with the prophet. I was careful to stick to authentic Christianity and leave the shenanigans to him. My duties consisted of opening the services, reading the scriptures, and passing the plate around during the offering. Since I was not ordained or a licensed lay minister, I didn't do any preaching. Occasionally, King Allen would give me a twenty-dollar bill, so I got along well enough with that and the constant food donations. For about two months I continued as the pastor's somewhat reluctant assistant until an evangelist, who was an ordained Elder, joined us. Not only did he *know the ropes*, but he also played his own guitar. As he replaced me as the prophet's trusted assistant, I resurrected my plans to leave. Things fell into place as my enthusiasm to go took form. I found a blue and white 1959 Impala on the used car row just East of *Sycamore Creek* on East Lancaster for fifty dollars down and ten dollars a week. My new wheels allowed me to get another machinist's job with my old shop on Main Street. Next, I took a single room at the YMCA on Jones Street, which was respectable enough for a single man of my status.

Chapter 20:

The Leaven in the Meal

The kingdom of heaven is like unto leaven [Baking Yeast] which a woman took, and hid in three measures of meal till the whole was leavened. (Matthew 13:33.)

It is important to note at this point in my spiritual growth that I knew that I was Saved (Reconciled with The Father) but I didn't feel as Holy as I thought a Christian should. The saintly folk around me had the air of someone whose feet were on the Earth, but whose head was in Heaven. I wondered if I would ever attain such a lofty bearing. Once more, it is crucial for me to clarify that one doesn't always witness the spirit's transformative effects firsthand. The work of the spirit in me as my consciousness became more in tune with the Kingdom of Heaven was like the leaven that transforms the meal in the jar.

One evening, on the way to my sister Jackie's house, I noticed the old fire station on Chambers Street had become the *"Durham Memorial Church of God in Christ"* (COGIC). Although I often drove past that corner to Jackie's house, I never noticed the church Before. But with the door ajar, the sounds of worshippers reached my ears, prompting me to enter with the Bible I kept in my car. The sanctuary was in the old fire engine bay. The inside doorway descended a few steps and showcased a line of eight or nine elongated mahogany pews, like the ones found at the *Temple of the Holy Ghost.* At the far end of the room was a stage with an ornate pulpit in the center. Eight people were sitting near the pulpit, discussing the night's Bible lesson. We nodded as I took a seat just opposite the door. I opened my Bible as someone called out the lesson scripture.

Sitting on the middle pew across from the door, I could hear the discussion clearly in the small area. They were having difficulty sticking to the subject, and there was tension as they continued the lesson. To the right and a few seats ahead of me, I noticed a little boy about six years old crying in a low voice. I could see the tears on his cheeks. I thought perhaps they didn't notice him because they were embroiled in the discussion.

I raised my hand and said, "Excuse me, this little boy is crying."

The pastor snapped back, "Yes, he has an earache," and refocused on the group.

I felt a bit chastised, but I looked up the verse in the Book of James that read:

"Is any sick among you? let him call for the elders of the church; and let them pray over him, anointing him with oil in the name of the Lord: And the prayer of faith shall save the sick, and the Lord shall raise him up; and if he have committed sins, they shall be forgiven him."

I interrupted them again with my raised finger and another excuse me.

This time, I had their full attention and read them the scripture, then said, "We are all here. Why don't we pray for him?"

Had I known they had prayed for the child earlier, I would have interpreted the looks they gave me with more anxiety.

Looking unsettled, the pastor rose again with both hands in the air and declared demonstratively, "He's right!"

Then he brought a bottle of olive oil with the brand still on it from behind the lectern. After anointing the boy, named Benjamin, we gathered around him, holding hands, touching, pointing, and praying. When the pastor, Elder Elijah Lee, finished the prayer, the child was no longer in pain and acting normal.

A warm sense of fellowship came with the boy's healing. It was as if a mini revival had broken out at that moment. Introductions were made with genuine smiles and. firm hugs; I knew I was home.

Note: I don't know why I never considered the Church of God in Christ before. It was the quintessential Black Holiness church and the largest major Black Christian denomination that didn't come out of a White church. While I never saw it written in COGIC literature nor heard it spoken by anyone, The Church of God in Christ from its beginning was the classical form of the Deliverance Ministry. In fact, after COGIC's founder, Bishop C.H. Mason attended the Azusa Street Revival in Los Angeles in 1907, the early church embraced sanctification through *The Holy Ghost* as its doctrine. With that came speaking in tongues, prophecy, and healing.

In her last days, Mama had joined a COGIC church. She heard the gospel of sanctification through the *Holy Ghost* from Sister *Thelma Todd*, a missionary from *Clark's Temple* in the *Riverside* community, and joined that congregation. I also had a history with COGIC: When I was a boy, we would peek through the open windows and doors of the tiny storefront Churches of God in Christ. We laughed as we watched the Sanctified Folk praising and glorifying God while moving in perfect harmony to the hypnotic jingle of their tambourines. But despite my giggling, I never quite forgot the seductive pull and the religious-like feelings as I was drawn to the charismatic rhythms. Later, when these things tried to enter my thoughts, I labeled them as grown-ups acting foolishly.

When Sunday morning arrived, I sat in my car outside the church as Pastor Lee and his wife, three boys and two girls, drove up and exited his White minivan. We swept the church and got things in order for the coming service. He and the boys ran a night janitorial service at a downtown office building. They made quick work of the job. His wife, Sister Mattie Lee, and the girls also did their tasks as efficiently as we did. Then, the congregants arrived almost as if spaced by some prearranged time slot. I remembered some of them from Wednesday night; the others seemed so familiar because of our common Spirit. Given our limited group size, waiting for the consistently tardy individuals was logical. Then began the most satisfying period of my life so far. I Spoke about three times in Sunday School but was eerily quiet during singing because of my raspy voice. Naturally, I joined that congregation when the call came at the end of services. That made our little group about twelve adults, and as many children. In these small family churches, sometimes the children outnumbered the adults.

About seven or eight new people joined the church in the next several weeks. I got to know them all as intimately as one knows their close friends. I was invited to after-church dinners by multiple families, and I loved the opportunity to socialize and eat amazing southern food. In retrospect, the glue that bound me tightly to a small, almost storefront-sized church was the finest fellowship I had ever experienced. Here were all the characteristics of goodliness. Every aspect of the religion in those days radiated pure goodness, and every experience was an exquisite sensation. Nothing plagued my inner spirit as I gave my all to this addiction. I was young and trusting anew. I believed my ways pleased God Himself.

I became known as a spirited worker and so the older saints (a common name for *Holy Ghost*-filled believers) offered valuable lessons concerning doctrine. They were always so self-assured that everything they did was the *Will of God.* I clung to their words and fulfilled their suggestions as an obedient child. However, I drew the line at wearing their conservative clothing. The young and older women were tastefully attired in long dresses with sleeves. The sister's dresses were classy enough, but the older preacher's baggy pants clashed with my generation's habitual dressing style. Still, I knew that starched and ironed khaki pants topped with a long-sleeved shirt were out of place in Sunday services. So, I bought a suit with a matching vest and one pair of added trousers off the rack at *J. C. Penney's* for $125.00. It was a light off-brown color with subdued darker stripes. This, and several inexpensive shirt-tie combinations, were the beginning of my church wardrobe.

Along with dressing like a regular church brother, I formed the opinion that Elder Elijah Lee was as good a preacher as any of them. He had the moves and the voice; his method of delivery was second to none. His sermons, whether Old Testament or New, were pure COGIC doctrine. I had only worked with Elder Smith and Bishop Allen before. Smith was a well-educated, dynamic preacher, and Allen was a salesman who never delved deeply into mysteries or doctrine. Elder lee was a down to Earth, gospel preacher who dealt with everyday people. From him, I learned the roots of the term *Holy Roller.*

When the Spirit was high, the tambourines jingled with fervor, and the congregation shouted. He shed his coat and got down on his knees. Tears flowed down his cheeks while he called on the *Name of the Lord.* I was fired up and with him all the way. We rebuked every demon and foul spirit that dared to raise its head. Above the near deafening religious excitement, Sister lee's rocking piano and high-pitched voice continually invoked the Lord to Have his Way. Sometimes, members with guitars and other instruments joined us and the level of our sounds went far beyond the walls. However, neighbors never complained, even though we carried on into the night. Perhaps, as they sat on their porches or opened their windows, our goings-on were the only church services they attended. This scene was cultural, and was repeated in COGIC churches everywhere, and in Holiness congregations throughout the Black community.

In these well after midnight services, men and women were slain in the spirit (passed out in ecstasy) on the floor. We carried on in an atmosphere of intoxication that can only be called *drunk in the spirit.* The morning stars sparkled, and the night was hushed when we locked the doors to the sanctuary. Unspoken was the vow that we would tirelessly do battle with the devil again and again.

I could have remained in our roles with him as the leader and me as a helper, but the rest of the congregation did everything to make me follow him. I knew from the outset that I couldn't because of my nonexistent singing voice and two left feet. But there was still hope if I was courageous enough to resist the church's eternal promptings to make me do so.

None of the preachers openly spoke of the spiritual mysteries of the *Kingdom of Heaven* as they were revealed to me during the periods of my consecration. The leadership's traditional unwillingness to explore beyond established boundaries may have been because of a history of education being racially oppressed. As a result, many charismatic preachers emerged, but their limited research skills made them average teachers. These fellows did not seem eager to expound on certain mysteries whose knowledge could be unlocked by much research of the old writings. But I had long been a student of ancient lore and had learned not to shy from the "dark sayings of the wise" wherever I found them. From the then-unofficial writings in the biblical Apocrypha and other books of wisdom, I embarked upon a keener understanding of how *The Great Mystery*, universally called God, forever transformed conscious mindsets into One with His will. I felt a kinship with these old, loyal to their calling, servants that I didn't with the rhythmic preaching brothers in the religion who were intensely faithful to the popular demands of the congregations.

Since God had not included a connection between me and music, then I was not called to be a traditional cultural preacher, but a spirit-filled Teacher. As if ordained by the Heavens, an opening occurred for a Sunday School Superintendent, when the pastor's daughter moved into a specific class to teach the youth. I settled into my niche as the director of education and number one teacher.

As always, I lay among my reading materials and put it all together. Our Sunday School booklet came from COGIC headquarters, but it had the same content as an interdenominational lesson series. I altered the generic subjects in the booklets, so they were perfect for our church's doctrine, and tied them together so that it was relevant to us at the local level. Before me, the little Sunday School, had in its less than forty-five-minute duration, been led by a teacher who read the introduction to the lesson and had let the students read two verses each with their comments. By the time they had finished reading the book, verbatim, it was time for the testimony part of the service followed by the main event, which was the sermon. Wanting to allow more personal input from the class, I set about reorganizing it.

Following the impersonal format for a less than average sized class, I held the sessions as a roundtable discussion group with me as chairperson or moderator. Instead of each member reading two verses, I read the introduction myself, emphasizing the memory verse, and split the lesson text between two readers. This way, we entered the discussion phase in about ten minutes. I encouraged people to share their thoughts and experiences about the subject, even if it didn't strictly follow the book. I would then expand on their remarks or answer questions that had arisen, with the pastor being the ultimate authority on the matter. Before, he didn't attend the lesson sessions but quickly became an active member of the school.

The school grew as more of the regular eleven o'clock members who got in on the tail end of the dynamic lessons began coming in at nine o'clock to take part fully. The roundtable format allowed each participant, including the pastor, to explain under the teaching anointing of the *Holy Spirit* when he spoke in Sunday School. As a result, the new spirit deepened and the class often extended beyond one hour. These glorious things went on for about a year. All this had me walking on cloud nine because I knew that God was using me. I developed a habit of sleeping in the church near the altar while undergoing a three days and three nights fast. I suppose I was trying to persuade God to send a more powerful anointing upon me, but He didn't buy into my mis founded zeal to become something greater than any other of His children.

In the Bible, Jesus' earthly ministry had mainly focused on reconciliation with the Father, healing, and teaching *"The Kingdom of Heaven"* through parables and allegory. So, I was on my own with dream interpretation. However, I was cautious not to challenge orthodox religious beliefs, since dreams were held sacrosanct in the ministry. But, because of a literal reading of the following section at Acts 2:17:

"And it shall come to pass in the last days, saith God, I will pour out of my Spirit upon all flesh: and your sons and your daughters shall prophesy, and your young men shall see visions, and your old men shall dream dreams."

my study of dream interpretation expanded as the night visions came with greater regularity. To understand them, I looked for similar symbolism in the dreams of other spiritually minded people around me. Many in our congregation believed, as I did, that dreams were messages from spiritual sources. So, there were always dreams told during the testimony services. Of course, the stories of dreamers in the Bible were the best examples of human encounters with *The Great Consciousness of the Cosmos* (God, as I thus understood Him). I saw a greater heavenly purpose behind these uncommon visions and prayed to understand in greater depth.

In one dream, I was alone in unfamiliar terrain. It had been raining softly, but now only the surrounding grass was damp. I thrust my right arm into a small cave and withdrew a blue book with the word ***Lord*** written in bold gold cursive letters on its hardcover. Then, I awakened. This message was so pleasing that it needed no further interpretation. It reaffirmed that I would find the ancient knowledge of God I sought, hidden in my inner mind. I just needed to learn to interpret it.

Because of the diverse night messages that came to me, I suspected the bulk of my dreams, although just as cryptic as the biblical ones, were not necessarily from the infinite. Driven to make sense of the mysteries that beguiled me, I also looked at reading materials of other religions and secular sources. All the while, the dreams themselves tantalized me. First, I would have two or three incomprehensible sets of nightmarish images from which I was glad when I woke up. Then one with some of the earlier dream's features that were easily understood in another dream.

I was being tutored by my subconscious!

ON THE BACK SHELVES OF THE USED BOOKSTORES, I discovered hardcover works by renowned psychoanalysts from around the turn of the twentieth century that explored the unconscious mind. I was captivated by the author's theories on the meanings of dreams in mental therapy. From them, I came to believe psychology could help me understand the non-spiritual aspects of my dreams. Armed with such an arsenal of techniques and methods, I pursued the source of my dreams as one pursues an addictive fix, and it did not disappoint. As I paid the sacrificial price of devotion to the craft, interpreting dreams brought immense satisfaction to me. The meanings of the dreams I interpreted proved to be correct. Later, as I learned to understand the connection of reoccurring themes and symbols, interpreting dreams became second nature. Combined with the healings and the in-depth teachings, my skill in revealing dream messages catapulted me further upward in the church.

Two dreams of great significance came to me then. In the first one, I rose upward in a swiftly moving elevator car of a tall building. I became apprehensive as we rose above the *thirteenth floor [Superstition]* and continued far beyond the physical height of the structure. But I calmed down as we finally came to a stop on a floor filled with peculiar devices. These, I recognized as some futuristic type of engine lathes and milling machines like the ones I operated on my job. Nearby in wooden boxes were the most perfectly finished parts I had ever seen. As I marveled at these parts, *a tall gray-haired man* came from somewhere and we spoke. He asked me if I could do work like this, further saying that he required work at this level from his employees. I told him I was not that good of a craftsman yet. He said, *"Go back, and when you are ready, I will call you."*

I awoke, understanding if I stayed true to my ministerial calling, my dream was a sleeping vision of personal power in the days to come. Although it isn't a heaven or hell issue with me, I still believe today I have never produced work of the caliber I saw in the dream.

The second peculiar dream came early in the predawn hours one Sunday morning. In the night vision, I was alone in an overgrown area on *The Hill* when I came upon an old machine that had sat on that spot from time immemorial. Although I knew in the dream it had been there for ages, no one who regularly took the shortcut to East Lancaster Street had ever seen it. It had the appearance of a street sweeper but without wheels. The unknown contraption was about seven feet high, just as wide, and approximately ten feet long. Suddenly, I was sitting on top in the operator's seat, which was somewhat like the cockpit of an airplane. I was surrounded by unfamiliar levers, dials, and gauges. When I lightly touched the control panel, the handles began moving on their own and various colored lights flashed as the *old gizmo* suddenly came alive and began to move. As a feeling of astonishment washed over me, I awakened. No quick interpretation came to me, but I vowed to figure it out later and prepared to go to church and my Sunday School class.

Approximately fifteen adults attended Sunday School, and halfway through, the group started asking personal dilemma questions. Each time one arose, I would ask, "Why don't we talk to God about it?" and then continued. After the third one, I asked, but did not move on, and insisted that we pray without delay. I was giving God praise and thanksgiving when the anointing came upon me. My eyes were closed, and my voice sounded strange as it rose and fell rhythmically as the spirit influenced me. Thoughts came to me fast, and I heard Elder Lee mournfully cry the words, "We surrender to Your will,

Lord" repeatedly while clapping his hands loudly. Similar sounds were coming from the congregation, but I dared not open my eyes lest the stunning effect pass. Eventually, the power of the anointing abated, and I brought the prayer to a soft completion. I returned to the moment. Some members were laying in the aisles, others in disarray on the pews, and most were still crying, thanking, and praising Jesus. The rest of the lesson was almost forgotten as those who were affected by the ritual visitation claimed victory over whatever had troubled them through shouting testimonies and tears and congregational singing.

After a spectacular worship service, we left to attend a district meeting at another COGIC church. I remember Elder Lee exuberantly told a group of other pastors in the parking lot: *"The Lord hit the Sunday School this morning!"* I listened but didn't hear my name, so I went into the building. Only this time, I was so hooked on the feeling of being the instrument of God, I went straight to where the other ministers were sitting and joined them.

I cleaned the church early the following Sunday morning and walked out to meet Elder Lee and his family's van at the driveway in the front of the building. The children were happy, and Sister Lee beamed as usual.

She piped up in a high voiced greeting, "Praise the Lord, Brother McKellar!"

"Good morning, Sister" I responded to the yellow dressed ball of energy that was the *First Lady* of our congregation. She tilted her head and looked at me affectionately, smiled and shepherded her two smallest up the two stairs and onto the porch. By this time Elder Lee was on the passenger side of the Van; his overstuffed brown briefcase in his left hand as he extended the right one to me for a handshake. I winced momentarily in anticipation of his painful grip.

As it came, he greeted me with a" Thank you Jesus" followed by "Do you have the word?"

"Yes sir" I responded softly. (Wondering what was up) "Anything wrong?" I continued.

"No everything is fine; we haven't heard from you for a while." [Code for wanting me to preach]

A slight bit of panic came over me because I hadn't expected to be called upon to be the principal speaker.

"Elder Drawhorn will teach Sunday School, and you take my place at the pulpit"

However, before things got underway, Elder Lee took me to his office and began filling out a local minister's Certificate. As he wrote, he explained the duties, rights, and privileges of a COGIC local minister. This scene was reminiscent of the time I received my ticket to fly solo in the T-34 so long ago. I suppose I looked just as flabbergasted each time. We went back to the sanctuary and sat behind the pulpit.

As the service proceeded, I asked God several times to send me much more faith so that my message would last longer than my customary fifteen-minute-long canned speeches. Of course, He didn't, but as the time for me to preach drew near, with what little faith I had, I decided when my message ran out, I would just give my testimony to save face.

And then, before I had time to put together a coherent message, Elder Drawhorn called me to the pulpit. When I began to speak my eyes watered in relief as the Spirit came upon me. As I delivered my message to the congregation, a was amazed as I saw some listened intently while other member's eyes were looking strange, almost guilty, as they both muttered their Amen responses.

After the sermon, when the prayer line (my favorite part) was concluded, I felt as if I had just taken a spiritual shower and was cleaned. I also felt a little proud of myself. But then, as I had said somewhere in the message. "None of us a perfect, God is still working on us."

Since I had begun my quest for spiritual excellence, I had been a celibate. However, one night when Spring of 1968 approached, a quiet, sweet, and charming young woman in the church appeared in my dreams. Her face appeared during some confused, incomprehensible chase scene. She told me things about her family life. Then her mother, one of the women that made the church workable, also appeared and handed me a rolled-up newspaper. I should have known at once what the dream meant, but I avoided acknowledging the interpretation until she caught me sneaking looks at her. Surprisingly, she didn't become offended as I had feared but smiled back at me. Eventually, I mustered the courage to speak to her in the presence of her mother and slightly older brother who accepted this tiny advance. Her mother welcomed it. So, a formal courtship began with me gently bragging at the after-church dinners in the family home about my relationship with God. Perhaps, through this subdued but still boastful talk, I hoped to cover up my former failure at marriage.

In the Fall of 1969, *Carolyn* and I got married! The wedding at the church was straight out of a storybook. When they first heard the news, the entire congregation was excited at the prospect of the coming union. By the awaited date they had decorated the building inside and out for the long-awaited event. Everybody was dressed to the nines. A friend of the family gave away the lovely bride, who was adorned in a beautiful White wedding gown. The bridesmaids were also dolled up for the splendid affair. Nothing formal had seemed right for me, but at last, I rented a blue tux outfit I was at ease wearing. I didn't know all the people who came that evening, but Billie from the alcoholic's recovery group, came with two of her female friends, whom I had met before. All this fuss and feathers made me somewhat unnerved, but I kept grinning. The sanctuary was so packed that some people couldn't get inside. It was only when the rice was thrown at us that I noticed someone had decorated my big White Buick with colorful paper streamers and written all over it. Amid this celebration, I thought, *"I hope this writing comes off cleanly."* Then we were off to my new fully furnished flat at the *Big Tex Morningside Apartments.* It was the first of several temporary homes in the beginning.

After a few vexatious years, we bought a two-bedroom house on the East side in *Stop-Six* to raise our two beautiful little girls. Vanda, the first one, was born a little after a year into marriage. Rachael, the second, came a year and a half later. Vanda was *daddy's little girl* from the outset, but I could not woo *independent* little Rachel into hero-worshipping one hundred percent of the time. Nevertheless, the two of us got along fine except for an occasional reminder of how much like me she was, which I still highly regarded. In the early part of these magical days, I walked on air, but it takes more than a lofty atmosphere to nurture a family and sustain a marriage.

But I am a little ahead of the way events fell. It comes down to this: Without each member of a joint effort fulfilling their role as the others agree it should be, there can be no true harmony.

Chapter 21:

Troubled waters

Despite the appearance of irrevocability in my personal and religious life, I was like the unfinished work of the leaven in the meal jar. Pride in the good changes taking place in me caused me to put my best characteristics forward as though I had already arrived at that stage in life. But, as they say, in the substance recovery group, *"I wasn't done yet."*

Looking back over my adult life, my failed relationships and alcoholism made me realize I wasn't ready to be a typical husband. After the children came into my marriage to Carolyn, petty squabbles sprang up over husband-and-wife role fulfillment. Unlike Pop, my father, I was never one to shy from a passionate debate in domestic disagreements. I kept pressing my point. The most troubling of these spirit-crippling arguments came on Sunday mornings before we left for church. The baby, Rachael, was too young to be troubled by these bouts, but I saw that they were affecting Vanda harmfully. Not having an effective sense of humility, I didn't know what to do!

As far as the church was concerned, I should have insisted strongly in the beginning I was not called to be a pastor. But my spiritual anointing and natural charisma made me seem like the other young hopefuls waiting to lead their own flocks. Method of delivery aside, I still had one imperfection. In COGIC's opinion, married men made better pastors. This conundrum set the older church sisters' minds to solving two problems. One, I needed to be married, and two, I needed to be the pastor. The first solution was fine and proper but considering the idea that I was pastoral timber rekindled the old rift that had plagued the congregation before I became a member.

I don't know what unresolved issue troubled a particular clique of the original members who founded the *Durham Memorial* congregation, or why they were not wholly satisfied with the new pastor. But, in ignorance, I wallowed in the praise they heaped upon me, never realizing how this was inferred by my mentor. This covert bickering between them was destabilizing. Just as our marriage contrasted with my belief of how such a relationship should function, I began to see the church wasn't one big happy family, either. This discordance began to invade my moments of spiritual concentration. I had, in the past few years, made minor progress with the *11th Step* of the *12-Step Program*, which read:

"Sought through prayer and meditation to improve my conscious contact with God, as I understood Him, praying only for the knowledge of His will and the power to carry it out."

Now that I was a member of the ministry, I needed to live the *11th Step* to the utmost. At the time, COGIC and many religious groups did not embrace the practice of the *12 Steps*. Reasons varied, but generally, adherence to *The Steps* were rejected because they were not biblical. Some denominations were more on tract, spurning them as just another religion. Initially working *The Steps*, I was led to Christianity. *The Power Greater than Myself*, I looked for, was revealed to me in the same manner as it had been since the beginning of ancient times. Simply put, with little faith, I prayed to a Higher Authority I had only heard about [Called on the *Name of The Lord*], who, moved by my sorrow, healed my infirmity. The touch of *The Living God* changed me, and now I couldn't settle for a distant deity in a tit-for-tat religion. Still, I needed to better understand God's will for me.

As I lost touch with my church, I started visiting other small congregations in different Black Holiness denominations. I found these country churches in the small rural settlements by driving on the back roads of Fort Worth. I was warmly received when I showed up early on Sunday mornings with my deep brown briefcase crammed with two Bibles, some research materials, and about ten Sunday School lesson booklets. I always had tasks to fulfill, ranging from teaching as a guest to praying and reciting scripture.

This quasi-evangelical lifestyle suited me mostly, but, like an old, rejected lover, I missed my days at *Durham Memorial.* While visiting a small church of about ten members in *Lake Como*, a Black suburb of Fort Worth, I was asked to bring the main message. With no small amount of apprehension, I accepted the invitation and taught an old Sunday School lesson from the pulpit. It went well, and before closing, I opened a prayer line. This went so well that the pastor, a slender gray-haired woman, said that God wanted to keep the revival spirit going. So, my first revival went on every night for over two weeks before I concluded it. This began a pattern of teaching one of Jesus' parables and opening a very fulfilling prayer line.

Even though I was not an ordained minister, I embarked upon the work. Eventually, I found myself traveling the highways further away from town. I slept in the car at roadside rest stops or other places I considered suitable. The roadside rest stops were friendly and sociable retreats in the warm summer nights. Many of the travelers were eager to meet and greet their fellow voyagers after a long day of solitude in their vehicles. I had ample time to reflect on how much like the *leaven* I had become.

It would take a thick double volume to tell the subtle nuances of lessons learned during my adventures that summer on the road, but space and time forbid such an undertaking. So, I will set down only the highlights and complete the first great spiral in my personal saga.

I went to El Paso and from there to Phoenix, Arizona, for another series of teaching revivals at Elder Ragsdale's *Church of the Living God.* (PGT). I was hooked, it seemed, working at day jobs, and visiting churches without respect to denomination. While the church work brought spiritual benefits to my ministry, it often fell short of meeting the financial goals of some pastors and leaders. In resisting their efforts to make money the principal reason, I grew dispirited. Different denominations claimed their own way of speaking in tongues was correct. Because most of it I found during the trip was unintelligible babblings, lacking a biblical basis, these and other differences in doctrine came across to me as fallacies rather than truths.

It sorrowed me to realize I was not in sync with the evolution of the religious body called the church. But I did not suffer guilt because a parting was in the offing. I believe now that it was important for me to be there in the days when the modern church's trajectory veered from the propagation of the gospel, as I knew it. I remember preaching the *Good News* as my first love, even though I couldn't fully embrace the programs and performances as a substitute for a soul-saving revival. With a heavy heart, I changed the focus of my journey and spent more time riding than visiting churches. Fortunately, the long stretches of me time between stops became periods of meditation. Although I observed my driving and enjoyed the sights and sounds of the world outside, the car was my secret place of prayer.

I WASN'T THE ONLY SEEKER TRAVELING THE HIGHWAY. This was still the era when White youths *(Hippies)* left their affluent homes. Like me, in my quest for the spiritual *Kingdom of Heaven*, they traveled the highways seeking their version of *Shambhala* (A spiritual kingdom). There, they hoped to reach *Nirvana* (A transcendent state in which there is neither suffering, desire, nor sense of *self*). Escaping the hypocritical circumstances of their upbringing, these adventurous, highly educated, unconventionally dressed, smiling *Flower Children* were just the people I needed to exchange my ideas and theories of higher existences with. So, riding on the road, whether in isolation or with companions, my old 1963 Pontiac was as close to anybody's Heaven as anywhere on Earth.

Coming back to Texas on Interstate 10, two young *Hippie* brothers flagged me down in Southern California. I, at once, knew them by their free and colorful style of dress. They introduced themselves as Zeke and Paul. We exchanged polite inquiries as to the other's condition. I half expected their speech would be in some counterculture dialect, but it was in conversational English. Perhaps they didn't engage me in their own style of *rapping* at first because I seemed to be an outsider. The taller of the young brothers played the harmonica [Zeke, I think]. The *hippie explosion* was filled with music, and although I was only familiar with a few of the songs he played, they were filled with emotion. As the fading light obscured the outside world, our rapping took on a more intimate tone. Somewhere in the night, in our discussion about Jesus, Paul, the quieter of the two had the questions about Christianity. It seemed he knew a lot about religion but had not delved deeply into the church. So, I told him what I knew about the mysteries of my faith.

Zeke said he had never been baptized and wanted me to do it. Since I was called by God to bring the good tidings of salvation, I agreed, but how? One Brother mentioned we were approaching a river (The Colorado River, I believe) on the California/Arizona border and could do the job there. Fear of going into an unknown and dangerous body of water gripped me for an instant because I couldn't swim. Simultaneously, the thought came, *"This is what you are here for!"* and my faith in my mission encouraged me. I pulled off the side of the road at the edge of the steel bridge and we found a pathway leading down to the river. A sense of peace washed over me as I observed the stillness of the waters, despite the obscurity of the night. Reassured by the taller brother who was in the river shirtless, that he would not let me drown should a mishap occur, I waded in barefooted to baptize him. To be sure I was using a good formula for the ritual, I clasped him around his back with my left hand, raised my right one straight up, and declared loudly, "On profession of your faith in Jesus Christ, I now baptize you in the Name of the Father, and of the Son, and of the *Holy Ghost*." When he came up from being totally submerged, we all shouted, thanked, and praised the Lord on the banks of the river.

In Arizona, I dropped the two off at an intersection that led to Lake Havasu City, where *London Bridge* is now located. I didn't know about the bridge construction project then or I would have surely gone with them out of curiosity. All the same, the baptizing ceremony was also a turning point for me. I was so reinvigorated that I went into the Phoenix/Tucson area to continue Teaching the Gospel as before. Sometimes, I stayed at the Phoenix

YMCA and worked pick and shovel jobs for independent contractors doing desert landscaping around newly built, large homes. I wasn't earning more than enough to simply live on, but I stayed at it for the rest of the summer. When it became too cold to sleep in the car, I started back home.

I came back through El Paso. Just West of Big Springs on U.S. Highway 180, I saw several White men in business clothes, running around a car off the left side of the road. They were panicking, so I pulled over, and asked if they needed help.

One man pointed to the driver, said, "It's his heart!"

I, too, became afraid, but I went over to the car to utter a prayer.

Curiously, at that moment, I felt embarrassed and helpless.

But I thrust my arm through the window and touched his chest. I don't remember what I said but felt relief as the sick man promptly recovered.

While talking to the group, I mentioned I was going to Fort Worth but was almost out of gas. The man I prayed for gave me a business card that said he was the *Commander of an American Legion Post* in El Paso. I followed them to a gas station down the road, where they filled my tank, and I continued home. Although I returned home with no money, my thirst for great spiritual power had been satiated, but it hadn't brought me the peace I looked for. Instead, the metaphysical successes, if anything, tempted me with feelings of loftiness.

A thorn in the flesh

My relationship with the churches I served in grew fractured. I could never hold membership in any of the denominations because I would not allow money to be paramount to what I perceived to be the spiritual obligations of the ministry. I wholeheartedly did my best in what I perceived to be God's work, but adhered to Jesus' mantra of *"Freely you have received, freely give"* for my labors. Consequently, I shied from the ever-growing, *Pastor and Wife Anniversaries* that were so cultish in tone. These were annual events of a week's duration, in which the doubtful virtues of the pastor and his wife were extolled beyond that of the *Savior*, Himself. I gained no traction in abolishing these abhorrent doings with the pastors. They felt they had scriptural backing to be doubly honored for their tireless service. Equally heart-rending, the principal members of the congregations, in their zeal to please the pastor(s), seemed blinded to what I saw as repugnant as *Golden Calf Worship*.

Months before the joyous event, the focus of the church became raising money to bless the couple. In the best of financial times, the small ten to twenty-member congregations could barely pay the church's normal expenses. But, during the anniversary frenzy, they raised exorbitant sums. Eventually, I broke fellowship on my own or it was made plain to me that I was no longer welcome, so I slunk from organized religion.

Note: The old-time doctrine I preferred was not strictly scriptural but had evolved from *Black Church* religious culture in the days before the *Azuza Street* meetings. The change of the narrow trajectory of church purposes from preaching the Gospel to seeking blessings through success motivation became widespread in the 1970s. Before that, a great many Believers literally followed *The Great Commission,* found in Matthew 28: 16. Those Preachers and Missionaries were like the believers in the Early Biblical Church. They carried out personal service through outreach action on street corners and in homes of the sick and suffering. These Servants of the Lord were empowered through their devotion to the *Holy Ghost*, whose indwelling they received in three phases. I mentioned these earlier in the chapter, "A seat at the Children's Table." I followed this ritual during my first days at *West Adams Foursquare Church*:

First: Being convicted of sin, the sinner received Jesus Christ as his/her personal Savior.

Second: The new believer underwent a period of personal cleansing of sinful behavior and habits. This was known as *Sanctification.* (Actually, Sanctification comes from God.)

Third: The new Believer received, through faith, the indwelling of the *Holy Spirit* that was promised in Acts 2:38. (Some churches used Acts 2:38 as the formula for water baptism)

As far as I know, the modern church at large no longer practices the above ritual. Most congregations find vocalizing the acceptance of Jesus Christ as one's Personal Savior to be sufficient for reconciliation with the Father and their church leadership responsibilities. While I do not argue doctrinal beliefs, I found that coming up in the old way set in motion the habit of knowing God for myself in a profound and deeper way. I cannot see how this intimacy with The Father, through Christ Jesus, can be accomplished by simply "Attending church" and repeating popular scriptures and other sayings.

Wandering alone, I mourned my relationship, which I believed was irretrievably broken, with *The Bride of Christ* (The Church). In the years that followed, I was like a battered lover who couldn't completely let go. I remembered the good times I had shared with my *First Love*. No matter that

I was no longer married to religion, I occasionally dropped by to warm myself with the fellowship of communal worship. But I didn't labor under feelings of guilt. Outside, I carried the message beyond a bench warmer's comfort zone.

I felt I was in no sense committing apostasy from the faith.

Still attached to my leaving was God's calling, as I believed it to be, then, and the dreams and fulfilling their interpretations that continued to enrich my spiritual life. I fervently ministered to those disenfranchised in secular settings. I never saw myself as the backslider former ministerial associates were wont to call me. I prayed at social functions and when I visited the sick in homes and hospitals.

Again, I wasn't the only one on the road. These were years of unrest for other old-time sanctified folk in the church as well. I saw the new doings of the church as a falling away from the faith. Enough of the new financial prosperity, brought by civil rights gains, made its way into church coffers. As a result, some of the dynamic COGIC Holiness ministers' highly educated and newly monetized congregations insisted on being more conventional and like mainstream church members elsewhere. For several reasons, a few of those who came up the old route didn't fit in with the modernization. Changes in how the church served the Black community were necessary and proper. But the church leaders should have kept those who adhered to the unadulterated holiness gospel, sacrosanct. However, the old *"Holy Rollers"* were simply allowed to leave. So, like me, they became uprooted and wandered from church to church, hoping to reclaim the old way. Some enterprising exiles found success as stand-alone pastors, incorporating aspects of the old COGIC way. Some fell in the wilderness! Thinking of myself as somewhat of a spiritual perfectionist, I trudged alone as time passed.

Chapter 22:

Thriving in the wilderness

In 1970, I was thirty-one years old, and worked with my older brother, Ray, building refrigerated trailer truck bodies for the *Fruehauf Trailer Corporation* near Fort Worth. I had about five years of sobriety at that time. About five or six of us workers would pray and discuss the Bible on the back loading dock during our lunch break. Our religious discussions turned to the upcoming, thorny contract negotiations. I was more than curious about them but couldn't get any substantive information from the guys on how labor unions worked. There were a lot of negative assumptions floating around that our negotiators "were going to let the company deny us a sorely needed pay raise, just as they did the last time." Of course, the union reps had no such idea in mind but the shop at *Fruehauf* had only been unionized for a few short years and the members did not understand how collective bargaining truly worked.

When many small non-auto workers first join large international unions such as the *UAW*, they expect to obtain the same wages and benefits as the big auto manufacturing workers. Fueled by misunderstandings, rather than a culture of union working, their frustrations defaulted to the belief that they were being cheated despite paying their dues. So, the guys in the plant gathered in small angry groups and bickered to the extent that a brawl was surely in the making for the upcoming meeting. Due to the high level of anticipation for the big meeting, I opted to attend with a group of individuals who intended to express their concerns to the union representatives.

When the day came, the meeting room on North Main Street, in the *Stockyards District*, was packed and the guys were rowdy. The meeting took place in a large room on the second floor of an old, converted office building. The wooden stairs leading up to the noisy gathering sounded like the heavy hammering of construction was taking place as the guys stormed up to the *battleground*. I didn't know what to expect from all the hullabaloo, but I became excited as if I was at a homecoming football game, but with a degree of trepidation.

The president of the local, *Cotton Copeland,* was banging the gavel soundly, and calling repeatedly for order as I entered the meeting hall. One of the most vocal of the welders named Stout, had the floor and rudely and vulgarly shouted above the clamor, "Mr. President, I asked for a copy of *them.* bylaws over a month ago." He made tough guy motions as the crowd chatter rose in intensity. The union officers running the meeting kept pleading for order, but the efforts to maintain decorum went unheeded. I had never seen such a rowdy crowd of people before and was somewhat saddened by the scene. The constant interruptions and rude behavior from the floor rose to a level where a coherent discussion was impossible. In addition to their threats and impatience, I noticed that the same anxious feeling I experienced during my alcoholism was now affecting the group. Moved with compassion, I saw myself as I raised my hand to get the chairman's attention. My leg shook inside my pants and my voice came out, measured and deliberate. The room felt eerily quiet as the members hung onto every word. I have never recalled what I said beyond: I, too, shared their uneasiness and something about family. A thundering applause broke the silence. After that, we conducted the meeting in an orderly fashion, although nothing was settled satisfactorily.

Meanwhile, on the strength of that one brief speech at the meeting, the shop wanted me to be the next president of the local. No doubt, other factors persuaded them, such as my minister's bearing, which was a part of my personality. Although I couldn't see my militancy then as clearly as I saw my responsibility to champion a righteous cause, it makes so much sense now.

So, after gathering a lot of reading material and listening to advice from the old union men in the shop, I told myself that this was *God's Will* for me. At least, I was convinced He would be with me in this worthwhile project. After ignoring the several soft suggestions of: *"Now, Van, I don't know if Texas is ready for a Black president."* This came from the union representative from regional headquarters who advised the locals.

Disregarding the Reps attempts to get me to see his reasoning, the guys and I went into full campaign mode. Relying on my intuition and logic, I put together a cadre from the *Black* and the *Mexican American* brothers. We visited the workers in the other eight shops during their off-clock hours and handed out flyers explaining my position. The *White* workers held a large majority of the votes and enough of them voted for me, but they didn't take part in my campaign. Nevertheless, I beat my White opponent, a former president of our local union, and also a former plant branch manager, by a landslide.

Then, I was off into a world that had only been shadowy before. This unfamiliar territory was not so much the sphere of bargaining collectively for the members, but the internal politics that was played on many levels. There was a legal as well as an ethical need to support fairness between members and nonmembers, regardless of their membership status. These abstainers wanted the benefits and protection of the union and would howl the loudest if their requests were not met. And, though the dues payers were concerned about their own predicament, this was no problem since I had long treated everybody's needs equally.

The next political level was like the first. My home plant at Fruehauf was by far the largest group of the eight shops in the local union. Still. I was just as much of a president to each one as to the other. Each independent shop had a chairperson of the shop committee, who oversaw the individual union stewards. A president deals primarily with the highest elected committee person in each unit called the *Shop Chairperson.* But like the good pastor I was becoming inside, I knew all the unit representatives. At the combined meetings of our local union. I ensured that the rights of the little shops were equally represented. In this way, we added three more shops during my term of office.

Meanwhile, I could not hold my home life together as well as I did the union. Things had gotten so bad between Carolyn and me that besides the kids the only consolation I found was in my outside duties. I knew it was just as distressing for my family, or worse, but I couldn't find the right solution to our problems. In the years immediately after our breakup, I often found myself looking back with guilt and self-condemnation. Presently, I am convinced, not because I lack any emotion, but after observing our respective paths, I can see clearly now that a viable marriage could not have flourished in such a climate. While I was at a union meeting in Denver, Colorado, Carolyn moved out of our little house in *Stop Six*, taking the babies with her. My solution to this tragedy was to bury myself in my newfound diversion, which I did by giving my all to the only family I had left: my work. Through my experience and the ability to master new situations, I didn't catch a case of the big head. My leadership style was that of a leadman with the ability to solve complex problems more than the average White-collar worker could.

The fellowship that came with these fruitful days kept me from returning to a worse addiction. It grew as my latent abilities came to the forefront during my meetings as president of the union with the chief executive officers of the companies. Even though the management types were all formal, I didn't change my style or behavior.

It was at these times I learned why the district union representative expressed his belief that "Texas is not ready for a Black president of the local union." Of course, there were other Black presidents of other unions in

Texas. However, these were not amalgamated organizations, which were represented by an outside Black Man, who negotiated on equal terms with The White Man. Although the country was in a new era of civil rights, these White alpha males did not suffer me and my supposed uppity attitude.

Since I always treated them with courtesy, but not acquiescence, the District Rep found their reluctance to meet with me a strong negotiation tactic. The result was some bosses would give in to some long-standing labor disagreements rather than face a Black Man's rebuke of their wrongly perceived values. Strides were made in this way. However, taking part in the grassroots level of politics was a surprise I had not imagined. One day, early on, the Rep and I drove to a large fancy motel in Houston for an election of officers meeting of the Region's *Community Action Program* (CAP), the *CAP Council.*

I was as green to the political goings-on as any country bumpkin!

On the way down to Houston, the Rep mentioned *Barbara Jordan* would be our keynote speaker. I didn't know who she was but mumbled something in the affirmative. The room was packed, and I was busy shaking hands and forgetting names. Distinct from the voices in the background, someone said, "She's here," as a long, brownish-colored Lincoln stopped in the sunlit front of the entrance.

A man from somewhere opened the car door and a Black American woman got out and walked in. The murmur picked up again in greeting and there was head-nodding as she passed by. Her talk was charismatic and the most inspiring speech I have ever heard. It stirred up a passion within me to perform the altruistic things she spoke about. It was reinforced in that instant that for me to do so would satisfy God as much as it would fulfill my purpose in this life. After a *short eternity*, as gracefully as she entered the room, she was gone, but her essence stayed as if to further inspire our doings.

Also unknown to me was that the union political groups comprised conservative and liberal factions that adhered to the style of the nation's political parties. The CAP *Council* was headed by liberals from the giant GM assembly plant in Arlington, Texas. When it came time for nominations for vice president, a very progressive minded, young brother I just met, named *Emillio Molleda*, stood up, looked at me with an inviting smile, and declared loudly, "I nominate Van McKellar for vice president."

I was delighted to learn later he was the past president of the organization and would win the new term as well. The nomination was seconded to applause from the floor. I don't recall who else ran for the position, but I accepted the nomination and won the vice presidency of the

Texas State CAP Council. Looking back, I can see that choosing me for VP was a marriage of convenience. The *Texas Liberals* needed the first Black president to be a member of their group as evidence of how forward-thinking they were. Alternatively, I needed to be an active part of an organization that worked to better the human condition to feel spiritually relevant. Again, I boned up on the requisite *National Labor Relationship Board* (NLRB) regulations, and other pertinent reading matters, which included a copy of *Robert's Rules of Order*, (Which I took as the definitive work on Parliamentary Procedure.)

Many were the minor victories in human relations that followed throughout my term of office as president of the local and vice-president of the *CAP Council.* Regardless of past practices of the office of VP being window dressing, I was into the business end of the organization to serve, and I did. Two notable adventures took place near the end of both terms. In the first one, the *UAW International Union* sent me to New Orleans for about three months to help convince the city bus drivers to choose the UAW as their representatives. We lost out to the *Amalgamated Transit Union* in the end. In the second job, I went to Austin, Texas to lobby the *63rd Legislature* to persuade the state representatives and senators to repeal the *right to work* on a union job without union membership statute *[Section 14(b) of the federal Taft-Hartley Act]*. This was during the *Texas Constitutional Convention of 1974*. That, too, was unsuccessful, but fulfilling.

Before I knew it, it was time for the reelection of officers in the local, but I was having second thoughts about continuing in the union business. Overall, the material gains during this venture called for another term as president. But the application of union techniques, while beneficial as a non-religious course of action, was not the live and let live methods called for in the ministry. The calling of Christ is about reconciliation with the Father and about agape love. Serving in the union, while fulfilling, was as far away from my calling as was the success motivation usurpation that was replacing the gospel in the Black Churches. By the time I informed the regional headquarters I wouldn't run again, it was too late to withdraw from the race against my opponent. I put up a half-hearted effort for a show and she won by about the same ratio as I did before. So, I left to do other things, eventually joining a track crew on the *Santa Fe Railroad.*

Section V: Conclusions

Chapter 23

Private Pilot

Sometimes, demanding work can become like a spiritual experience, so it was with the arduous work on the Tie Gang in the blistering Texas sun. There was a certain peace in the pounding, arm-burning, even-tempered rhythm of the spike mall. It was much like the blues cadence that carried me to the day's end in the fields so long ago. The only qualm that tried to enter my thoughts was the small copperhead snakes that liked to hide in the shade beneath the replacement crossties. Now and then, these venomous creatures would dart out when the tie was moved. My hefty calf high, steel-toe boots afforded me sufficient courage until we moved from the flat country south of Fort Worth to an area north of town.

Soon, we were *laying* track across from *Meacham Field,* a large general aviation airport. As the brightly painted single-engine airplanes swooped low in front of us when landing, improbable thoughts tantalized me. For some quasi-pragmatic reason, I had accepted the notion that piloting planes again was beyond my financial reach. Yet, I kept telling the crew that I was once a pilot and would fly again someday, which brought forth doubtful comments and smiling faces as they sized me up in my greasy work clothes. Then, one day after work, I drove over to the most prominent building near a side gate of the airport and went inside.

I was bathed in familiarity as I entered an airplane hangar after sixteen years. Recalling the taste of the pretty treats sitting in the middle of an immaculate space in front of me, I felt as dejected as a kid in a candy shop with only pennies in his pockets. I walked over to a group of men standing near some offices off to the right. They had the air of those who fly. After speaking with them, I sauntered across the floor to the *Cessna Pilot Center*, where I met the owner, *Bill Vieroski*, whom I liked instantly. I was pleased that Bill was a few years older than me. He reminded me somewhat of Mr. Kessler, my old primary flying instructor. I would enjoy his guidance and friendship for years thereafter. After the lengthy talk strangers engage in to assess the other's abilities, I memorized the prices of everything. But more importantly, I learned that if I already had a private pilot's license, with the G.I. Bill, I might qualify for aid to get further training at a rate that I could easily afford.

I felt my heartbeat quicken as the blood rushed through my temples.

Because of my prior flying experience, I could get my *Private Pilots License* as soon as I was ready for the test. If I studied for the written test on my own, it would be monetarily workable. We scheduled a flight to assess my skills, and I left with all the books and manuals I could afford at the moment. With all the panache of a salesperson who skillfully inserts his foot in the door, I walked over to a red and white airplane and peeked inside the cockpit before leaving.

Humbled by the enormous task before me, my thoughts turned to God, not adhering to a formal prayer, but informing Him I intended to use the faith and self-confidence I had gained as a minister for something other than His work. Of course, I knew it was not a sin, but I still had not spiritually matured. For that reason, I needed to justify this frivolous desire in my mind.

Since I had sorted out the financial and spiritual obstacles, I focused on overcoming the mental barriers as I drove home to my apartment on Tucker Street. Being near the planes had reinvigorated a sense of belonging to more than the adequate recreational lifestyle I had been living since I left the Air Force.

The enormity of the project ahead demanded excellence!

On April 3, 1977, I completed the *Preflight* walk-around inspection, draining the accumulated water from the fuel petcock below the high wings of the *Cessna 152, N150RA*, rented from Red's Aircraft. The cockpit was small but not tight. The engine cranked smoothly on the first try, and my excitement rose. After clearance from Ground Control, I taxied northward. By the time I reached the beginning of the active runway, I felt at home. From the top of the cabin, the tower barked back my request for a left turn out from runway One-Eight-Zero. Moving my head from side to side like a crane, I pulled the little plane to the center of the runway and advanced the throttle to its highest limit. There was only a little of the inevitable pull to the left as we began the takeoff run. The nose came up as I increased pressure on the wheel. Once again, I felt the gentle buffeting of the air currents as we rose into the air.

Delighted with the realization that I had not lost my pilot skills and was only a little rusty, I knew I would be ready for the examination much sooner than I originally thought. I remember *Jo Anne's* puzzled look because unexpected; I explained that I wouldn't be able to see her as often as usual because I was studying for my pilot's exams. This lifelong friend knew I wasn't sneaking around on her, but didn't like the idea of being suddenly shifted to second place in my affairs. Nevertheless, I put everything, except my visits with Vanda and Rachael, on the back burners and hit the books.

I flew with one of the center's other instructors for 5 hours, and 1 more with Bill, who released me for solo flights on April 21st. Between lessons, I passed my Private Pilots written exam with a score of 90%. Then, in two months, I was awarded my PP License on June 11th, 1977, my birthday.

I was approved for the G.I. Bill, but since I waited so long before using it, I only had 4 months left to earn my *Commercial Pilots License*, so the race was on. The helpful thing about this was that the FAA allowed me to self-certify my earlier flying time. I passed the *Commercial Pilots* written test with a score of 77. Just two months later, I passed the flight test with flying colors on August 26th. The plane I flew was a sleek, blue and white *Cessna Cardinal*, which was required because of its high-performance engine, adjustable propellers, and retractable landing gear.

By the time my G.I. Bill monies ran out, I secured a job at *Oak Grove Airport* as a general machinist, fabricating parts for the *Bell Helicopter Corp*. I relieved the owner, "Pappy Spink's" son, Hunter, in the control tower on weekends so that he and his wife, Jean, could ride with his *Moto Guzzi* motorcycle club. I also worked the refueling truck and did other things around the airport. These were magical days because *Oak Grove* was far enough from the city to host airshows. I loved to fly aerobatics in the Air

Force, but I was more cautious about many things now. I wasn't tempted to do daredevil maneuvers so close to the ground that just the tiniest error could spell disaster. But there were those who dared to do that type of flying professionally. Despite my reluctance to show off my skills in this manner, I admired and envied the show pilots who did.

What a deceitful disease is covert racism, slumbering in long-forgotten places of the heart.

I was pleased now that I was no longer struggling with the old issues of open bigotry and back with the planes. But there were still almost imperceptible barriers to the freedom I hoped for. I met no outright slurs as I flew to the popular places frequented by White pilots in the 1980s, yet segregation roused its serpentine head in the words of the most innocent conversations. Often It was only a sly humorous remark whose true meaning was so deteriorated by age as to be unrecognizable to younger generations, but its gatekeeping intent was unmistakably remembered from the past. But I watched where I stepped. Sometimes, I was so accustomed to my supposed place in our biracial society that it took a while to hear the *dog whistle* plainly. One day, I was in the lounge at the tower. We were recounting moments we had experienced in aviation [Hangar flying] and getting acquainted. An outwardly innocent event took place that, much to my consternation, would reoccur all too often. When I was introduced to anyone, the conversation stopped, and a staff member piped up, *"This is Van. He's a commercial pilot."* We all smiled, and the socialization continued. However, when a White pilot was the new guy, introductions were simply, "This is Bob or whomever." No mention of qualifications or accounting for presence, just a simple greeting. In prior days, this revelation would have caused me to be uneasy or less accepting of attempts to heal. As I thought about these things, from somewhere in my mind I recalled when I or my friends had made similar comments regarding the introduction of people outside our circle. This time, like the times I took little *leaps of faith* in God, I was willing to receive the good that was in humanity without being unduly swayed by pain and hasty generalizations. It is important to note that I was close to forty years old, almost 200 lbs., and showing gray in my temples. These were the years when the title *Mister McKellar* didn't feel as overdressed as a Sunday suit. Nevertheless, with that stage of life came the moral maturity that attaches itself to spiritual growth. I spoke so authoritatively about the interpretation of dreams and other mysteries that friends often came to me seeking meanings and answers.

UNRESTRICTED BY MONETARY CONCERNS, I FLEW at every opportunity that didn't clash with my regular responsibilities. In my teen years, when the airplane was new to me, my flights had been for a particular reason. I needed to perfect a maneuver or to wing off to some far destination to practice navigation. Now that I was licensed and flying to gain hours of experience, I had time to tour and investigate the well-ordered world that lay below. My practice area was over the sparsely populated countryside southeast of Fort Worth. While airborne, I saw the expansive farming areas near small towns like Waxahachie and Venus, where I once worked in the hot weather.

Keeping well clear of the fast Jet traffic leaving and entering *Naval Air Station Dallas* to the North, I leisurely circled the fields below. Once, while aloft, I tried to work up emotions about injustices I had known through the years. I could only manage a sniffle for the *little boy's* sufferings in the cotton patch so long ago. No tears now, for his inconceivable yearning to escape to a world among cottony clouds high over the green and gray checkerboard countryside. This lack of remorse wasn't from the victory of having overcome the years of feckless oppression that did not kill the daydreams of a child. My feelings now were something not born of strife. Neither was this the satisfaction of having escaped worldly ties and being nearer to God's (supposed) home in the sky. Sad old memories, though still somewhere in the background of my mind, paled before the joy of tranquilly sitting alone far above the hustle and bustle of life. As I made incremental corrections to the flight controls and scanned my surroundings for changes, I appreciated I had endured the ruthlessness time had dealt to me.

What had been the vehicle of change responsible for my serenity?

This near-magical inner harmony came from the spirit that, as a matter of course, matures the soul of the seeker just as the leaven inevitably transforms the meal.

One late summer morning, a few years later, I dressed and left the house grumpy because I had a scheduled flight that day. I was well down the road before it hit me that the sacred relationship between me and flying had garnered enough fruit to satisfy my lifelong craving and never return. My halfhearted desire to be a professional pilot faded when I realized there was something else, I wanted much more than to achieve the dream that transformed me from a poor, paranoid, uneducated boy into a master of the inaccessible skies. The hard practicality of operating in the crowded environment of modern flying instilled in me that there were no *kingdoms in the clouds*. And I knew from my years on the road the wonders of the world firsthand. Now something higher commanded my devotion. I was unwittingly drawn into a new quest to explore the limitless possibilities of my very soul.

In the early 1980s, more and more job opportunities became available for Black Americans in middle-class professions. Until then, I had clung tightly to my childhood dream as if it would someday disappear. Fewer racists were proud to be singled out as such, and the lives of Black heroes and leaders were accepted as American success stories. During these days, I still attended church now and then to keep my hand in *The Lord's* business. I was acutely aware I was not perfect and free from sin. Since I didn't say I was someone of greater status, I rose no further within the ranks than a lay minister. Regardless of my many human frailties, the *Holy Spirit* was my constant companion; chastising, guiding, and blessing me through it all. I would see Vanda and Rachael in these religious settings when they came to services with their grandmother, *Dorothy*, who remained faithful to *The Calling*. The kids and I skipped the airshows and opted for tourist attractions, carnivals, and amusement parks every weekend. Unfortunately, I wasn't mature enough to demand access to Vanessa. Even decades later, I still carry the weight of my failure as a parent and not being able to form a close relationship with my first-born daughter.

In the years that followed, everything slowed down after I was injured while removing a heavy chuck from an engine lathe. I couldn't do hard work after November,1982, and the road to recovery was long but not overwhelming. After three years of rehabilitation, I flew for a brief period in 1985, and then the FAA denied my Medical Certificate, because I took necessary pain meds. This brought my life as a pilot to an end. Many pleasures that called for physical exertion were forsaken along with the flying. Some withered away because I no longer needed to achieve my ego's gratification.

Chapter 24:

The Common Aspects of God

With these sedentary days of physical recovery and the approach of middle age came a more in-depth reflection of what had driven my outward behaviors. This was not just a turning over of past events in my mind. I had time to fill in the gaps I passed by, by continuing to perform running personal inventories. Much, but not all of the long recovery from my injury was spent contemplating a realistic future. I spent just as much time pouring over volumes of the thoughts of other men who had written about God (As they understood Him.)

In time, I came to see that a few of the writer's thoughts about the nature of a great power that influenced the state and movement of humankind were the same as my thoughts on God (As I sought to understand Him). I never imagined what my *Higher Power* looked like because I thought I couldn't comprehend the Infinite with my limited abilities. But, like an African tracker on The Savanna, who skillfully identifies his quarry by the unique evidence left of his comings and goings, I knew the occasions when God had been at work in my life and other events around me. On this basis, I continued giving my all to further investigation of people directly involved in these matters and written works from the library delivery van. Principal among these were great teachers such as *Jesus*, who, in the Bible, taught the love of God and our fellowman above all things. I searched *The Holy Quran*, which was sent down to *Prophet Mohammed* (Peace and Blessing be unto him) until I found similarities with what I understood. I also found familiar evidence of the inward man, in the writings about *Siddhartha Gautama, The Buddha Nature*. The list goes on beyond *Lao Tse's* teaching of *Tao.*

Humankind, like Moses, in Exodus 33:13-34, yearns to see the infinite Glory of the *Name above all Names* (Which, because of Its complexity, cannot be spoken), but is given only the basis of God's relationship to him. This, *The Great Mystery*, reveals as the *Name of the lord.* While Moses was on the rock, safe from death with God's protection, I realized that God loves us and wants to mend our relationship. The study also showed me that different religions emerged from a central figure who had a revelation about a deity whose existence was unclear, but certain. In the ensuing religion's effort to keep their relationship with God (As they understood Him by hearsay), within their grasp, these social-cultural systems, imposed limits upon the invisible divinity as to what He would or would not be, or do. *My explanation of the basis of religious systems and doctrines in no way is an endorsement or criticism of them individually or collectively.*

As much as I craved to understand the nature of God, albeit in a minuscule way, my efforts shed little light on the mysterious appetite that affected me. My need to understand the unseen essence of humankind and its relationship to the universe naturally took a different tack than that of highly educated, pre-twentieth-century European and Eastern philosophers. It seemed to me they sought understanding for the sake of understanding, while I needed a working relationship with powers greater than those of an oppressed and highly inhibited high school dropout.

I concluded that the direct path that led to the knowledge I looked for did not exist to me in my corporeal state. However, through reconciliation with the *Father of All*, I was eternally secure. To continue in a general direction would be enough. Despite everything, I concluded that religious bodies' altruistic goals were the ideal way for me to continue my obligations to God's calling. Through my religious nature, I realized my reason for existence in a way that grappling with the further study of metaphysics could not.

The upshot of this was that I lessened my mental quest in supposed paranormal realms. I came to appreciate God's handiwork from what I saw in the old *Black Culture* around me when I was a child. Although they could not read their Bibles so well, they, like my considerations of *Tao Te Ching*, they also believed "*The Lawd* moved in mysterious ways. When stressed and needy, they spoke in a distinctive, cultural idiomatic dialect of the God who knew our sufferings as *The Way Maker*. What God's form was, was as incomprehensible to them as to the prophets, yet they too spoke with unshakable faith. The faith which is spiritual and unseen. But whose healing touch is evidence of God's unfailing Love.

Upon recalling these things, I acknowledged that because of God's children still in servitude, I shared a bond with the mission of the wayward church. But I also wrote:

FELLOWSHIP WITH INFINITY

I am at ease in the universe,
philosophically, I have worked it out.

Not to say that I am intimate with all mysteries.
just not in awe of the depth of its magnitude,
nor clothed in darkness by moving majesty,

I am one with the pageantry in the heavens,
as familiar as the dawning of God's ecstasy.
Stars confined within their constellations,
rapturously held in endless delight.
I hear "church bells on Earth ring together,
and choirs sing with Heavenly joy."
The patterns of light and Love are unfailing.

Though the cycles try my every moment.
I see seasons pass in their instants of time
and the changes, ever-changing, which alter not
their outcomes through the generations.

I am microbic, yet a vital part of the fellowship.
I am joined to these phases by the Creator's Hand.
Intervals meshed with infinitesimal progress,
Sure steps… locked to the rhythm of life.

I am at ease in the Cosmos.
Mother Earth's Eternal Child.
Fashioned in the Mystery that permeates.
Consecrated at the dawn of Creation. □

Trials in the wilderness

Despite my unfinished spiritual quest, I stayed conflicted about attending church due to its shift in focus from preaching the gospel of salvation to building a believer's kingdom of prosperity on Earth. Like the Israelites that left Egypt, I wandered in circles through the promised land. I didn't realize there was a matter of absolute trust in God yet to be fulfilled. Nevertheless, now and then, I suffered some small amount of guilt when I remembered the dream of Jesus anointing my hands. Even though I was convinced that ministering to people who did not attend church was within my calling, I would find myself going to one of the houses of worship. On these occasions, I put aside certain Christian-like lay mannerisms. I wanted to appear as inconspicuous as any visitor to the various congregations. There, I hoped I could absorb a much-desired communal warmth spirit of the services without having to take part in the goings on. At once, upon choosing an end seat somewhere behind the bulk of the worshippers, the ministers sitting in the pulpit would beckon for me to join them.

Even the Ushers were prone to whisper, *"Are you a Minister, Sir?"*

Then, after nodding in the affirmative (I couldn't do otherwise) I was directed to a more prominent seat up front.

No matter how much I wished to appear the same as the regular visitors, my ministerial roots came to the forefront. As usual, there was work for me to do, so I surrendered to the Spirit's will (As I understood it to be) and was received warmly. I was a popular speaker thereafter until my anointing carried my brief talks into the area of repentance and becoming a new creature in Christ Jesus. The leaders and principal members that put forth airs of sinless Christians became uncomfortable by the implications that they were less than perfect. Whenever this happened, I could see my talks on repentance were becoming tiresome, and I believed it was time to leave, and did so. At other times, a spirit of revival fell upon the congregations, and I would be asked to teach a series of lessons accompanied by prayer lines.

I HAD DEVELOPED INTO A LONER, but not because of my fragmented relationship with the church. I recognized my prior inability to cope with the unhealthy residual habits of my former addictions were responsible for a less than desired relationship with my children and the loss of a family. The irrational behavior brought on by my alcoholism was the reason that Merle and I couldn't remain together. With Vanessa's mother, Frankie, my inability to be a provider because of alcoholism was also the major reason our relationship never got off to an adequate start. In my failed marriage with Carolyn, there was a deficit of interpersonal skills that never ripened during my drinking years. This made me immature as a husband and father. All the same, during these unbalanced times between devotion to the church and flirting with other religious mindsets, I had a dream that I met a fascinating woman from the south. This caused me to reconsider my celibate mindset and realize that I had been in the wilderness too long and was human after all. True to form, such a person, accompanied by a mutual friend, came to my apartment in Fort Worth a brief time thereafter. Her name was Rasheedah!

When her name was spoken, my poetic soul heard soothing music as well as rhapsodic verse.

There were obstacles to pursuing this lovely and younger in-process divorcee. To begin, she was a devoted member of *The Nation of Islam*, which was under the leadership of Imam Warith Deen Mohammed, one of the founder's sons. I was a follower of the teachings of Jesus. It should have been no problem, since each religion was an offshoot of the *One God*, and we both saw our respective Black worship styles as instruments for the betterment of Black people. The snag was that I was in my mid-forties when some moderately successful men try to recapture their squandered youth by wanting cars and women that are beyond their ability to handle. Being so strongly attracted to her, I gave-in to my addictive personality until having her was within reach. I was so hooked; I fought against all reason until I became a willing slave to unbridled romantic love.

The whirlwind days of our courtship began with all the ingredients of any sugary romance. At times, I appeared to be running back and forth like a football receiver, with his eyes fixed on the moving ball. I bought a two-year-old, White *Buick Le Sabre* that had gray patterned cloth upholstery. In addition to the car, more youthful dress attire pushed my outmoded casual clothes to the corners of my closet. I didn't change my style of speaking, but I updated a few formerly rejected romantic cliches into my conversations with her.

Rockie's friends excitedly recounted the happy changes I brought into her life. We were the newest couple on the way to eternal bliss, and they reveled in our romantic antics. We were so mesmerized by each other that we never finished the exquisite meals in the intimate little dinner spots we slipped away to. Every place my big Buick carried us was enchanted. If there was evil in the world, I couldn't see it through the eyes of love.

Eventually, we got married and moved to Colorado. After a year, my fourth pretty daughter, Roslyn K., AKA *Roz*, came into my family. Like my other daughters before her, loving *Baby Roz* became the most devoted to of all my addictions. Life was good for a few months thereafter. But alas, all too soon, Rasheedah and I were embroiled in arguments stemming from differences we did not display before we *tied the knot*. Being only a few months old, *Roz* couldn't articulate to those outside her most intimate space the trauma the arguments were having on her. However, once again, I grew to see the emotional strain being brought into this unusually quiet child's only world. But this time, I took slow but effective action to alleviate, I thought, little *Roz's* stresses. After long weeks of potential give and take solutions that needed legal force, Rasheedah and I called it quits in 1992 when *Roz* was about five and a half years old. There wasn't a nasty custody battle with the amicable divorce and *Joint Custody* regarding *Roz*. Since I was retired from work and could devote more time to a child showing all the signs of the dreaded McKellar's (Hereditary) asthma, it was agreed through the courts that I was best suited to be the *Primary Physical Custo*dian in raising *Roz*.

I WAS FIFTY-THREE YEARS OLD and believed I was beyond the influences of the pitfalls of the past, when I rented an older two room, garden level apartment in Aurora, Colorado, with little *Roz*. I was strong enough to make it work, but other aspects of life would test me mightily anyhow. At that time, I ran a complex, numerical controlled machine, for *Alcoa Packaging Machinery* Operations, a manufacturing shop just south of Denver. As a Boring Mill machinist (A top position). I also ran for and won the vice-president of the *Local Machinists Union* and also the chairperson of my company's shop committee.

Unrealistically, it seems now it was providential that another back injury sent me home to be the full-time parent I needed to be. However, this new faith walk was not easy in the beginning. Soon, my machinist salary withered away, and the daily trials of poverty assailed me. Still, I knew that God was watching me, even though at times I felt spiritually disconnected from his oversight. But I carried on with my spiritual affairs just as I did when I was actively involved in the ministry. Financial trouble began as the rent became due, or the car needed expensive repairs.

To add to all this, serious medical issues for both *Roz* and I became more intensified. In about 1994, I received a diagnosis from the *Denver VA Hospital* doctors that I could not accept, so I refused further investigation or medical treatment for the problem. As always, I endeavored to trust that my faith as a man of God would pull me through. Yet, fears of impending doom came to the forefront as I realized I might have to leave *Roz* to the cruel mercies of the world, just as so many other good people had left their innocent children behind. My first reaction to this calamity was an attempt to remake an already fragile child into a superwoman, able to thrive no matter what came. I became impatient, and demanding as any *Drill Sargent.* How much of these capricious tantrums was because seven-year-old *Roz* not becoming a fully functioning adult or my frustrating efforts to find a solution to the dreaded killer stalking me, I didn't know. But the damage was done. I became like so many religious parents who drive a wedge between them and their children before God revealed to me "Exactly where I was missing the point." Having regained a modicum of sanity, I sent *Roz* to a stern female psychologist (who had me pegged as the problem from the introductions), so she could have someone to listen to her feelings about the insanity at home. Then, I turned my attention to my *Old Friend,* God. My protestations to *My Higher Power,* centered around the belief that, since He ultimately was going to work this mess out to mine and Roz'*s* benefit, why not reveal to me His plans. I knew that I was pushing the limits as far as religious beliefs were concerned, but nothing came to comfort me.

Before my turn at practicing trust in God when the chips were down, my strong faith in my ability to get a prayer through was accompanied by feelings of the presence of the spirit upon me. Now these assurances disappeared as if God had deserted me. But to save dignity (pride), when dealing with others, I was a fount of scriptures and sayings relevant to overcoming each obstacle. Truthfully, it was akin to *Hell*! Throughout the attacks of anxiety, I was careful to put forth the image of the towering man of God I had convinced myself I had become over the years. As my now unnecessary repetitive prayers went unanswered, I searched deeper within for the reasons for my predicament. During this period of uncertainty, I knew that it was me that was out of kilter and that it was important that I did not blame God directly for the negative things that had come upon me. To do so would be to personally sabotage relief by the fulfiller of all faith. Sadly, my mental state was such that again. I tried to see myself as a modern-day version of the Old Testament patriarch, Job, who was severely tested by Satan through sickness. But this comparison wasn't an exact fit, because unlike Job, there was a chink in my armor. I had not used my ministerial gifts to heap up money and earthly treasures for myself, but I allowed pride to usurp dignity in comparing myself to other people, in whom I did not see God working in their lives. Also, I knew that I was far from perfect and had considerable guilt for the suffering caused to others by my past drunken deeds. My dreams were dark and negative again. In two of them, a graveyard and a cemetery figured prominently, but to my relief, when interpreting them, I only drove by the graveyard and found my way out of the cemetery maze.

In my waking hours, I borrowed library books and studied statistics and all sorts of research material on my condition. But the information I found yielded nothing that eased my mind completely. These worrisome things went on for about forty-five fearful days after the discouraging diagnosis. I didn't understand it then, but I was in no danger despite my feelings of doom.

Our relationship with God is secure through the unchanging love that binds us through The Spirit. It is a sure anchor of our souls that our fleshly constitution can't understand. So, I worried needlessly.

During these trying times, God still delivered me from the grip of poverty and lesser troubles, always coming through just in time to prevent us from going under. But my pride, in who I took myself to be, was being deconstructed through fear.

When I served God through the ministry, and the Two of Us were a closely bonded Team, I had unwavering faith because of who I felt I was in Him. Now that I believed I no longer fulfilled those ministerial obligations, I feared the possibility of a crack in our relationship. Of course, I should have trusted God with the matter, and believed in His Grace, alone, during the onset of my new sickness. However, just the opposite took place. I needed one of the old signs that He was there to heal me. Distressingly, while I never said it, I had coupled my imperfect works to God's blessings. After much suffering, I remembered that God (As I understood Him) would not torture His children, so I refused to ask, *"What am I doing wrong?"* The question seems to suggest that I was being punished by God for something I couldn't comprehend. Additionally, I realized that my healing did not depend on receiving an answer to my prayers. Understanding the mechanism of God's healing was unnecessary for me. Neither was feeling the presence of the *Holy Spirit* proof of my salvation. This too comes by trust in God's Good Grace; sensation being quite unnecessary. Realizing these things, I acknowledged my wavering faith and knew that God would protect Roslyn, just as He had protected me from my earliest childhood. Nevertheless, I went into the kitchen of our Lansing Street apartment and opened the Bible I had in my hand. This time, I received the clearest sign I have ever had as my finger fell directly on Philippians 2:27 as I began reading; I felt immediate relief as I read:

"For indeed he was sick nigh unto death: but God had mercy on him; and not on him only, but on me also, lest I should have sorrow upon sorrow."

It was not a perfect fit for my situation, but it was enough to convince me I had heard from God, Himself. After that, the pain continued for about seven days and then ceased. At last, I agreed with my heart that the greatest faith was believing in God's Faithfulness when all the natural evidence showed just the opposite. Going forward in power, I sensed I was unstoppable with God's *Holy Spirit* redefined as my companion.

Homeschool

Credit: istock.com/Paper Trident

IN THE ENSUING YEARS, *ROZ* AND I HAD MANY PROBLEMS, but nothing insurmountable. Notably, because of asthma, *Roz* had to be homeschooled for high school before attending college at the *University of Colorado at Colorado Springs*. The most eventful of those times was *Roz's* and my college years. At the beginning, I structured the framework for homeschooling uniquely for *Roz* and me as two students studying together. I, the older, more diligent of the two, made sure of all the preparations for class sessions and decided on the curriculum. I called the Governor of Colorado's Office and obtained the actual high school curricula from the *Colorado Department of Higher Education* (CCHE). Then, I combed the public libraries and homeschool stores for books and other teaching aids, making networking connections all the while. *Roz* and I were no strangers to regular school homework. Asthma had forced us to FAX daily classroom work between home and *Lansing Street Elementary School*, since the second grade. To make matters worse, *Roz* became impaired by social phobia and retreated into severe depression. Somehow, we carried on. Much of *Roz's* coping strategy came by way of a lovable, near decrepit but precocious white teddy [Polar] bear named *Roger* who became her interface with the world. We studied when *Roz* wasn't having medical issues, and she excelled in learning. However, *Mrs. Rybek*, and the *Lansing* teaching staff taught Roz to read [Which was beyond my ability], and consulting with them, I built upon that foundation.

Rasheedah bought several expensive science and mathematics volumes and surprisingly helped in other more necessary ways, such as believing in our undertaking. Soon, we were materially set. All that was needed was to do it. To this end, I structured the class sessions along the lines of the *Socratic Method* because a parent knows their child's strengths, when the child, because of competitive socialization, may not appreciate their mental aptitude. So, I would propose situations above what her grade was studying, and *Roz* would quickly find weaknesses in my assertions. Our standard of understanding anything was: *If you can't explain it, you don't know it.* Make no mistake, the homeschool class became heated as *Roz* sometimes lost patience with me when I was slow to catch on to the new [Since the 1950s] math. Since *Roz* was better than me in math and current subjects, my ignorant responses taught her how to teach as well as appreciate my old familiar learning style. From our discussions on Mythological beliefs, I foraged into metaphysics and its relationship, if any, to the spiritual realm. Somewhere in her pains, *Roz* discovered her own unique relationship to the God of whom I so glowingly spoke. The upshot of it all was that as we plumbed the depths of possibilities, we both became better thinkers.

In the beginning, when homeschool was just an idea, I feared I might not have the temperament to tutor my sensitive young child. But she passed all the exams the regular students took, and thereafter, *Roz* was accepted into several good colleges, both in and out of state.

Also, I suspected that *Roz* had not fully believed homeschooling could recover the lost opportunities she had as a *National Honor Society Candidate.* I sensed this in the second year of classes and arranged for us to attend a recruitment gathering put-on by the *University of Colorado* at its downtown Denver Campus. *Roz* feebly mustered sufficient excitement to please me, or at least get it through my thick skull that all was in vain.

On a sunny Denver Day, the Presentation was an elaborate affair with lots of people milling around decorated booths. Modern elevator music floated throughout the venue. It was a splendid metamorphosis as *Roz* saw that one impressive, well dressed, scholarly Dean was actively trying to enroll her, there, on the spot. As they spoke, a great weight was lifted from me also, and I sniffled under my breath. When we were home again, I tore-up the Web and internet searching for both schools and scholarships to get *Roz* a first-class college education. Those efforts bore fruit and soon *Roz* was off to the *University of Colorado's* mountain college in *Colorado Springs* after receiving a full-ride scholarship. [This story to be told by *Roz* of her own journeys.]

Move-in Day came, and I was a proud father, walking through *Roz's* dorm wing. Remembering *Prairie View A & M College* so long before, I began the thought of "Boy, I wish I could go to coll...," and at once accepted the proposition that I, also, would get a college education.

Again, there is no need to belabor the point that after my studies in the homeschool, I was a diligent student despite the mounting physical pains and impairments. Before I knew it, I was a seventy-two-year-old college graduate receiving my BA *cum laude* in *African American Studies*, minoring in *History* from *Metropolitan State University of Denver.* The local TV and newspapers loved it; so, did some of the big, syndicated media. As such human-interest stories go, the media carried it until the next college graduating senior took the limelight. Although my college education restored significant self-esteem, I lost due to poverty, prejudice, and alcohol addiction, there still seemed to be something left undone in my life's journey through uncharted worlds of thought and being. In those settings, I championed worthy causes as they came to me. Skirmishes with the Spirit of *Ol' Jim Crow* remained vexing and intractable throughout. Most centered on "the inherent inferiority of The Black Race." I overcame these because they were stupid. Then, misfortune assailed me with terrible fury, and I spent about three to five days in the *Denver VA Hospital* annually. I clung to life for many reasons but mostly out of pure resolve [Stubbornness] because I felt it was not time to close the books.

Epilogue

DURING ONE OF THESE HOSPITAL TRIPS, when I was eighty years old, the *Hospital Chaplain* stopped by my room and introduced himself.

Suddenly I was filled with the need to tell this fellow minister about my life. "God has carried me through an adventurous life," I began.

But he looked rather distant, while making motions with his hand from the sky, down to his waistline, as if writing, while saying to me three times as I continued speaking, *"From Him, to you, write it down."*

Several weeks later, I was recuperating at home and began the task of *"Writing it down."* But not so fast, first came the remembering of how God was intertwined in the adventures and misfortunes that I had lived through. I thought of beginning with my cloud vision while at *Clarks Hotel* in Los Angeles. After many starts, I recollected how God (Unknown to me before then) had been the architect and unseen support behind my life and that this was His story as well, of how He, through Godly patience, and daily endeavors, is reconciled to His errant children. So, recalling when I was a boy, the pains of poverty affected me mostly during the times we had no food for several days. People all around us had money and food to spare, but no one offered any help even though they knew that poor families were in distress. I considered how they would not share, as Mama always had when strangers in need knocked at our back door for a handout. Pop had come through the years of *The Great Depression* and told stories of nationwide hunger. Our periods of hunger were the result of oppression by those in the upper rungs of society. More than the hunger, it pained me that people could be unaffected by others' suffering.

At these times, Grandma prayed, but nothing happened at once. So, I came to believe that God was only a figment of our imagination. Eventually, things got better as I began to read. It hurt less when I learned that other people in the world shared our plight of poverty.

Although I was not low-spirited in my personal approach to life and my surroundings, I grew to see mankind, *generally*, as inherently selfish and uncaring for anything but their own circumstances. I saw it in the black people on *Baptist Hill* as well as the whites. I saw the way the world embraced the concept of material gain over fairness, and it negatively affected me.

I didn't physically distance myself from the church and other people, yet I took notice that they had, to me, a much more boisterous sense of self-esteem. To be sure, I had my moments of swagger concerning personal accomplishments, but I am speaking about how other people act as if they were the greatest just because they were themselves. Not feeling the need for unwarranted pride, I was one of the "Poor in spirit" of whom Jesus said "...for theirs is the kingdom of heaven." When I *received* [Awakened in me] the "*Holy Spirit*" in Los Angeles, in 1957, I knew that God was watching over me and would not let me fall. In that moment, I became so spiritually rich that the pain of having less material wealth than others forever vanished from my mindset.

Except for the cadet incident, prejudice never caused me sufficient mental anguish to be thought of as personal pain. Although I faced prejudice in my early years, I was intelligent enough to see through the lies and stereotypes. When I worked the *12 Steps Inventory* during my coming to grips with my own form of defensive bigotry, I understood that my oppressors were also flawed in the same and similar ways. Again, after trying to live in harmony with the *Holy Spirit*, I took up the practice of forgiving others as God forgave me. I am not near what I should be in this, but I sincerely try despite emotional flare-ups.

My propensity for addiction is not a thing to overcome with me because I understand why I have an addictive personality. I see now that my troubles with alcohol and marijuana were I used substances as a quick fix for my emotional and social inadequacies. I didn't understand that my social shortcomings had nothing to do with fulfilling my true destiny. My ability to go all-in to achieve a workable solution is an innate capacity that empowers me to succeed in any endeavor. But, without the guidance of the *Holy Spirit* in understanding my motives, I turned the blessings into an accursed pursuit. In so doing my good inner faculties tried to stop me by tripping me up. After I understood myself better thanks to my work with the *12 Steps* of recovery, I mastered baseless fears and was at peace with myself.

Still, being shepherded through life as I had lived it under the eyes of my *Higher Power* [God], was not a lesson for me alone, but for all who yearn for inner peace in this unloving world we have created. It is we, humanity, that are the architects of destruction to our society. Many say that the Creator [Against His Nature] is the root cause of our many calamities, because of the level of power needed to bring it all under control again. That assumption flies in the face of the *Creation Story.* In it, God made mankind from the atomic elements of this dimension and breathed life [His Spirit] into us. Despite our many negative entanglements with our Creator, ancient writings, including the Bible, plainly show He never took His power from humanity. Since He never revoked His gift to those He set over the Earth [Men and women], it falls on us to correct the errant spiritual orbit of our world before the Landlord does evict us.

Our innermost feelings bear witness that my words here are true. Our works upon this Earth also bear witness to us that we are like Our Father in our ability to create wonders, and like Him, what we can conceive in the material world, we create. So, all is not lost. The power for good in us outweighs the power of evil because we were first created to do good works on Earth. It has long been said that peace on Earth begins in each person's heart. There we must muster the courage to dare to break with what goes against our loving nature and seek God's awaiting Spirit of Redemption. If we are willing to sit and dine with our neighbors, we will find that the *Master of the Household* has set a feast of Love for us to enjoy in an Eden of our own making. On the menu is faith, from which the tiniest seed grows into longsuffering so that we may be reunited with God and our fellow siblings in gentleness and goodness. These sprouts, in time, mature into love, joy, and inner peace. However, if we continue with wars and segregation of our common heritage, and do not turn from our current path, we will starve our original loving natures. We will go into oblivion without partaking of God's feast of life. History will conclude that we neglected so much, and that in our existence on Earth all we had were *Crumbs from the Master's Table.*

LAMENTATION FOR MOTHER EARTH

Hushed in the still of night, I feel my Mother's crying,
Tears o'er the plight of sons and daughters dying.
Her days are in December, with movements old and slow,
I weep when I remember her beauty of long ago.

We children were her pride, near Eden, her favorite spot,
She was a tender young bride, and we… a quarrelsome lot.

Great kingdoms rose and fell; Nations grew wicked and wise,
But ignored the Prophet's death knell, beneath the clouded skies.

A deluge of Heaven's tears fell upon the crimson land,
Reseeding with hope—new years—sown by the Master's hand.

His rainbow said, "Never again will the sky open and flood;"
So, we parted on Shinar's Plain to a heritage soaked in blood.

Marching through the ages, we slaughtered as we came,
History has untold pages of killing in Humanity's name.

The flora, we have burned; the fauna, we put to sword.
All living things have learned to fear the trampling horde.

Behind deceitful faces, we trap our fellow men,
Whether of different races or of the selfsame skin.

With stiff wills unbending, we live with bated breath,
While moving toward an ending; composing a song of death.

Now, is the lamenting heard; with bitter tears is it sung;
Brotherly love is only a word flowing from a crafty tongue.

Weep for sylvan slopes…weep for crystal lakes,
Weep for forlorn hopes…oh, weep...for Man's mistakes…
Copyright Van McKellar, 1979

About the Author

VAN, A RECOVERING ALCOHOL ADDICT, has lived alcohol free for 59 years and has not smoked anything for over 38 years. He is a former local minister of the *Church of God in Christ* Inc. He is an accomplished writer of rhyming poetry and has a Commercial Pilots License. The author's BA in African American Studies from *The Metropolitan State University of Denver* enriches his intimate knowledge of the *Black Experience* in 20th century, *Jim Crow America.* This memoir is Van's initial offering.

www.ingramcontent.com/pod-product-compliance
Lightning Source LLC
Chambersburg PA
CBHW021222090426
42740CB00006B/343

* 9 7 9 8 2 1 8 6 1 0 2 1 0 *